Impression Manageme

Impression management – our ways of controlling what others think of us – is central to our working lives. So central, in fact, that we often use it automatically. *Impression Management* is an integrated study of this often overlooked aspect of organizational life. Among other topics, the authors discuss:

- psychological, organizational and communications-oriented approaches to impression management
- our ways of building, enhancing and protecting our reputation at work
- the influence of impression management on recruitment and selection procedures, and so on

Covering theory, measurement and current business practice, the authors illustrate the practical effects of impression management on organizational life and companies' performance through research studies and examples drawn from recent business history.

Impression Management will make an important addition to the library of any organizational psychologist and human resource manager. It will also appeal to anyone interested in the dynamics of organizational politics and in the exercise of power and influence strategies.

PAUL ROSENFELD is a personnel research psychologist at the US Navy Personnel Research, Studies, and Technology (NPRST) Department of the Navy Personnel Command. Dr. Rosenfeld is currently the NPRST Washington, DC liaison.

ROBERT A. GIACALONE is the Surtman Distinguished Professor of Business Ethics at the Belk College of Business, University of North Carolina-Charlotte.

CATHERINE A. RIORDAN is Assistant Vice President and Professor of Psychology at Central Michigan University. She is also Interim Vice Provost.

Psychology at Work
Series editor: Clive Fletcher

This series interprets and examines people's work behaviour from the perspective of occupational psychology. Each title focuses on a central issue in management, emphasizing the role of the individual's workplace experience.

Books in the series include:

Creating the Healthy Organization
Well-being, Diversity and Ethics at Work
Sue Newell

Impression Management
Building and Enhancing Reputations at Work
*Paul Rosenfeld, Robert A. Giacalone
and Catherine A. Riordan*

Managing Employee Performance
Design and Implementation in Organizations
Richard S. Williams

Managing Innovation and Change
A Critical Guide for Organizations
Nigel King and Neil Anderson

Managing Teams
A Strategy for Success
Nicky Hayes

Recruitment and Selection
A Framework for Success
Dominic Cooper, Ivan Robertson and Gordon Tinline

Psychology
at Work

Impression Management

Building and Enhancing Reputations at Work

Paul Rosenfeld, Robert A. Giacalone and
Catherine A. Riordan

THOMSON

™

LEARNING

Australia • Canada • Mexico • Singapore • Spain • United Kingdom • United States

Impression Management: Building and Enhancing Reputations at Work

The Thomson Learning logo is a registered trademark used herein under licence.

For more information, contact Thomson Learning, Berkshire House, 168–173 High Holborn, London, WC1V 7AA or visit us on the World Wide Web at: http://www.thomsonlearning.co.uk

British Library Cataloguing-in-Publication Data
A catalogue record for this book is available from the British Library

ISBN 1-86152-970-8

First published 1995 by Routledge, under the title
Impression Management in Organizations: Theory, Measurement, Practice

This edition 2002 by Thomson Learning

Typeset by LaserScript, Mitcham, Surrey
Printed in Great Britain by TJ International, Padstow, Cornwall
Cover design by Metamorphosis
Text design by Malcolm Harvey Young

Contents

Figures

Tables

Boxes

Series editor's preface

Understanding the psychology of individuals and teams is of prime importance in work settings as rapid and far-reaching changes continue to occur. Organizational structures are shifting radically to the point where individual managers and professionals have far greater autonomy, responsibility and accountability. Organizations are seeking to reduce central control and to "empower" individual employees. These employees combine in teams that are frequently cross-functional and project based rather than hierarchical in their construction. The traditional notion of careers has changed; increasingly, an individual's career is less likely to be within a single organization, which has implications for how organizations command loyalty and commitment. The full impact of information technology has now been felt, with all the consequences this has for the nature of work and the reactions of those doing it.

The capacity of people to cope with the scale and speed of change has become a major issue and the literature on work stress only increases. The belief in the importance of individuals' cognitive abilities and personality make-up in determining what they achieve and how they contribute to teamwork has been demonstrated in the explosive growth in organizations' use of psychometric tests and related procedures. Perhaps more than ever before, analysing and understanding the experience of work from a psychological perspective is necessary to achieve the twin goals of effective performance and quality of life. Unfortunately, it is the latter of these that all too often seems to be overlooked in the concern to create competitive, performance driven, or customer focused cultures within companies.

It is no coincidence that the rise in the study of business ethics and increasing concern over issues or fairness paralleled many of the organizational changes of the late twentieth century. Ultimately, an imbalance between the aims and needs of the employees and the aims and needs of the organization is self-defeating. One of the widely recognized needs for the twenty-first century is for a greater emphasis on innovation rather than on simply reacting to pressures. However, psychological research and theory indicate that innovation is much more likely to take place where individuals feel secure enough to take the risks involved, and where organizational reward systems encourage experimentation and exploration which they have signally failed to do in the last century. Seeking to help organizations realize the potential of their workforce in a mutually enhancing way is the business challenge psychology has to meet.

The central theme of the *Psychology at Work* series is to interpret and explain people's work behaviour in the context of a continually evolving pattern of change, and to do so from the perspective of occupational and organizational psychology. Each of the books draws together academic research and practitioner experience, relying on empirical studies, practical examples, and case studies to communicate their ideas. The reader, whether a student, manager or psychologist, will find that they provide a succinct summary of accumulated knowledge and a guide to how to apply it in business. The themes of some of the books cover traditional areas of occupation psychology, while others focus on topics that cut across such boundaries, tackling subjects that are of growing interest and prominence. They are directly relevant for practitioners, consultants and students of HR and occupational psychology but much of what they deal with is of great value to managers, and students of management, more generally. This broad appeal is demonstrated by the fact that an earlier version of the series, the *Essential Business Psychology* series, was highly commended by the Management Consultancies Association book award. The *Psychology at Work* series shares the aims, and some of the titles, as the original series but the individual books have been substantially updated and the range of titles is expanded. Although the books share a common aim and series heading, they have not been forced into a rigid stylistic format. In keeping with the times, the authors have had a good deal of autonomy in deciding how to organize and present their work. I think all of them have done an excellent job; I hope you will find that too.

Clive Fletcher

Acknowledgements

The publication of this our second book on Impression Management renews a commitment to an area of interest that began when we met as graduate students in the late 1970s. It was in those days at the State University of New York (SUNY) at Albany that we first formulated the idea of applying the impression management perspective to organizational life. Although the challenges of the moment (e.g., getting our dissertations done, finding a job) initially prevented us from acting upon these ideas, our resolution to develop this area now brings forth our second book born of a notion that the theatrical metaphor is as appropriate to the workplace as it is to daily social interaction.

As with our past works, we wish to thank our families, friends, and colleagues for their love, support, and encouragement. Being good impression managers, we wish to apologize for ignoring them during the period necessary to get this book done!

In particular, our sincerest thanks to our parents, Abraham and Judes Rosenfeld, Frank and Theresa Giacalone, and Beverly and John Riordan. We are also greatly indebted to Mary Sellen, our favorite librarian; Karen, Andrew, Joshua, and Elizabeth Giacalone who make the work worthwhile; and to Jack, Phil, Amy and Katie Thompson for their inspiration, patience and sharing the family PC with Mom during the final stages of this book.

Special thanks are reserved for people who helped along the way. We thank Clive Fletcher for his very positive feedback throughout this and our previous impression management book. We also are very pleased to have this book published by Thomson and our editors there Anna Faherty and Jenny Clapham have been wonderful to work with. They have done a great job keeping the book and its authors on schedule. We greatly appreciate Marcy Scott's assistance and Lance Haynes' comments on an earlier version of this book published in 1995 by Routledge.

We owe a special thanks to our colleagues, students, friends, and relatives for their influence on our thinking, careers, lives, and impression management skills: Renatte Adler, David Alderton, Jamie Archer, Stephanie Booth-Kewley, Steve Butnik, Sad Carino, Jack Edwards, Bob Ford, Willie Harbart, Jean Henry, Laura Jarvis, Steve Knouse, Farrell Malkis, Trina Moten, Luce Myers, Carol Newell, Steve Payne, Gary G. Peer, Hinda G. Pollard, Sharon Scott, Jerry Stevens, Laura Stoll, Marie Thomas, Pat Thomas, Tom Trent, Zannette Uriell and the entire Shanske family (Ruth, Warren, David, Neal, Susan, and their wonderful children). Finally, we note the passing of Jim Tedeschi who first introduced us to impression management at SUNY-Albany and died during the writing of this book.

Paul Rosenfeld
Arlington, Virginia

Bob Giacalone
Charlotte, North Carolina

Catherine Riordan
Mount Pleasant, Michigan

1 IM in Organizations: An Introduction

Forever Changing Jobs

> Jobs is an irresistibly charming man who can turn on a dime to cruelty
> (Poniewozik, 2000, p. 38).

One of the better-known business figures over the past quarter century has been Steve Jobs, a cofounder and later reviver of Apple Computer Company. A recent biography described Jobs' tumultuous career by saying he was the first businessman who could be considered a rock star! (Deutschman, 2000). While the remarkable struggles, persistence and intermittent successes of the various companies he has led alone might have led to Steve Jobs' notoriety, his skillful and sometimes less than skillful use of *impression management* (IM, pronounced 'I-M') also made him both famous and infamous in the business world.

Press accounts of Jobs' life and career have consistently made reference to the way his appearance and behavior created a very distinctive public image. As a way of introducing you to organizational IM, we rely on a biography by Lee Butcher (1989) and several more recent accounts, to analyze Jobs' public identity and give you an idea of what IM is, and how it is critical to success in the business world and to building and enhancing reputations at work.

One thing is clear about Steve Jobs: he did not initially use IM to create an image of someone who would 'fit in'. In both his early life and with the image of Apple products, he seemed to resist what, as we shall see in Chapters 2 and 3, are often common goals of IM: to be liked by others and to be seen as normal. Jobs seemed to thrive on being perceived as 'strange'. Though the son of devoted parents, Jobs 'wanted to look and feel like an orphan who had spent a few years bumming around the country, hopping on freight trains or riding in eighteen-wheelers' (Butcher, 1989, p. 41). Jobs did not change his haggard appearance even when he took his first job at the Atari Computer Company. 'While at Atari, Jobs was following Ehret's mucusless diet, eating yogurt and fruit. He believed that the diet eliminated the need for bathing. Others disagreed' (Butcher, 1989, p. 49).

We don't claim to know exactly why Jobs really did some of these weird things, but it is clear that he was devoted to and very effective at managing the impression of being an eccentric. Although it is possible that his strange behaviors may have been the result of being oblivious to reality, we think that Jobs, like many up-and-comers in contemporary organizations, was actively trying to cultivate an image so as to create a particular identity. Consider the following example of Steve Jobs' approach to conducting interviews. When recruiting prospective employees, he would take them to lunch at a nearby restaurant, put his feet up on the table, and proceed to 'attack them mercilessly' (Butcher, 1989, p. 119). Jobs clearly seems to have been using IM to create an identity as a peculiar nonconformist.

Even when Jobs was desperate for start-up money for Apple computers, he refused to conform to the traditional standards for making a positive impression in the business world. 'Thin, somewhat grubby, with long hair, he ran around either in sandals, or barefoot' (Butcher, 1989, p. 68). Though the dress standards were somewhat relaxed in California at this time, most bankers and financiers were still accustomed to entrepreneurs wearing ties, suits, shoes and taking showers when they came to request significant investments in their businesses.

As Apple became more successful, Jobs' appearance and brazen self-confidence offended a lot of people on Wall Street. Jobs had two qualities that allowed him to overcome these deficits, at least in part: He was persistent and had a knack for convincing people he was smart and competent. After hounding an advertising representative Jobs wanted to represent Apple, he got him to visit their operation. The representative said that within three minutes he knew that Jobs 'was an incredibly smart young man' (Butcher, 1989, p. 82). This ability to manage an impression of great intellect may have been responsible for Jobs' success at persuading others. Later in his career, Jobs is said to have 'pulled off an almost impossible deal when he convinced a software supplier to accept a small fee instead of royalties. The supplier said Jobs made it seem that he was providing a service to humanity. "He made me feel like I should pay him for letting him use my software", the supplier said' (Butcher, 1989, p. 219).

Jobs' success demonstrates that though physical appearance and other nonverbal cues are important when we present ourselves to others, skillful verbal IM can often overcome them. Jobs used presentations of his products to impress audiences about his own intellect and his products' potential. He could create a good first impression, and was not shy about claiming credit for success or for accomplishments within the company; tactics known as **acclaiming** that we describe in Chapter 3. Ironically, according to a business partner, Jobs lacked engineering know-how. Jobs' identity outside the company was not consistent with his partner's assessment. He successfully used IM to create a much more positive image of himself as a highly creative engineer.

As we shall see in Chapter 3, **intimidation** is an effective form of IM. Once in power, Jobs used intimidation as a management style. 'He ruled by intimidation, yelling and screaming at people' (Butcher, 1989, p. 96). When he later became head of Pixar, an animation company, Jobs would sometimes scream at subordinates until he hyperventilated. He fired one of his consultants and refused to pay for her completed work. Jobs would even park his car in the company's handicapped spaces (Poniewozik, 2000). This use of the IM technique of intimidation may be why Jobs managed to retain so much power despite the fact he was not as knowledgeable as some and more disliked than most.

In summary, we can see in Steve Jobs someone who appears to strategically select identities he wants to manage and goes about doing so. Some of the identities chosen were effective for him and his products. He pulled off many good sales jobs by masterfully controlling his public image. However, not all his strategies worked. As we shall see, the indiscriminate, nonjudicious use of IM can backfire. Jobs' use and abuse of IM through fabrication and intimidation led to hostility, noncooperation, and doubts about the truthfulness of what he said. Jobs' was eventually stripped of his managerial responsibilities at Apple.

However, just as bad IM can lead to failure, good IM can be a key to redemption. In 1996, the forever changing Jobs returned to Apple and reestablished himself, 'turning the company from a has-been into a profitable trendsetter and restoring his reputation as a visionary' (Poniewozik, 2000, p. 38). However, there were aspects of the Jobs character that didn't change as much. He continued to vigorously use

IM to influence perceptions of reality. In the fourth quarter of 2000, Apple suffered a 57 per cent loss in sales, the worst it had done since Jobs had returned to control of the company. To Jobs, bad news was just an anomaly. After the bad financial results appeared he said, 'We're starting this year with a bang' (Markoff, 2001, p. 4).

Steve Jobs' use of IM may seem bizarre and excessive. That is because of the identities Jobs chose to create and his inappropriate and inconsistent use of IM in critical situations. But while everyone does not use IM as indiscriminately as Jobs did, they do use it often to help achieve their own social and organizational goals such as being liked and valued by friends, co-workers, and supervisors. Thus, we are all 'forever changing Jobs' because in our own lives we play many roles, assume various identities, and are different things to different people, both at work and elsewhere. The how, what, why and where of IM in organizational settings is the topic of this book.

Introducing IM in Organizations

Getting along with other people at work, school, or home is often a daily struggle. In many parts of our lives, there are no longer clear guidelines for how we 'should' behave. Even the expectations we thought we understood quickly change. To an increasing extent we are interacting with others, not in conversation in an office, business, or living room, but remotely over handheld computers, through wireless communications, and on the Internet. Each of these factors makes relations with other people harder. Today it is even more important to understand who is playing which role, how we should act, and why other people are doing what they are doing. The focus of this book, IM, is the *process whereby people seek to control or influence the impressions that others form* (Schlenker, 2000). We impression manage in many different ways – what we do, how we do it, what we say, how we say it, the furnishings and arrangement of our offices, and our physical appearance – from the clothes and make-up we wear to nonverbal behaviors such as facial expressions or posture. All these behaviors in some way can help define who and what we are. They convey an identity and what we want and expect from other people. These **social identities** constitute how individuals are 'defined and regarded in social interaction' (Schlenker, 1980, p. 69).

What is IM?

Sociologist Erving Goffman wrote one of the first books devoted specifically to the area of IM. In *The Presentation of Self in Everyday Life*, Goffman said IM involves attempts to establish the meaning or purpose of social interactions, guides actions, and helps us anticipate what to expect from others (Goffman, 1959). IM is a **mutual ritual** that helps smooth and control social relations and avoid embarrassment. Even actions that at first glance appear to be meaningless might actually be strategically performed to show the social actor in the best possible light. People are performers who play many different roles to construct their **social identities**. When these social identities involve information related to the self, the term **self-presentation** is sometimes also used (Schlenker, in press; Schlenker & Pontari, 2000). Some of these IM behaviors are consciously controlled while others, such as eye contact and posture, often are unwittingly expressed. We attempt to control our IM behaviors because they are a primary means of influencing how other people treat us. Goffman describes the reasons for, and the consequences of, IM:

> When an individual enters the presence of others, they commonly seek to acquire information about him or to bring into play information about him already possessed. They will be interested in his general socio-economic status, his conception of self, his attitude toward them, his competence, his trustworthiness, etc. Although some of this information seems to be sought almost as an end in itself, there are usually quite practical reasons for acquiring it. Information about the individual helps to define the situation, enabling others to know in advance what he will expect of them and what they may expect of him. Informed in these ways, the others will know how best to act in order to call forth a desired response from him.
>
> *(Goffman, 1959, p. 1)*

Let us see how Goffman's vision of IM would apply to an important component of building and enhancing reputations at work: the performance appraisal. Assume that Chris is an employee who will be evaluated by Bill, his supervisor. Bill begins the appraisal interview with a brief greeting and outlines his intent to discuss Chris's performance over the past year. Chris sits stiffly, and acts aloof and uninvolved. Bill had intended to include a number of criticisms of Chris's tendency to miss project deadlines, but now, noting Chris's defensiveness, he hesitates in order to avoid an unpleasant encounter (and the negative impressions of him as a supervisor that might result). Instead Bill tries to calm Chris's fears by communicating the positive part of his evaluation but avoiding the critical portions. Chris awkwardly smiles and makes eye contact. Bill continues the performance appraisal, emphasizing Chris's contributions. He wants Chris to see him more like a helper or coach than critic. He suspects as long as he is able to maintain this identity, Chris will listen to what he has to say, believe he is trying to help, and respond positively to his suggestions. Chris, upon hearing his praises, relaxes, realizing that because he has a positive identity in his supervisor's eyes, he will probably not be blamed for missing several key project deadlines during the past year. Consistent with this positive identity and perceived support from Bill, Chris acts like the cooperative productive employee his supervisor is describing. He senses Bill's interest in improvement in certain areas and willingly participates in a problem-solving dialog about how improvements might be achieved so that he is able to deliver projects on time in the future. Bill and Chris have successfully negotiated a **working consensus** of their identities and roles in this situation. The working consensus says that in order for social interactions to proceed smoothly people will tend to support each other's identities and are reluctant to say what they really feel (DePaulo & Bell, 1996). At some level, they both know that Chris is not really as good as Bill says he is, but through this process of mutual IM, both 'go along' with the positive evaluation and avoid the negative in order to smooth a potentially rocky, awkward interaction (see Chapter 7, for further discussion of IM in the performance appraisal process).

Research on IM has gradually accelerated over the years since Goffman's groundbreaking work. IM can be found in the fields of sociology, management, organizational behavior, social psychology, communication, criminology, and political science, to name just a few. In this book we draw on research from all these areas to focus on applications of IM to organizational life.

Since Goffman, some authors have defined IM negatively, as a form of interpersonal manipulation occurring in a limited number of settings or as applying to a small set of social behaviors. This view supports a common misperception: that IM is something basically bad, involving actions performed primarily to gain the upper hand, or to deceive.

However, more recent perspectives see IM as a very broad and common phenomenon; a fundamental part of all interpersonal interactions (Rosenfeld, Giacalone, & Riordan, 1994).

IM: the expansive view

Barry Schlenker and colleagues (Schlenker, Britt, & Pennington, 1996; Schlenker & Pontari, 2000; Schlenker & Weigold, 1992) labeled this optimistic perspective the **expansive view**, while considering the more limited, nefarious, Machiavellian perspective, the **restrictive view** of IM. The restrictive view was popular among social psychologists when we were graduate students during the late 1970s, and still exists to a lesser degree today. We reject this approach and adopt the broader, expansive view in this book. The expansive view sees IM as a universal feature of human behavior where people constantly attempt to 'package' themselves so as to communicate their desired images and identities to significant others. This perspective assumes that people carry out IM in ways that help them achieve their objectives and goals, both individually and as members of groups and organizations. Sometimes IM is done consciously and deliberately, while other times it may be unconscious, automatic, and habitual (Schlenker & Pontari, 2000).

When interacting with others in the workplace we typically have many things on our mind, including a number of goals we hope to achieve in the same situation. Each of these goals is associated with particular **scripts**, **plans**, and **agendas** that operate in the background and guide actions most likely to lead to the desired impression. Scripts are for routine responses while plans accommodate more novel situational or identity demands. The combination of a goal and its associated script or plan is called an agenda. Agendas work like many of today's PCs: multiple computer programs are running simultaneously, and some programs run in the background without our awareness. Similarly, when we interact with our co-workers, customers, or contractors, we are assumed to have multiple agendas, with some operating even though we may not be aware of them (Schlenker & Pontari, 2000).

At times, the impressions that are managed in this way serve to bolster or protect the impression manager's (who we call an 'IMer'and pronounce 'I-M-er') self-image; other times impressions are managed with the hope of pleasing significant audiences. Sometimes IM is truthful and accurate. However, other times it involves 'false advertising' through the use of exaggeration, fabrication, deception, or outright lying. As Kashy and DePaulo (1996, p. 1037) note, 'Lying is a fact of social life rather than an extraordinary or unusual event. People tell lies to accomplish the most basic social interaction goals such as influencing others, managing impressions and providing reassurance and support.'

At times the target of IM is a stranger, sometimes a former co-worker, sometimes a boss, sometimes a jilted lover. There are times when the target audience is real, while on other occasions the audience is only imagined, as in Robert DeNiro's classic 'you talking to me?' soliloquy in the movie *Taxi Driver*. Thus, there are many faces to IM. Within this expansive view, IM is seen as *a goal-directed activity of controlling information about persons, objects, ideas or events, to audiences* (Schlenker & Pontari, 2000, p. 201). IM is a broad phenomenon in which attempts are made to influence the perceptions and behaviors of others by controlling the information they receive. In our opening example, we showed how Steve Jobs used IM by controlling what he said, his demeanor, and his clothing so that he would appear eccentric and intimidating.

The expansive view contends that we not only engage in IM for other people, but that our IM behaviors may affect what we think about ourselves. Our views of who we are often reflect the public roles that we take on (Schlenker & Pontari, 2000). This is particularly the case when a person freely chooses an identity and is publicly committed to it. Then IM on the outside becomes the self-concept on the inside as people change their self-concepts to match their IM behaviors (Kelly, 2000). So you become a boss by acting like one, a president by acting presidential and an author (we hope!) by writing a book. Thus, 'If one wants to become a certain type of person, one should try to publicly act like that type of person' (Schlenker & Pontari, 2000, p. 224). We have seen a shy employee become self-confident after she successfully described the results of an employee opinion survey during her first major corporate presentation. It was almost as if she observed her outstanding performance and concluded, 'Hey, I'm pretty good at this!' and left with a more positive self-image than she started with. In IM terms she had done such a good job persuading the **external audience** of her competence that she also persuaded her **internal audience** as well.

With this broad-brush background about the scope of IM behaviors, we now provide more details on IM theory and research to lay the groundwork for the information presented in later chapters. Following this brief overview, we pose and answer some general questions that students of IM often ask when first introduced to the field.

Historical Background: IM Metaphors

A number of different metaphors have been used to describe individuals as they engage in IM. In his classic *Principles of Psychology*, William James (1890), used the **metaphor of multiple selves** to describe human behavior. Rather than having a single unified self-concept, James argued that people have multiple selves of which they show different sides in various situations. He wrote that a person, 'has as many social selves as there are distinct groups of people about whose opinions he cares. He generally shows a different side of himself to each of these different groups' (James 1890, p. 294). James' notion that we have multiple social selves that are strategically presented to gain favor with different audiences greatly influenced later theorists, including those known as **postmodern psychologists**. Postmodern psychologists believe 'that we have no single, separate, unified self. They maintain that we contain many selves and that the proper response to the suggestion, 'Get in touch with yourself', or, 'Be yourself' is: 'Which one?' (Stephens, 1992, p. 40). This contemporary view is actually not that different from one advocated by James over a century ago: 'We do not show ourselves to our children as to our club-companions, to our customers as to the laborers we employ, to our own masters and employers as to our intimate friends' (James, 1890, pp. 46–7).

Within sociology, beginning in the early part of the twentieth century, there was a perspective referred to as **symbolic interactionism**, that popularized many of the concepts used in contemporary IM theory. Within this framework, the **dramaturgical metaphor** was elaborated and refined. The dramaturgical metaphor implies that social and organizational life are something akin to a theatrical play, with people playing a set of roles, coordinated with each other at times, and adjusted to maximize their effects on important audiences. William Shakespeare captured the essence of the dramaturgical metaphor when he wrote in *As You Like It*, 'All the world's a stage, and all of the men and women merely players. They have their exits and entrances, and one man in his time plays many parts.'

Take for example, Stephanie, a successful manager at a software development firm. At work, Stephanie is a cool decision-maker and tough taskmaster. At home she is a tender mother whose response to her son Andrew tripping and cutting his lip would never be called 'cool'. At the market, Stephanie screams at a clerk who drops her groceries. In the community choir, she is fun loving and spontaneous. To survive, to succeed, to excel, Stephanie is different things to different people, a busy actress in the drama of everyday life.

While Goffman felt IM served as a **social lubricant** greasing the skids for smooth interactions, some later work characterized IM as serving more specific, goal-oriented purposes such as gaining power and influencing others. The **metaphor of the yes-man** emerged in the 1960s and was seen in the work of Edward E. Jones on the IM technique of **ingratiation** (see Chapter 2). The yes-man uses ingratiation tactics such as opinion conformity to get others to like him. Since we tend to reward those we like, the successful yes-man uses liking as a stepping-stone to power and influence.

The 1970s saw the IM perspective become increasingly popular among laboratory-oriented experimental social psychologists. Indeed, during the late 1970s the three authors of this text first became interested in the role played by IM in social and work settings. The IM theory we encountered then used the **metaphor of the manipulator**. IM was seen as being performed to control other people, to dupe an audience, often for nefarious reasons. Schlenker and Pontari (2000, pp. 199, 200) described this earlier view of IM. 'To most social psychologists, it evoked negative images of superficiality rather than substance, and deception rather than authenticity... The connotations of superficiality, pretense, deceit, and immoral manipulation persist, giving it something of the status of the black sheep in the social psychological family.' Today we see this metaphor as too restrictive because it included only a small subset of IM behaviors and assumed that most people had sleazy motives for their IM actions.

The **organizational politician metaphor** also was developed in the 1970s and still exists today (Harrell-Cook, Ferris, & Dulebohn, 1999). It characterizes people as having a diverse set of objectives in social interaction, often related to power. People in organizations use IM in political ways when it will help them accomplish their goals. Today, the politician metaphor is still apt for some IM behaviors, but the focus of IM has broadened to include an ever-increasing range of organizational behaviors that go beyond viewing people as amateur politicians (Giacalone & Rosenfeld, 1989).

IM in Organizations: A Journey From Extreme to Mainstream

Even though Goffman emphasized that IM was a common, very normal feature of most interactions, not all subsequent theorists adopted this broad perspective. In social psychology, for example, IM was originally characterized as being an 'extreme' form of behavior for several reasons. During the 1960s, IM was seen as a contaminant or artifact of laboratory research that needed to be eliminated or controlled so that important, 'real' relationships among variables could be observed. During the 1970s it was gradually acknowledged that IM was not simply an artifact of laboratory research but that it played an important role in social behavior. However, the consensus was that it was a form of deceptive manipulation. IM was seen as a conscious attempt to deceive and manipulate others about the true characteristics of the self.

Although popular management books recognized that IM processes were crucial to organizational success (Korda, 1975; Molloy, 1978; Ringer, 1976), the academic side of organizational research was slower to accept IM as a viable theory, again perhaps because it was viewed as too sleazy or extreme (Rosenfeld & Giacalone, 1991). In the mid-1980s, more organizational studies using the IM framework began to appear (Giacalone, 1985; Giacalone & Rosenfeld, 1984, 1986, 1987; Ralston, 1985; Zerbe & Paulhus, 1987). In 1989, two of us edited *IM in the Organization* (Giacalone & Rosenfeld, 1989). It was the first attempt to systematically apply an IM framework to a wide spectrum of organizational processes. *IM in the Organization* was directed primarily toward scholars and researchers. Two years later, we edited *Applied IM: How Image-Making Affects Managerial Decisions*, a book focusing on organizational and practitioner applications (Giacalone & Rosenfeld, 1991).

Together, these two volumes served as sourcebooks for what has become a rapidly growing and now distinctive field called *organizational IM*. These two edited books integrated previous IM research conducted by leading social psychologists like Barry Schlenker, Mark Snyder, Roy Baumeister, Bob Arkin, Rick Snyder, Robert Cialdini, and Mark Leary, with organizational and business applications of IM associated with the work of noted organizational scholars such as Gerald Ferris, David Ralston, Mark Martinko, Jerald Greenberg, and Robert Bies. In retrospect, it is difficult to see how IM could have been overlooked in many theoretical discussions of the job interview, employee theft, substance abuse, career strategies, performance appraisals, exit interviews, negotiations, conflict resolution and many others (for discussions of these topics see Giacalone & Rosenfeld, 1989, 1991). Incorporating IM in today's research and practice is beginning to yield a better understanding of how organizational processes are substantially affected by individuals' concerns over how they are seen by others. Box 1.1 describes a good example of how a finding from a laboratory study in psychology is now being used to suggest how managers can be more effective.

Today, as IM has become more popular among organizational researchers and practitioners, it also has come to be viewed as more

---

| Box 1.1 | **IM and the Self-Fulfilling Prophecy: Out of the Closet and Into the Live Arena of Management Applications** |

The phrase 'out of the closet' used in the title above comes from a chapter by Dov Eden in *Applied IM* (Eden, 1991, p. 37). He is referring to the emergence of IM from being studied primarily in highly controlled laboratory experiments in social psychology to use by practitioners trying to improve the exercise of management and make organizations more effective. Eden's focus is the **self-fulfilling prophecy**, the finding that when people expect something to happen, they act in ways that make the event more likely to occur, and thereby increase the likelihood of the event actually happening (Merton, 1948). While the self-fulfilling prophecy was once considered a form of IM that could harm the validity of laboratory experiments, Eden's work has shown that it can have positive organizational benefits.

Eden's extension of this work into education and organizational training derives from the famous study *Pygmalion in the Classroom* by Rosenthal and Jacobson (1968). It was shown that students' academic performance could be increased by merely leading their teachers to expect that those students were 'late bloomers' and would show significant increases in performance during the ▶

year. Since the original study, expectations have been shown to increase performance in organizational training programs and many classroom settings.

According to Eden, the self-fulfilling prophecy can be a powerful management tool. '[T]he practical implication ... is that anything that raises managers' expectations concerning what subordinates are capable of achieving can lead to improvements in subordinates' performance' (Eden, 1991, p. 15). Eden points to ways an employee can use IM to raise a manager's expectations for her performance. If she suspects, for example, that the manager doubts her ability in certain areas, she could manage a contrary impression by completing some exceptional work in those areas and being sure the manager hears about it. If the manager changes his expectations to be in line with the new information, the raising expectations make it more likely he will act in ways that aid the employee's higher achievement, making her higher achievement more likely to become a reality. An interesting application of this theory occurred in the US Navy when low performing sailors who were taught to manage more positive identities actually increased their performance and their supervisors' evaluations of them (Crawford, Thomas, & Funk, 1980).

Managers can use IM to be sure they are conveying high expectations to those who report to them. Eden suggests a number of ways managers can communicate expectations to their employees: explicitly stating their expectations; setting difficult but realistic goals for their employees; giving employees tasks on which they are likely to succeed so they can build up their own self-confidence; and suggesting interpretations for employees' successes and failures that reinforce employees' motivation. A poignant example of the last strategy is an executive who said to one of his managers who was afraid he would lose his job because he had just made a mistake that would cost the company $100,000, 'Why should I fire you when I've just invested $100,000 in your development?' (McCall, Lombardo & Morrison, 1988, p. 154; cited in Eden, 1991). This statement clearly conveys the executive's confidence in the manager's ability and probably helped the manager to see the mistake as a painful learning experience rather than as a failure revealing his inadequate ability.

'mainstream' than 'extreme'. We view IM, as many others now do, as a commonly occurring and very 'normal' part of many aspects of organizational life. IM, in this contemporary perspective, is seen as being essential to effective organizational communications and interactions. To understand organizational life we need to understand IM. As we shall see, the range of phenomena it helps to explain includes all aspects of organizational behaviors, from the job interview to leadership, from ethics to organizational surveys, from performance appraisal to issues of diversity.

Organizational Politics and IM

> Politics is, like it or not, the way things get done in most organizations
> (Kathleen Kelley Reardon, quoted in Rosenstein, 2001, p. 6B).

The study of organizational politics developed in business in parallel to the development of IM in social psychology. Organizational politics refers to engaging in political behavior that the organization has not sanctioned, is often harmful to the goals of the organization, and seeks to maximize the organizational politician's self-interest (Harrell-Cook, et al., 1999). Organizational politics has been associated with increased work stress, less job satisfaction, and increased desire to leave the organization (Harrell-Cook, et al., 1999). While IM typically focuses on the individual, the organizational politics approach looks to larger groups such as **coalitions** that compete with each other to achieve political influence in an organization (Abdullah, 1997).

There are different 'triggers' for organizational politics and IM. The IM literature tends to consider both internal (e.g., personality) and external (e.g., environmental) triggers for IM behavior, whereas organizational politics traditionally has focused more on the external triggers in the organization. One such external trigger is **uncertainty**, resulting from the lack of clear objectives, poorly understood decision processes, strong competition, unclear performance measures (Beeman & Sharkey, 1987), or change (Raia, 1985). Uncertainty fosters more political behavior. Moreover, when people work in highly politicized environments, it affects them negatively. A study of nurses found that being around a lot of political behavior was a source of job stress and reduced job satisfaction, and it also led to more political behavior as a coping mechanism (Harrell-Cook, et al. 1999). Organizational politics begets organizational politics.

How, When, and Why Do We Use IM?

Before beginning our journey into the specifics of organizational IM, we first address some common questions that individuals new to the study of IM often ask. The first is 'How, when and why do we use IM'? If you were to ask university students why they chose a particular career or college major, they might list a series of reasons, or motives, for their behavior. Similarly, people carry out IM behaviors for a number of reasons. Just like a particular career could serve multiple ends – travel, opportunity, wealth – one IM behavior can serve several purposes. Take for example Emily, a young engineer at her first staff meeting trying to manage the impression she is an expert on applications using the World Wide Web. While we might initially think that Emily is acting the role of Web expert only to impress others, some theorists have argued that Emily may also be trying to impression manage herself as well (Baumeister, 1982). In Emily's case being seen as an expert might boost her own self-confidence and self-esteem concerning her professional abilities. To be an expert may signify for her that she is closer to the type of person she ultimately wants to be (her 'ideal self'). Emily may be managing the impression of Web expert for another reason – during her job interview she claimed to be a Web expert and two of the interviewers are sitting in this meeting. Thus, she needs to be consistent with her previous statements. Finally, Emily may be claiming the identity of Web expert as a way of influencing how others will treat her at work in the future. Convincing others that she is a Web expert will increase her chances of being assigned Web-intensive projects that would allow her to get choice job assignments and increase her job security and future promotion opportunities. For Emily, managing the image of expert could result from trying to accomplish all or any of these goals at the same time. Moreover, her motivation to manage the image of expert could change over time and in different situations as might be the case if the people who had interviewed her left the meeting, or as she gained more confidence about her ability and place in the organization.

As Emily's case study illustrates, people engage in IM for many reasons that are influenced by social, personal, and situational factors.

Some theorists explain how we choose when and what impressions to manage by characterizing individuals as engaging in a quick **cost-benefit analysis** (Schlenker, 1980). People are simultaneously assessing the benefits they might achieve from successfully presenting one image versus another, at the same time they are estimating the costs involved in portraying that image. They also figure in the likelihood that they will be able to carry off the IM, because if they can't, they risk being perceived as a fake, phony, or charlatan. To return to Emily, she is likely to manage the expert image if she feels she knows enough about the Web to carry it off and she sees more benefits than costs resulting from being perceived as a Web expert. In her case, benefits seem to exceed costs. However costs might exceed benefits if the Web application being developed was fraught with problems she might not be able to fix, so that she might be viewed as a lowly computer 'technician' rather than a multiply-talented Internet engineer.

We have defined IM as the attempt to influence the impressions that others form by controlling the information they receive. Therefore, it is not surprising that IM is more likely to occur in public, when other people are around. There are times, however, when we engage in IM even when no one is around. Sometimes we rehearse an IM attempt to fine-tune its potential effectiveness or to better anticipate its impact on an audience. A nervous employee may anticipate being questioned concerning her knowledge of a prank that caused the office voice-mail system to play the first line of the song 'Take this job and shove it' when incoming callers wanted to leave a message. She may imagine the interaction with her boss, formulate an explanation for why she was working late on the night of the episode and responses to follow-up questions he might ask, while carefully noting her facial expressions as she practiced responses to questions he might ask her the next day.

A three-component model

Leary and Kowalski (1990) proposed a theoretical model designed to help us better understand how, when and why we engage in IM. The three components in the model are **impression monitoring**, **impression motivation**, and **impression construction**. These can be seen in Figure 1.1. Impression monitoring occurs when individuals are conscious of the impressions they are making, either because of the particular situation they are in, or because they are the type of people who often are aware of the impressions they make. If people see IM as a way they can attain important goals or change the way they are perceived in a more desired direction, they will be motivated to engage in IM. The types of impressions people choose to construct depend on their self-concept, the type of identity they have or would like to have, the values they assume the audience has, and the setting for IM.

To see how this model might work, let us take the case of Steve Jobs as he started up a second computer company, NeXT, after being forced out of Apple in the late 1980s. It is very likely that Jobs did a lot of impression monitoring. The turmoil at Apple had taught him well that his every public action could be grist for the international media. Additionally, during his ouster from Apple, the press portrayed him

Figure 1.1	**Three Component Model of IM**

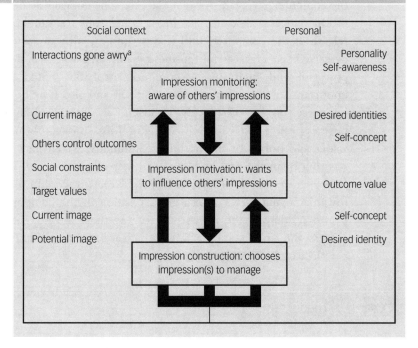

Source: Based on Leary and Kowalski, 1990, Leary 1993
Note: [a]Social context and personal variables are placed at points in the process they are most likely to influence

much more negatively than it had previously. Certainly, Jobs would have wanted to change this very negative image and so he would have been carefully monitoring how his actions were being perceived.

The second process in Leary's model is impression motivation. It seems safe to assume that Steve Jobs recognized a key to the success of his new company was improving his public image and ensuring his product was perceived positively. Thus, his impression motivation was high.

The selection of an image to construct is the final process in Leary and Kowalski's model. Jobs needed to be perceived as an effective businessperson and his product as useful and reliable. In contrast to the eccentric image he presented in Apple's early years, Jobs became very conscious of his physical appearance. It was written about him at that time, 'Rarely is he seen in jeans and sandals and never in the office in such attire; instead he wears elegant European suits tailored to fit his slender frame and he looks like a successful executive' (Butcher, 1989, pp. 216–17). The image of the NeXT computer also seems to have been carefully constructed. About $100,000 was spent on a logo long before the computer was ready for manufacture. The critical role of quality for product success in consumer markets led Jobs to want to delay the release of the computer until it was running without failures. To be perceived as a successful businessperson and to have developed a powerful and high quality computer probably would have been important for Jobs' personal sense of self and also how he wanted to be perceived by others. By choosing an image of an orthodox businessperson, our 'forever changing Jobs' was conforming to the values and norms of the business community, which may have made securing financing and building customer relations easier. If he could construct the image of high quality for NeXT, it would go a long way toward moving NeXT into a good position in the computer market. However, despite the intense use of IM there are no guarantees of success: the NeXT computer was a much admired powerful PC that few people actually purchased (Poniewozik, 2000).

Cybernetic model of IM

Bozeman and Kacmar (1997) proposed a **cybernetic model** that also tries to explain the how, when, and why of organizational IM. The model offers a goal-oriented, information processing view of IM, cybernetic model says people choose the particular identities they manage by looking at a combination of the value they assume will result from that particular IM behavior and how likely it is that they will be able to execute the behavior and obtain the desired outcome.

The cybernetic model assumes that IM behaviors are often aimed at achieving a certain identity that involves accomplishing a goal or **standard**. Individuals are assumed to have a standard for their behavior in mind and they judge whether they reach that standard based in part on feedback they receive from others. The model also assumes a **monitoring function** that allows people to regulate their IM to match the feedback they receive from an audience.

The cybernetic model assumes that in ongoing interaction individuals monitor whether they are achieving their desired identity. The desired identity feeds in to a comparison process in which the desired identity is compared to the current identity. When individuals feel there is a good match between their desired and current identities, their IM behaviors will be sustained to maintain that identity. If they need to adjust the current identity because there is a discrepancy between the desired and current identities, people will change their behavior. That information is fed back into the desired identity and the process continues.

To help you understand the cybernetic model, take the case of Zack, who after being laid-off when his company downsizes accepts a new position at a firm located near Detroit, Michigan. Zack is looking forward to making a fresh start and wants to get off on the right foot. He has an initial idea about how he is being perceived and a rough idea of what he should be doing and acts along those lines even though he has some uncertainty about how he should actually behave. He seeks advice (i.e., feedback) from many sources, including colleagues, workers, bosses, support staff, and his old buddy Norm who he used to work with at his previous job. Based on the feedback Zack gets and how he interprets it relative to how he wants to be perceived in the company, Zack continually adjusts his behavior and sees what effect it has on those he works with. In this way Zack's behavior is consistent with both the cybernetic model and research on employee adjustment to new work situations. This research indicates that as newcomers' conceptions of their roles, their job, and the effectiveness of their behaviors becomes clearer, they still watch for subtle cues about how they are being perceived, but as time goes on they stop asking for direct feedback from everyone but their supervisor (Callister, Kramer, & Turban, 1999). This makes sense since supervisors usually control key rewards.

Is IM Good or Bad?

The term IM as used in everyday conversation implies something disturbingly Machiavellian. However, researchers and practitioners who look beyond this commonsense understanding of IM see the pervasive and sometimes even beneficial effects of IM for social interactions and organizational life. Although IM surely can be used for unprincipled ends, we are coming to appreciate that it more frequently serves benign and even beneficial aims (Schlenker & Britt, 1999; Weatherly & Beach, 1994).

As we shall see in Chapters 4 and 5, some of the most interesting examples of IM at work are instances when it is used to extricate someone from problematic situations at home, with friends, or on the job. The field of IM is much broader, however. Each of us, even those not 'in trouble' of some sort, engage in IM as a normal part of our daily lives. Self-interest is only one of many motives for IM. People's IM can be used to help others as much as exploit them. Mike, for example, may agree with the opinions expressed by a potential benefactor to his university (an IM technique called opinion conformity, discussed in Chapter 2) so that the benefactor likes him and subsequently donates money for scholarships that assist students from low-income back-grounds. Both the interests of the benefactor and the students who will benefit from his philanthropy are well served by Mike's IM.

In our view, IM is neither inherently good nor bad but rather is a fundamental part of social and work lives. Whether IM is good or bad, ethical or unethical, really depends on *why* it is used and *what* effects it has; a decision that requires a judgment of the motives and consequences of the IM as used in a particular situation. Consider the case of Elizabeth, who appears to be considerate of the personal and professional needs of those who report to her as part of playing the role of being a good supervisor. If Elizabeth were being considerate so that her employees model her desirable behaviors and become a more effective and productive workgroup, few would call her IM immoral or bad. If she were using the trust gained from being a considerate supervisor to try and convince several employees to agree to an unfair early retirement package, that would be another story! In these two situations although the IM behaviors (being considerate) are the same, it is the motivation behind them and their desired effects that determine whether the IM used in these situations is good or bad.

Does IM Imply We Are Social Chameleons?

> A man will boast to one person of an action – say some sharp transaction
> in trade – which he would be ashamed to own to another
> (Cooley, 1964, p. 217).

Are we merely social chameleons constantly changing our identities depending on whom we are with, regardless of who we really are? Or, do we engage in IM to 'accurately' convey the type of person we are? The answer to both of these questions is 'sometimes, yes; sometimes no.' Mark Leary has pointed out that as more and more depends on the outcome of successful IM, the tendency to present images that would have a desired effect on an audience increases, even if the images are not accurate (Leary, 1993). Alternatively, when certain images are central to our sense of who we are, we are more likely to try to manage an impression consistent with our self-image, regardless of the situational constraints. Let us use the example of David, a would-be digital electronics expert, to illustrate how these factors interact. As the prestige of those in attendance at an important professional meeting he attends in Ithaca New York increases, so would David's desire to manage a good impression also increase. If he suspected the prestigious audience members would value his knowledge of new digital electronics components, he would be more likely to share that knowledge; if they seemed to view digital electronics experts as overly specialized nerds, he would probably choose to downplay his talents. Alternatively, if David felt he had invested much time and effort in becoming a digital electronics expert, and this was an important part of his self-concept, he would be more likely to present that image, regardless of the audience. If his expertise was just something David had picked up and cared little about it, he would not be as likely to try to present that image. Thus, in certain situations, we act like chameleons and change the identities we present to fit our surroundings. In other situations, especially with traits we consider important to our self-image, we are less chamelon-like.

It should be noted that consistency in IM is also important because inconsistency can lead an audience to question the accuracy of all of our communications. We previously noted that some at Apple felt Steve Jobs was not a good manager. He would say one thing and do another, which made them feel they 'couldn't believe a thing the guy said'. Thus, consistency in IM is important to managers of organizations. One way managers can make IM be seen as consistent and credible, is to make 'actions speak louder than words', as described in Box 1.2.

Box 1.2	**Consistency in IM: Actions Speak Louder than Words**

Many of us have heard from our parents that 'actions speak louder than words'. Manufacturing companies recognized the wisdom of this saying and are managing an impression of quality both in advertising and in their actions. In the eighties, one of the factors leading to the decline in market share of the US car industry is said to have been the poor perceived quality of American cars relative to those manufactured by the Japanese. Some American car companies responded with marketing campaigns that focused on the quality of their products. Yet their old negative image remained and that kept people from buying the cars.

One car company, then called the Chrysler Corporation, now called the DaimlerChrysler Corporation, realized that it would take more than verbal claims of increased quality. Instead, they said they would back up their claims with action. An advertising campaign they had at the time said, 'Buy one of our cars. . . Take it home, and within thirty days, if you don't like it for any reason, bring it back and we'll refund your money' (Iacocca, 1984, p. 181). Certainly, backing the claim of quality up with a promise of this type of action is a lot different from just making the claim.

At about this same time, Chrysler's financial troubles became widely publicized. While those in the company felt the problems would be turned around with the increased quality of their product, the sales had yet to arrive. However, the company's suppliers were becoming reluctant to ship parts for the improved products because the bills were not being paid. 'At the same ▶

time we had to keep the suppliers shipping their stuff to us, even when we didn't have enough money to pay them. The first thing we needed to do was convince them that we weren't heading into bankruptcy. You can't fool suppliers. They know your business very well. We brought them in. We showed them our future products. We let them know we were here to stay. We asked them to stand by us' (Iacocca, 1984, p. 186). This strategy was effective, presumably because, even though the company's claims that they would soon turn the financial picture around were easy to make, actually becoming familiar with the product and its performance carried more weight. IM words are more effective when bolstered by IM deeds.

In another example of how actions can make for effective IM, Eleuthere Irenee Du Pont, a creator of the huge DuPont corporation, built his family's house next to the powder yard as a way of convincing workers and the community that the danger from the production of gunpowder was not serious. Later he backed up his claims of being committed to his employees by caring financially for the survivors of a blast that leveled the powder mills.

(DuPont de Nemours and Company, 1952, p. 22)

Does Everyone Use IM?

Most interaction goals are mediated by the actor's attempts to manage
the general impressions others form of him or her as a person
(Jones, 1990, p. 168).

Concerns with face are salient in virtually all encounters
(Holtgraves, 1992, p. 141).

Although there are cultures in which its occurrence is less prevalent than in the United States or Western Europe (Hu, 1944), IM, in our view, is a universal phenomenon. As we shall see in Chapter 6, while everyone uses IM, there are individual differences in the form, frequency, and success of IM attempts. Certain people are more likely to try IM. Certain people are better at it than others (Turnley & Bolino, 2001). For example, while you might think that the authors of this text are themselves expert at managing impressions in their own lives, one of us is really a much better IMer than the other two (we won't say who except that it rhymes with a common lunch meat!).

According to a perspective called **evolutionary psychology**, IM behaviors are universal and evolved as a way of regulating human relationships. This perspective maintains that friendship relationships serve to support human survival through a **norm of reciprocity**: we help others and expect that they will help us in return. However, the give and take of reciprocity will be damaged if it is suspected that one of the parties has not or might not carry through as expected. IM can serve as a signal that one is sincere about giving to others and helps detect when others may be insincere. As Pinker writes, 'In humans, the talkative species, long-term reciprocity creates an arms race of IM. Everyone tries to show signs of integrity (exceeding that in actual behavior) while developing hypersensitive radar for such hypocrisy in others' (Pinker, 1994, p. 3).

Do We Consciously Manage Certain Impressions?

There is no compelling psychological reason why impression management must be either duplicitous or under conscious control. Impression management may be the product of highly over learned habits or scripts, the original functions of which people have long forgotten (Tetlock & Manstead, 1985, pp. 61–2).

The entire process of self-presentation gradually becomes over learned, automatic, and hence unconscious (Baumeister & Hutton, 1987, p. 72).

Certainly some IM behaviors are conscious. We may plan and rehearse our IM in preparation for important interactions like a job interview or first date. However, the reality is that much of our behavior including our IM is automatic; it occurs without awareness or with very little attention being devoted to it (Baumeister, 2000). Some of the most automatic behaviors are those we perform very frequently in the same situation, that are not of great difficulty, and are the ones we have performed successfully in the past. Because many of our behaviors fit in this category – like showing respect toward authority figures, not making rude gestures when obnoxious customers can see us, and keeping our shortcomings to ourselves – we may not be consciously aware of much of our IM. This may explain why when asked, very few people acknowledge the amount of IM they do on a daily basis. Research is beginning to make clear that people often are engaging in IM, even though they are not aware of it (Bozeman & Kacmar, 1997).

We can consider IM behaviors we do automatically as being our **IM habits**. Many nonverbal behaviors such as grimacing when a co-worker tries to take credit for our work, or smiling when receiving a compliment from 'the big boss' might fall in this category. As we shall see in Chapter 3, even though nonverbal behaviors often occur without our awareness, studies have shown that when we are consciously trying to create certain impressions, we use nonverbal behaviors effectively to accomplish our objectives (DePaulo, 1991).

We go off 'automatic pilot' and pay closer attention to our IM when we think the consequences of our behavior could be very good or bad. This would be the case when making a formal presentation at a business meeting, or when we suspect the image we are trying to present may be challenged, as might happen if we said something stupid during a job interview (Leary & Kowalski, 1990). In these situations we think more about IM tactics, their performance, and how the audience might react to them. Apparently, this contemplation of IM renders us more cautious in the images we choose to present, making us reluctant to present overly positive images. On the other hand, when we are managing impressions automatically, research has shown the impressions tend to be more positive (Paulhus, Graf, & VanSelst, 1989; Schlenker, in press).

Does IM Really Work?

Given all the time, money, and effort people and organizations put into IM, it seems clear they think it will work. Although the times we have failed in our IM attempts probably stick out more in our minds – the muffed job interview, getting caught shopping on a 'sick day' – most of the time we do it pretty well. Research has shown that people are quite good at using IM to communicate their internal experiences (DePaulo, 1992).

As we shall see in Chapters 4 and 5, IM not only works to make people view us more positively, it also is remarkably effective at damage control when we screw up. In a scenario study of US Senators charged with illegal actions, it was found some explanations given by the accused were quite effective in altering the way they were perceived (Riordan, et al., 1983). In fact, participants in that study were very forgiving of those who gave 'the proper' explanations for their behavior. How forgiving people are willing to be, however, may depend on how directly the perceiver is affected by the screw-up. A study of people's reactions to the mistakes of telephone solicitors and discount store baggers showed that when people were directly and negatively affected by the employee's errors, they evaluated them more negatively (Greenberg, 1996). This study demonstrates an important point about whether or not IM works: It depends on many factors. An example of one such subtle factor is consistency. A study of accountants at a New York accounting firm showed when they were inconsistent, their images were very negative (Crant, 1996). As we shall see throughout this book, whether IM works or doesn't often depends on more than just the IM itself. The situation in which IM occurs and the people involved are important parts of the equation as well.

Does IM Affect the Impression Manager?

It is easy to think about IM focusing only on how it affects others. After all, a primary purpose of IM is to influence the impressions others have of us. Yet, engaging in IM also affects how we think about ourselves. To illustrate the effect of IM on the impression manager, consider a study of people who reported 'playing dumb' across a variety of situations (Gove, Hughes, & Geerkin, 1980). The researchers found the people who played dumb the most often were also the ones with the poorest mental health. In the long run, portraying negative images may not be good for our health. Similarly, Tennen and Affleck (1991) concluded that people who are quick to blame others for their failures (a common form of defensive IM) are often not very well adjusted. This means the employee who always says 'it's not my fault' or 'it's not my job' may ultimately suffer for blaming others.

IM can also have positive effects on the impression manager. Training in the self-fulfilling prophecy, as described in Box 1.1, is a good example of some very positive effects of IM. In fact, the impact of IM probably falls on a continuum of adaptive to dysfunctional. It is also true that a total lack of IM would be seen as maladaptive. A friend involved in career counseling retold in amazement the story of a student who refused to dress up for an interview or to think about those things he might mention to an interviewer to present himself in a positive light. In fact, he felt it would be wrong of him to give answers that had been premeditated in any way, or even to hold back something an employer might want to know. As you might suspect, this individual is still unemployed!

A Concluding Note

We hope this introductory chapter has given you a sense of what the rest of this book holds in store. We will discuss many aspects of organizational IM not included in this chapter. The questions we raised will be addressed in greater detail. You will come away with an understanding of what organizational IM is, and is not; the various tactics and strategies of IM, the reasons they are used, and when they are most likely to occur; and the effects IM has on audiences and IMers. First we will deal with IM strategies for looking good, followed by strategies to avoid looking bad. Differences among individuals in their tendencies to engage in IM and how to measure those differences will follow. Applications of IM to the area of human resource management will be outlined. We conclude with a presentation of new, emerging, and future areas of IM research and practice. We hope you will come to share our enthusiasm for this exciting area of organizational behavior and gain a clear understanding of how influencing the impressions of others is an integral part of organizational life.

2 Ingratiation

Willy was a salesman. And for a salesman, there is no rock
bottom to life. He's a man way out there in the blue, riding on a
smile and a shoeshine. And when they start not smiling back
– that's an earthquake
(Arthur Miller, 1969, *Death of a Salesman*).

Winning Friends and Influencing People

He was a poor Missouri farm boy, shy and not very athletic. He
suffered from feelings of inferiority and eventually sought public
speaking so that people would notice him. The poor farm boy became
a teacher of public speaking and, in 1936, published a book outlining
his recipe for success. Neither the author, Dale Carnegie, nor the
publisher, Simon and Schuster expected the book to sell much; the
original printing of *How to Win Friends and Influence People* was just
5,000 copies. Much to their surprise, the book became one of the great
bestsellers in world history! At the time of Carnegie's death in 1955
the book had sold nearly five million copies, eventually being second
only to the Bible in nonfiction sales. By 1987, *How to Win Friends and
Influence People* had sold 15 million copies, had been translated into
over 35 languages, and the motivational course inspired by Carnegie's
writings had graduated over three million students in 69 countries.
The Carnegie course became very popular in the corporate world with
many management professionals and trainees completing the basic
course as well as targeted courses in customer relations, sales, and the
'executive image' (Abrams, 1991; Johnson, 1987). One measure of the
popularity of Carnegie's message in the corporate world is that 80 per

cent of the Fortune 500 companies have paid for Carnegie training for at least some of their employees (Abrams, 1991) The Dale Carnegie Institute currently grosses about 100 million dollars per year (Stengel, 2000).

While Dale Carnegie's success was phenomenal his message was simple: 'Never find fault, never argue, flatter people at every opportunity, appear sincere, and smile, smile, smile' (Stengel, 2000, p. 203). Like Willy Loman, the salesman in our opening quote, the key to success often rides 'on a smile and a shoeshine'.

Carnegie stressed the importance of praising others and noted that one of the most effective selling techniques is to make other people like you (Schlenker, 1980). Like the expansive view of IM, Carnegie believed that one could both be sincere and expert in interpersonal influence; that while social influence could be used deceptively, it did not necessarily have to be so.

Dale Carnegie's formula for success shares much with the focus of this chapter, **ingratiation** – tactics and strategies aimed at making others like you. Carnegie's common-sense analysis of ways of winning friends and influencing people, although appealing, has been largely unexamined (Abrams, 1991). Like Erving Goffman's views of IM described in Chapter 1, Carnegie's are based on his own insights and experiences rather than systematic research. In contrast, ingratiation tactics described in this chapter have been the subject of much scientifically oriented research by organizational and management scientists as well as social psychologists. We summarize this research and systematically apply its findings to work settings.

As did Carnegie, IM theory assumes that a basic human motive, both inside and outside of organizations, is to be seen by others in favorable manner and to avoid being viewed negatively (Rosenfeld, Giacalone, & Riordan, 1995). These attempts to be seen favorably or positively are called **acquisitive** IM while defensive tactics that seek to minimize deficiencies and avoid disapproval are called **protective** IM (Arkin, 1981; Palmer, Walker, Campbell, & Magner, 2001). Both acquisitive and protective IM tactics can be **directly** applied by the parties involved or occur **indirectly** through association (Cialdini, 1989). In this chapter we describe the most studied acquisitive impression tactic – ingratiation. Other acquisitive tactics, both direct and indirect, will be reviewed in Chapter 3. We present the various protective IM tactics in Chapters 4 and 5.

Ingratiation: An Overview

And in our faults by lies we flattered be
William Shakespeare, *Sonnet 138* (quoted in Stengel, 2000, p. 18).

Performance is important; you've got to perform. But ingratiation does
something more. It gives you an edge
Psychologist Ronald Deluga (quoted in Odom, 1993, p. E–12).

Ingratiation is the most common and most studied of IM techniques. Edward E. Jones (1964), one of the pioneers of IM research first described ingratiation. Dr Linda Ginzel, one of Jones' students, provides a 'behind the scenes' look at his profound influence on her career and IM research.

Ingratiation refers to a set of related IM tactics that have as their collective goal making the person more liked and attractive to others (Jones, 1990). We might call ingratiation 'attraction management' (Pandey & Singh, 1987) and view it as the scientific study of behaviors related to what more commonly is known as flattery (Stengel, 2000). As originally conceptualized by Jones (1964), ingratiation was defined as 'a class of strategic behaviors illicitly designed to influence a particular other person concerning the attractiveness of one's personal qualities' (p. 11). The ingratiator subscribes to the philosophy that, 'you can catch more flies with honey than vinegar'. During the 1980s, a popular anti-drug slogan in the United States was 'Just Say NO!' The ingratiator's slogan might be 'Just Say HELLO!'

While Jones' original view was that ingratiation was inherently illicit ('ingratiating actions are illicit because they are directed toward objectives not contained in the implicit contract which underlies social interaction', Jones, 1964, p. 11), organizational researchers have increasingly destigmatized these various forms of attraction management. They have argued that ingratiation is a common, often effective and acceptable means of social influence in organizations (Ralston, 1985; Ralston & Elsass, 1989). As Liden and Mitchell (1988, p. 574) note, 'the use of ingratiatory behaviors may not always involve devious methods to manipulate others... In fact, an individual may not be consciously aware that he or she is using ingratiatory behaviors.' Like other types of IM, ingratiation may be an automatic response triggered by certain social or environmental cues, in particular those that

Behind the Scenes
Linda E. Ginzel

It is impossible to describe how I became interested in the topic of IM and the nature of my research without knowledge of the profound impact of my advisor and mentor Edward E. Jones. As a Ph.D. student at Princeton, Ned taught me how to think about interpersonal perception within the framework of experimental social psychology. He introduced me to both the study of attributional logic (how do people infer the causes of behavior?) and its flip side (how do people elicit desirable attributions?).

My first experiments, with Ned Jones and Bill Swann, explored people's intuitive understanding of attributional reasoning and investigated the conditions necessary for people to behave as attribution theories predict they should. The results demonstrate how difficult it is for people to identify accurately the impact of their own behavior in shaping the behavior of others. Since that time, I have been intrigued by this powerful notion: What we observe in others is often shaped by our actions, yet we tend to treat these reactions of others as independent of our own influence.

As I became more and more interested in understanding the reciprocal nature of interpersonal perception and social interaction, I also shifted my focus from attitude attribution to judgments of task performance and ability. I took time off from my Ph.D. studies and worked as an internal management consultant for Mutual of New York. It was there that I discovered the relevance of social psychology in an organizational context and began to develop the idea of a dynamic evaluator-performer feedback sequence. I returned to graduate school and conducted an experiment which demonstrated that evaluators underestimate the impact of their own behavior, resulting in biased performance judgments (Ginzel, 1994). A second related experiment focused on the active role that performers (i.e., targets of evaluation) play in conveying a desired impression to the evaluator. Research in this area has interesting implications for the different strategies employed in managing impressions of competence versus likability in performance-relevant settings.

I took my first job at Stanford's Graduate School of Business and made the transition from social psychology to organizational ▶

behavior. It was during this time that I became interested in organizational IM due in large part to my colleagues Bob Sutton and Rod Kramer. During my two years there, we had lively discussions about the role of the organizational audience in shaping the IM process. Ultimately, we developed the idea that organizational IM is a process of reciprocal influence and conceptualized IM as a negotiated 'settlement' involving organizational actors (top management) and the targets (members of the organizational audience) of their influence attempts. I also became interested in what I refer to as **self-presentation by proxy**, involving situations when a third-party makes competence claims on behalf of another.

For the future, I hope to better understand the attributional reasoning that underlies interpersonal relations and the strategic use of attributional logic for IM. By studying the reciprocal nature of interpersonal perception and social interaction, I am returning to a theme that Ned Jones (with John Thibaut) introduced us to 40 years ago.

highlight differences in social status (Gordon, 1996). A character on the 1960s TV show, *Laugh In* used to scream, 'Here come da Judge'. For many organizational members, knowing that 'da judge' 'da boss' or others higher in status are coming is more than enough to turn on an **ingratiation script** without lots of planning or premeditation,

Rather than being illicit, we believe that ingratiation can have positive benefits in organizations and should be sanctioned under certain circumstances. Judiciously used, ingratiation can facilitate positive interpersonal relationships and increase harmony within and outside of the organization. In Chapter 8, we suggest that IM techniques such as ingratiation may be crucial to members of racial/ethnic minority groups, women, immigrants, and expatriates who often need to please majority group members in positions of greater social power. By generating liking and feelings of good will, ingratiation may counter natural cognitive tendencies to stigmatize, stereotype, and devalue people who are different (Allison & Herlocker, 1994). In achieving his or her goal – increasing liking and attraction – the successful ingratiator becomes familiar, activates norms of reciprocity, and goes from a stereotyped outsider to a liked insider. Viewed in this way, ingratiation can be a useful work skill rather than a sleazy, deceptive tactic (Strutton,

Pelton, & Lumpkin, 1995). Although organizations can suffer if they only reward yes-men and disdain criticism (Odom, 1993), ingratiation, in proper doses, is a binding and unifying force, melding diverse subgroups in the face of tendencies that seek to divide them. As Ralston (1985, p. 478) has written, 'In fact, it may be argued that moderate levels of ingratiatory behavior are beneficial to the organization in that it may be a form of social glue that builds cohesive work groups in the absence of compatibility.'

Ingratiation creates **compelling illusions** (Clark & Salaman, 1998) that help persuade employees that they like each other. This liking can enhance workplace cooperation, teamwork, and ultimately productivity. In many organizations, a little deception goes a long way! The truth may set you free, but in organizations it can be costly. That ingratiation pays – literally – was the conclusion of a study of supervisor-subordinate pairs (described by Odom, 1993). That study found that ingratiation gives an employee a 4 to 5 percent edge in their salaries over those who depend only on job performance. Additional 'food for thought' was obtained in a study of tipping behavior in restaurants. Rind and Bordia (1996) reported that servers who smiled, wrote 'thank you' and drew happy faces on the back of customers' checks received higher tips than those who didn't.

Of all IM tactics, ingratiation may be the one most immediately translatable to the workplace. Many organizations themselves engage in ingratiation through their advertising campaigns, promotional events, and annual reports (Mohamed, Gardner, & Paolillo, 1999). At the individual level, because the need for ingratiation and likelihood of its occurrence rise with increasing power differentials (Schlenker, 1980), the hierarchical organization is the breeding ground of ingratiation and the employee–supervisor relationship – one built on power differences – its most prototypical example (Deluga & Perry, 1994).

During the Total Quality movement of the 1990s and followed by other empowering employee approaches of the twenty-first century, many business models moved away from the hierarchical management style, gave employees greater decision-making responsibility and even referred to them in more embracing terms as 'team members' or 'associates'. We believe that ingratiation exists even in the most quality oriented organizations (Knouse, 1996). In our experience, the chain of command is still alive and well – whether in a formal way as in the Vatican or the military, or informally – even in so-called flat organizations, those where the terms 'supervisor' and 'subordinate' are forbidden 's' words.

Our view is that power differences are why ingratiation is common in the workplace. The employee, often a person low in power resources, may have few other options except for ingratiation to influence the more powerful supervisor. A successfully ingratiating subordinate who has been able to make the supervisor like her, has achieved a great deal since the supervisor is now more likely to reward and less likely to punish her (Schlenker, 1980). In this way, the ingratiating subordinate has achieved a measure of social influence over the powerful superior. By manipulating supervisors to like them, successful ingratiators limit their supervisor's options to punish and control. Employee ingratiation is therefore **power enhancing** in that it restricts the 'degrees of freedom' or control that the target has over the subordinate (Kumar & Beyerlein, 1991). If successful, the ingratiator pulls off a subtle power shift, undetectably moving power from the target to him or herself, leaving the interaction with a better 'face' than when they started (Stengel, 2000). Skilled ingratiators, it has been said, are masters of 'immaculate deception'.

Nearly 40 years ago, this organizational dynamic was brilliantly described by Edward Jones,

> he [the ingratiator] may try to amuse his boss with a joke during a conference thus taking time which might have been spent in fulfilling the stated conference purpose of detailing market conditions in the Dubuque (Iowa) area. Insofar as such 'extra-curricular activities' succeeded, he becomes attractive to the target person's eyes; and an important consequence of this gain in attractiveness is an enhanced ability to control the target person

> *(Jones, 1964, p. 11).*

In applying these notions to the workplace, Wayne and Ferris (1990) have suggested a **cognitive information-processing model** whereby subordinate ingratiation attempts lead to a cycle of events that positively bias the nature of the employee-supervisor relationship.

> [T]he successful use of ingratiation by a subordinate may lead a supervisor to form a positive impression of that subordinate and to attribute desirable qualities to him or her. On the basis of these positive attributions and impressions, the supervisor may categorize the employee

favorably; doing so may influence the supervisor's immediate responses to the employee, such as affect, and later decisions about the employee, including performance ratings and behaviors related to exchange quality

(Wayne & Ferris, 1990, p. 488).

Given the dynamics of most organizations, it is safe to say that ingratiation is an everyday occurrence. One study found that more than one quarter of managers indicated that they encountered ingratiation on a frequent basis (Allen, Madison, Porter, Renwick, & Mayes, 1979). Furthermore, this occurrence of employee ingratiation may be expected to intensify when: (a) resources are scarce; (b) individuals are very dependent on each other; (c) job criteria and performance appraisal criteria are subjective; and (d) objective personnel policies are few or not well enforced (Liden & Mitchell, 1988). These all seem to be characteristics common in many twenty-first century organizations.

Far from being a simple prescription, however, successful ingratiation is an interpersonal minefield that requires skill to prevent backfiring (Crant, 1996) and avoidance of the dreaded attribution that one is a deliberate manipulator. Research on ingratiation suggests a number of methods, techniques, and strategies associated with increased probabilities of success. The nature of ingratiation, its specific forms, and implications for the workplace are discussed below.

Types of Ingratiation

Opinion Conformity

When Aristotle said, 'birds of a feather flock together' he intuitively saw what social scientists have extensively documented: similarity breeds attraction. According to Donn Byrne's law of attraction (Byrne, 1971), the greater the proportion of similar attitudes that two people share the more they will like each other. Ingratiators often capitalize on the similarity-attraction relationship by becoming 'social chameleons' who are experts in the art of opinion conformity. These modern-day Zeligs express opinions or act in ways consistent with another person's attitudes, beliefs, and values so as to increase liking (Bohra & Pandey, 1984; Ralston, 1985). An organizational example was provided by Lee

Iacocca, the noted former US auto industry executive. According to Iacocca (1984, p. 98), conformity to the proper executive image really mattered to Henry Ford, II when he was the CEO of Ford Motor Company: 'If a guy wore the right clothes and used the right buzz words, Henry was impressed. But without the right veneer, forget it.'

There is research supporting the effectiveness of opinion conformity in the workplace. According to the results of a study of 152 supervisor/subordinate pairs (described by Odom, 1993), opinion conformity is a common and effective form of ingratiation. The conclusion was that opinion conformity and other forms of 'kissing up' to the boss work, even though the tactics themselves are sometimes transparent to co-workers and the bosses themselves. As Odom (1993, p. E-12) writes, 'They [ingratiation tactics] work because it is human nature to appreciate compliments, to want reassurance that your attitudes are correct and to like the people who admire you. So even when the boss knows you are kissing up, it still pays off – literally – in positive job evaluations, promotions, and higher pay.'

Like other forms of ingratiation, opinion conformity thrives on power differentials such as those between bosses and subordinates. In an early ingratiation study, Jones and his colleagues showed that opinion conformity occurred when a supervisor had the power to evaluate a subordinate's performance (Jones, Gergen, Gumpert, & Thibaut, 1965). They had respondents rank the effectiveness of advertising slogans in increasing sales. Respondents later overheard a supervisor express either the value of group cooperation or of independence in accomplishing work tasks. The supervisor was either to have the power to evaluate the respondents' performance on the task or not. On an attitude survey completed after they found this out, respondents expressed opinion conformity only when the supervisor had the power to evaluate their performance.

In general, the greater the difference in power between two people in an organizational setting the greater the likelihood that the lower status individual will imitate the attitudes and behaviors of the higher status person. An applicant being interviewed for a job by an avowed vegetarian may offer that she eats very little red meat and fears Mad Cow disease. A male employee transferred to a female supervisor may claim he deplores the prevalence of sexual harassment. A graduate student seeking a dissertation topic may cite evidence supporting her mentor's pet theory. In a study demonstrating organizational opinion conformity, female job applicants tailored their nonverbal and verbal behaviors to match the views of women held by their interviewer (Von Baeyer, Sherk, & Zanna, 1981). When the male interviewer was known to hold views congruent with the traditional female stereotype, female applicants gave more traditional responses to questions about family and relationships, spent more time on their physical appearance and were less assertive in their verbal and nonverbal behaviors than when the interviewer held less traditional attitudes. We will have more to say on IM in job interviews in Chapter 7.

As with many workplace IM tactics, opinion conformity is often strategically applied to fit the ingratiator's goals. A study by Jellison and Gentry (1978) illustrates this point. In a simulated job interview situation, some role-playing applicants were informed that the interviewer hired people he liked while others learned that he hired individuals he did not like. Applicants had access to information about the job interviewer's attitudes. On a later selection test, applicants adjusted their attitude statements to the hiring philosophy of the interviewer: they matched attitudes when the interviewer hired those he liked and expressed divergent views when they thought the interviewer hired those he did not like.

In addition to power differentials, availability of resources in an organization affects the occurrence of opinion conformity. The more limited resources are, the more ingratiation tactics such as opinion conformity are likely to occur (Liden & Mitchell, 1988). Pandey and Rastogi (1979) supported this contention. Individuals participated in a hypothetical job interview in a situation that was either competitive (20 job applicants available for 10 jobs) or noncompetitive (20 job applicants available for 40 jobs). More opinion conformity occurred in the competitive situation.

The boss's illusion

While managers and other organizational leaders are often rewarded with higher status, pay, and more control over what they do, there is a downside as well. The further one advances in an organization the more they may become the target of scrutiny and criticism. Expressions such as 'it's lonely at the top' also suggest that managers may become isolated from the realities of their employees' lives. Roy Baumeister

(1989) has described a phenomenon called the **boss's illusion** that illustrates how opinion conformity can lead managers and supervisors to have distorted views of reality. According to Baumeister, the behaviors, attitudes, and values of leaders often become standards that are followed by others. One example is the popularity of red ties in the US because many political leaders favor them. As Baumeister (1989, p. 65) notes, 'If bosses present themselves as energetic, athletic persons, for example, the subordinates may start to drop remarks about their weekend jogging marathons or after-hours racquetball conquests. If bosses present themselves as casual mavericks – or as strict, staunch adherents to organizational policy and prestige – the subordinates may follow suit.' This matching of attitudes and behaviors to those of the boss is, of course, classic IM, and textbook opinion conformity. The boss, however, thinks that a subordinate's actions reflect real views rather than being strategic IM. 'Bosses may think that subordinates are really similar to themselves, when in fact the subordinates' behavior is simply a reflection of their influence' (Baumeister, 1989, p. 65). The boss's illusion refers to this misreading of a subordinate's real views by their superiors.

The boss's illusion may have negative consequences when a subordinate leaves for another job. Freed from the influence of the former boss they may no longer act like the boss does. The boss may be predictably dismayed by this sudden turnaround. 'If they [subordinates] revert to other patterns when the bosses' influence ends, and the boss learns this, the boss may perceive them as disloyal and hypocritical' (Baumeister, 1989, p. 65). The boss's illusion may be one reason why once close mentoring relationships (e.g., graduate students and dissertation advisors) often sour and end on a discordant note (Baumeister 1989; Levinson 1978).

Successful opinion conformity

A number of strategies has been associated with successful opinion conformity.

1. Mixing disagreement with agreement

Because all ingratiation tactics risk backfiring if too obvious, successful opinion conformity is best if disguised and complicated. When obviously tied to a reward, or close in time to important events such as performance evaluation or promotion requests, the best advice is not to use it (Stengel, 2000). To make opinion conformity work, one approach is to mix agreement and disagreement with the target's attitudes (Jones, 1990). Disagreement should be given unsurely on trivial issues while agreement is given confidently on important issues. Disagreeing with the boss over who is going to win the Wimbledon tennis tournament (a trivial issue) serves to enhance the credibility of later agreement with the boss's plans for a new marketing strategy (an important issue). Given previous disagreement, conformity appears to be sincere rather than feigned IM. Jones, Jones, and Gergen (1963) showed the effectiveness of mixing agreement and disagreement. They found that someone who occasionally agreed with a powerful target was liked better by the target than a person who agreed consistently.

2. Yielding: expressing initial disagreement and gradually changing to agreement

The consistent 'yes' man – someone who always agrees with the boss – runs the risk of being viewed as gutless or weak. One way to augment opinion conformity is to initially disagree with the boss's views on an issue but gradually over time be 'persuaded' as to the wisdom of his or her beliefs (Wortman & Linsenmeier, 1977). Yielding allows a person to simultaneously reap the benefits of opinion conformity – increased liking – while also managing the impression of autonomy: the kind of person who thinks for oneself.

3. 'Lick-up, kick-down': agree with the boss while publicly disagreeing with others

It has been said, that one definition of hell is middle-management. The middle manager is caught between the need to ingratiate the boss while also maintaining an image for those he or she supervises. One way the manager in the middle can enhance her own opinion conformity with her boss is to disagree clearly and publicly with others, usually peers or subordinates, while still agreeing with the boss (Stengel, 2000). As with yielding, an illusion of autonomy is maintained and conformity with the boss is enhanced.

While 'lick-up, kick-down' may help win kudos with the boss, it can prove costly to one's image among those being kicked – subordinates.

Vonk (1998) called the behavior pattern of kissing up to superiors while being disagreeable to subordinates, the **slime effect**. In studies with Dutch students, he found that the 'lick-up, kick-down' pattern resulted in very negative ratings of the manager among those being kicked. A middle-manager who kisses up to the boss by agreeing with the boss's views, arouses suspicions among subordinates that the behavior is simply done to impress rather than to express a true view, especially since observers of ingratiation are more skeptical than are its targets (Gordon, 1996). Kicking-down by disagreeing with subordinates only confirms their worst suspicions – the middle-manager will say anything to get ahead.

4. Pre-emptive conformity

Timing is everything, both in the entertainment world and the world of the ingratiator. Stengel (2000) suggests that a way of making opinion conformity work is to anticipate a target's views and express them before they do. In the workplace, we might call this sort of educated guessing, 'beating the boss to the hunch'. Say that Niles knows that his supervisor Sarah tends to look down on the firm's HR department but has high regard for outside consultants. When Sarah calls a meeting to discuss the firm's annual Diversity training, Niles pipes up, 'No one much fancies what our HR department puts out, but I hear that the consulting firm, "Diversity Costs" really gives a whiz-bang presentation.' 'Brilliant' says Sarah, 'just what I was thinking!'

Favor-doing

The second major form of ingratiation behaviors capitalizes on the simple truth that a good way to instill liking is by doing favors for others. The favor-doer hopes to capitalize on the **norm of reciprocity** which is a universal rule of social behavior suggesting that we should help or pay back those who help or do favors for us (Gouldner, 1960). Favor doing – especially when the favor is unrequested – instills liking and an obligation to 'try to repay in kind what another person has provided us' (Cialdini, 1993, p. 17). Many charitable organizations have found that donations increase when the original solicitation contains an unrequested gift such as customized address labels (Cialdini, 1993).

The ingratiator, however, typically seeks liking rather than a reciprocal exchange of gifts. This leads to an intriguing possibility: From an ingratiator's standpoint the most effective type of favor is one which *cannot* be readily reciprocated (Jones, 1964). The favor-doer seeks to 'trigger a feeling of indebtedness' (Cialdini, 1993, p. 30) which can be exploited as a powerful means of social influence. So if you loan the boss ten Euros to buy lunch, he can easily repay the money later. However, if you install a new CD player in the boss's car (something the boss cannot do himself), the favor may be 'repaid' in increased liking and subsequent organizational rewards such as favorable performance evaluations and promotions.

One of the few organizational studies that looked at favor doing as a form of ingratiation assessed the various tactics used by modern-day Willy Lomans – salespeople (Strutton, Pelton, & Lumpkin, 1995). They found that in their interactions with customers, salespeople do indeed get by on a 'smile and a shoeshine' as well as other ingratiation tactics such as favor doing.

Other-Enhancement

> Buttering up the boss is celebrated in folkways and in the literature
> as the royal road to organizational advancement and success
> (Kipnis & Vandeveer, 1971, p. 281 as quoted by Aryee,
> Wyatt, & Stone, 1996, p. 100).

> Brownnosing goes on every day and everywhere simply because
> it is functional to establish a favorable impression with those
> that can potentially affect one's outcome
> (Vonk, 1998, p. 861).

Dale Carnegie preached that, 'the average man is more interested in his own name than all the other names on earth put together, (quoted in Stengel, 2000, p. 197). To Carnegie, honestly praising others and using their names, were the keys to being successful. Research has shown that these forms of strategic praise called **other-enhancement** are an effective type of ingratiation behaviors. We tend to like those who like us, praise us, give us positive evaluations, and bolster our self-esteem (Ralston & Elsass, 1989). Since most people have a need to be liked, other-enhancement works whether the target is your bosom-buddy or your boss. Other-enhancement tells us that others like us and helps validate our self-image. It benefits both parties: the ingratiator who gains social power through being liked, and the target, who gains enhanced self-esteem when others come to praise him (Stengel, 2000).

The ingratiator exploits the simple and powerful social rule – that we like those who praise us – to increase the target's attraction towards her. An other-enhancer may manage the impression that she thinks the world of her boss. The boss's positive qualities such as efficiency, intelligence, and appearance are stressed, emphasized, and exaggerated, while negative traits like impatience, temper, and short-sightedness are minimized, distorted, or ignored. If properly disguised and strategically employed, other-enhancement can be a powerful means of getting ahead in an organization. Wright (1979, discussed in Ralston, 1985) claimed that successful executives at General Motors were those who most skillfully flattered their bosses.

Several studies have demonstrated the effectiveness of other-enhancement in organizations. In a classic work, Kipnis and Vanderveer (1971) placed research participants in a situation where they thought they were supervising workers manufacturing products on an assembly line. The participants were told they could send messages to and receive messages from the workers. In actuality, the nature of all the messages was controlled by the researchers to establish the experimental conditions. The messages were manipulated so that one of the hypothetical workers was clearly superior to the other two who both were average performers. One of the two average performers sent other-enhancing messages to the 'boss'. The messages indicated that the boss was a 'nice guy' who could count on the subordinate for help and faster work if needed. Kipnis and Vanderveer found that the use of other-enhancement influenced ratings of the subordinate by the boss-respondents. The average other-enhancer received performance evaluations as high as that of the superior performer and better than the average noningratiating worker – even though their actual performances were the same as the noningratiating workers. Other-enhancement had the rather profound effect of making the ratings of an average worker the same as someone whose actual performance was clearly better! Thus, performance is important, but so is ingratiation. All things being equal, it gives those who practice it well an edge.

Other-enhancement was also found to be effective in a simulation study by Pandey and Kakkar (1982). They had role-playing work supervisors send 'subordinates' a note explaining a job that the subordinate was to learn. The subordinates replied to the note in either an other-enhancing or nonenhancing manner. It was found that subordinates who sent supervisors the flattering replies were subsequently rated by the supervisors as more attractive, intelligent, and viewed as being more successful and promotable. They were also offered more help and recommended for higher wages. Independent of performance, other-enhancement offers the potential for dramatically improving a person's organizational outcomes. This is particularly the case when people of similar performance apply for a job, have their performance evaluated, or are up for a promotion. Ingratiation in the form of other-enhancement may then serve as the tiebreaker (Stengel, 2000).

Successful other-enhancement

While other-enhancement may seem plausible in theory, it is not always effective in practice. Because there are negative labels associated with obvious or excessive other-enhancement (see Table 2.1), the technique runs the risk of backfiring.

What makes for effective other-enhancement? Several approaches increase the likelihood of success.

1. Use of third parties

The risk of detection can be minimized if a third party is used to deliver the flattering message (Liden & Mitchell, 1988). Linda Ginzel (see 'Behind the Scenes') has aptly called this **self-presentation by proxy**. Stengel (2000) recommends complimenting a person behind their back. As Wortman and Linsenmeier (1977, p. 145) note, 'If a manager is told by one of his colleagues that another colleague made favorable remarks about him, he is unlikely to conclude that the remarks were made to obtain his affection'. Say Robert wants to tell his boss Anna that he really likes her and she is the best boss he has ever worked for. Rather than telling Anna this directly, Robert instead praises Anna to her secretary Tina. The hope is that eventually Tina will pass this on to

Table 2.1	**Risks of Ingratiation: Some Negative Terms Associated with Blatant Other-Enhancement**

1. apple-polisher
2. back scratcher
3. boot-licker
4. brownnoser
5. butt-kisser/ass-kisser
6. cajoler
7. fawner
8. flunky
9. kiss-up
10. panderer
11. suck-up
12. sweet-talker
13. sycophant
14. toady
15. yes-man

Based on: O'Brien (1993); Stengel (2000)

Anna, and Robert will gain the benefits of other-enhancement without risking its dangers.

2. Making compliments credible

To be effective, other-enhancement must be credible. To maintain credibility, factors such as **timing**, **frequency**, and **discernment** should be considered. **Timing** means that the delivery of other-enhancement should not be linked to a desired goal. Asking for a promotion right after telling the boss how bright she is may make the strategic nature of the compliment obvious and counterproductive. The **frequency** of other-enhancement is also a factor in its likely success. In general, other-enhancement is a tactic best used sparingly. When dealing with the boss, it's a good idea not to bury Caesar with praise! If Tanja gains a reputation as one who uses compliments all the time, this will likely undermine the effectiveness of her future attempts at flattery. When Henry is intent on ingratiating his supervisor, he is best advised to limit how often he compliments other people in the supervisor's presence.

Lastly, effective other-enhancement should be **discerning,** since indiscriminate other-enhancement is likely to fail. An effective approach is to mix flattery with criticism – the compliments should be in important areas and the negative comments in trivial areas or in **acknowledged areas of weakness.** For example, when Catherine points out to her boss Ralph, that he is driving too fast, the credibility of her also saying that Ralph's presentation at the company's annual sales meeting was fantastic is enhanced. Additionally, one should not compliment everyone in the same manner, but should compliment others on characteristics that are not obvious and offer compliments about things that targets are uncertain about (Stengel, 2000). It has been found that other-enhancement is more likely to be effective when it stresses the target's personal effectiveness (Ralston & Elsass, 1989) or is for characteristics the target finds desirable but is unsure that he or she possesses (Schlenker, 1980).

Self-Enhancement

The fourth and final type of ingratiation is self-enhancement – directly using IM to make oneself be seen as more attractive (Schlenker, 1980). Through self-enhancement the ingratiator's best characteristics are made apparent to target audiences. The goal of this form of ingratiation is to find out what the target thinks is attractive and claim it for oneself.

In organizational settings, self-enhancement is commonplace in job interviews (see Chapter 7). The candidate who really wants a job in a sales department may stress how good he is at relating to people and how persuasive he is in conversations with others. This technique of playing up one's strengths may be effective. It has been found that job applicants who used IM tactics that focused on themselves were rated higher than applicants whose IM tactics focused on the interviewer (Kacmar, Delery, & Ferris, 1992).

That successful self-enhancement may be as important as actual performance in determining organizational outcomes has been suggested by the popular linguist Deborah Tannen (1994) as a reason for why men are often more successful than women in many work settings. In studying how men and women differ in their language patterns, Tannen has claimed that men in work situations tend to engage in more ingratiating behaviors than women do; the impact being that men benefit more even though they aren't necessarily better performers. As Shapiro (1994, p. 59) summarizes Tannen's view, 'she describes men in the workplace who boast and brag, take credit for others' accomplishments and shamelessly court the boss. It works: they get promoted. The women Tannen writes about are far more modest; they concentrate on doing a good job in the belief that it will be rewarded. They're wrong: it isn't.' There is research suggesting that women's lack of self-enhancement may act as an 'invisible career barrier' (Singh & Vinnicombe, 2001, p. 183). Male salespersons were more likely to use self-enhancement than were women salespersons (Strutton et al., 1995). Men had higher scores on a measure of their tendency to use ingratiation (Lee, Quigley, Nesler, Corbett, & Tedeschi, 1999). Conversely, even when women's performance does not differ from that of men, they tend to be more modest in describing it (Heatherington, Burns, & Gustafson, 1998). Thus, while men readily, boast, brag, shout their own praises and get rewarded for it, women in work settings often sell themselves short, hoping that they will be judged on the basis of their performance. While in a perfect world, good performance would speak for itself, in the real world of work it rarely does.

When individuals do engage in self-enhancement to please significant others, reality serves to constrain overly self-aggrandizing presentations. If information exists that could repudiate an overly positive claim, individuals will present themselves in a more accurate fashion, one that is closer to what they really believe (Schlenker, 1980). Cascio (1975) found that exaggeration in resumés and application blanks was less likely to occur when the information could be verified by previous employers.

When reality constrains self-enhancement in one area, individuals may engage in **compensatory IM**. Baumeister and Jones (1978) found that respondents who scored poorly on a personality test did not contradict this to an observer who knew of their poor performance. However, they engaged in compensatory IM by exaggerating their personality descriptions for characteristics that the audience had no direct information about. Therefore, one factor associated with successful self-enhancement is how much information the audience has about the claim and how easy it would be for them to check. The general rule, as stated by Schlenker (1980, p. 188) is, 'the more difficult it is for the audience to check the veracity of a self-presentation the more likely people are to self-aggrandize'. In practice, the successful self-enhancer will acknowledge known weaknesses but make overly positive claims for things the audience knows little or nothing about. Box 2.1 presents several examples of overly positive claims that were later repudiated when more information came to light.

The Ingratiator's Dilemma

The use of ingratiation is more skill than science, an interpersonal minefield fraught with constant danger and the risk of unpredictable explosions. Bosses are not buffoons who passively accept all manner of employee ingratiation. Rather, they may ignore or discount obvious, excessive, or poorly presented ingratiation attempts (Rao, Schmidt, & Murray, 1995). If the boss comes to believe that Sam's compliments and kind actions are simply attempts to win her favor, she may react negatively and come to dislike Sam more. The consequences of failed ingratiation are not neutral but may place the ingratiator in a far worse IM predicament – being disliked – than when he or she began (Arkin & Shepperd, 1990).

These dangers illustrate the concept of the **ingratiator's dilemma**. The greater the person's need to engage in ingratiation, the more likely it is that the ingratiation attempts will be detected and fail (Jones, 1990). Rather than being used blindly, ingratiation often requires a person to engage in a complicated decision process. Jones and Pittman (1982) suggest that this decision to engage in ingratiation involves the consideration of **motivational**, **cognitive**, and **ethical** factors.

The motivational component of ingratiation is called **incentive value**. It refers to how important it is for a person to be liked by the target. Incentive value goes up as the power difference between a person and a target increases. There will be a greater incentive value for Moe to ingratiate himself with his boss than his peers. Moe's incentive value will be particularly high if he needs the boss's support to get a promotion he really wants.

The cognitive aspect of the ingratiation decision is called **subjective probability**. It refers to how successful a person thinks an ingratiation attempt will be. The higher the subjective probability of success, the more likely it is that a person will attempt to ingratiate a target. Tara is more likely to compliment her vain management instructor on his lecture than her contentious business ethics professor. The vain

| Box 2.1 | **Exaggerated Self-Enhancement: Real-World Examples** |

An interesting example of the dangers of unchecked self-enhancement that came to light in the wake of the break up of the Soviet Union is the claim of longevity by residents of the former Soviet republic of Georgia. During the 1970s, Dannon yogurt had a successful advertising campaign based on claims that residents of Georgia regularly lived past 100 years of age on a diet consisting largely of yogurt. A US Census Bureau study utilizing greater access to the former Soviet Union (and a greater ability to check the veracity of these contentions) found that the claims of longevity were due largely to the inaccurate reporting by the Georgian residents of their age (Geier & Hawkins, 1993).

There also seems to have been some exaggerated self-enhancement regarding the performance of US made Patriot missiles in shooting down Iraqi Scud missiles over Israel during the Persian Gulf War. *Newsweek Magazine* reported that the US military claimed that the Patriot missile had a 40 per cent success rate over Israel ('Anti-Scud Duds', 1993). This despite an Israeli defense official informing the US President in February 1991 that Patriots successfully intercepted only about 20 per cent of incoming Scuds. Several days later, the President claimed that the Patriot performed nearly perfectly. *Newsweek* reports that in 1993 Israeli defense officials acknowledged that the Patriots had knocked out one Scud at best and none at worst.

During the 2000 US presidential election campaign George W. Bush was able to successfully paint his opponent Al Gore as a serial exaggerator. Gore gave his opponent lots of ammunition. At one time or another he claimed to have invented the Internet, that he and his wife Tipper were the role models for Eric Segal's novel, *Love Story*, and that medicine for his mother-in-law cost more than the same prescription for his dog. While there was an element of truth to all these assertions, under the scrutiny of a political campaign, they were seen as stretching the truth even beyond what is usually expected of a politician. Why would a successful, experienced politician like Al Gore engage in such exaggerated self-enhancement? Henneberger's (2000, p. 3) explanation will seem familiar to students of ingratiation: 'And when he tells a lot of these stories ... he seems above all to be looking to be liked'. ▶

Politicians might be expected to engage in exaggerated self-enhancement but there was widespread shock and outrage when in June 2001 it was revealed that Pulitzer Prize historian Joseph Ellis had distorted his past (Tyre, 2001). For years Ellis had described his experiences as a platoon leader in the Vietnam War during his classroom lectures at Mount Holyoke College. The truth was that he had taught history at West Point and had never served a single day in Vietnam!

management instructor is more apt to appreciate and agree with the flattering statement and reciprocate with increased liking of Tara. The contentious business ethics professor is more likely to see the compliment as intentional ingratiation and discount its sincerity. There is a higher subjective probability associated with ingratiating the management instructor than the business ethics professor.

The ingratiator's dilemma can be thought of as the dynamic interplay between these motivational and cognitive components. As a person becomes more dependent on a target, his or her need or motivation to ingratiate the target increases. However, because dependency increases the **salience** of ingratiation attempts, the cognitive part – the subjective probability of success – decreases as the motivational aspect increases. As Jones and Pittman (1982, p. 237) note, 'the dilemma for the ingratiator is that the more important it is for him to gain a high-power target's attraction, the less likely it is that he will be successful'. In practical terms, the greater the difference in status between ingratiator and target the more subtle and disguised ingratiation needs to be; the greater the status similarity, the less disguised and subtle the ingratiation (Stengel, 2000).

Assuming that a person resolves the ingratiator's dilemma and concludes that it is worth the risk, one final aspect must also be considered. This is the ethical or moral justification for using ingratiation in a particular situation. This factor – known as **perceived legitimacy** – is the degree that ingratiation is considered appropriate in particular settings. For instance, a husband might avoid using ingratiation with his wife, a worshipper his minister or Rabbi, a client her therapist – not because they are incapable of the act, but because perceived legitimacy is low. Ingratiation in these settings violates norms stressing authentic IM.

Just as there are situations that constrain the use of ingratiation, there are settings where it is more appropriate. The perceived legitimacy or ethics of ingratiation depends on the situation or environment one encounters. We contend that organizational environments are settings that sanction ingratiation as a means of building and enhancing workplace reputations. In the business world, salesmanship and trying to make others like you are legitimate ways of operating. Power differentials are inherent in the structure of most organizations and those low on the 'food chain' often have few avenues of social influence other than 'kissing up' through ingratiation. As Jones and Pittman (1982, p. 238) insightfully write, 'Ingratiation is likely to be perceived as legitimate in settings where self-salesmanship is sanctioned by the individualistic norms of the business world.'

Resolving the Ingratiator's Dilemma: Factors Associated with Successful Ingratiation

1. Avoid blatant ingratiation: adopt a complicating strategy

Although successful ingratiation can never be guaranteed, our analysis of the ingratiator's dilemma suggests that blatant ingratiation may be worse than doing nothing at all. Blatant ingratiation is often easily detected, leading targets to view the ingratiator as having ulterior motives (Jones & Pittman, 1982). A more successful approach is to adopt a **complicating strategy**. The ingratiator may act modest or even denigrate herself to even things out. The key is to be modest and self-denigrating on things that are trivial or unimportant while being self-enhancing on core issues (Schlenker, 1980). The aim of this complicating strategy is to use modesty and self-denigration to increase the credibility of subsequent ingratiation attempts. While describing to his boss all the extra hours he has logged on the road selling insurance, Bill jokingly suggests that one reason he needs a raise is to pay for several speeding tickets he got. 'I guess I'm a lousy driver but a great salesman' he says, in effect bolstering the validity of job-relevant ingratiation – selling insurance – by admitting a flaw on a job-irrelevant characteristic – driving ability.

Is a complicating strategy enough to make ingratiation work? Are some bosses so blind that they can't see ingratiation attempts for what they really are? The answers to these questions are often surprisingly, 'yes'. Because targets – bosses, supervisors, CEOs, etc. – have a need to be liked (we all do), they are more likely to view ingratiation attempts as sincere than others (often incredulous co-workers who can't believe the boss is buying that!) observing the same interaction. It has been found that targets are more hesitant to attribute ingratiation attempts to ulterior motives than are other observers (Jones & Pittman, 1982). Gordon's (1996) meta-analysis found support for this in the published ingratiation literature: targets judge ingratiation attempts aimed at them more positively and like the ingratiator more than those who simply observed the interaction.

Although on first glance this lack of discernment on the part of targets of ingratiation may seem perplexing, we must remember Goffman's notion of the **working consensus** mentioned in Chapter 1. People involved in social interactions will strive to maintain each other's face so as to avoid the embarrassment associated with interactions that break down. Targets of ingratiation get caught up in the 'social dance' and follows rules that stress politely maintaining the other's face in interactions (Brown & Levinson, 1987). Once the ingratiator locks-on to the target, it's hard for the target to question what is going on because that would damage the social interaction by threatening the working consensus. Observers of this social dance are not part of the interaction, their face or ego is not invested in it, and they tend to be more skeptical and question the ingratiator's motives (Gordon, 1996). Even though all his colleagues view Reg's conversations with his boss, Deborah, about the latest exhibits at the art museum as blatant 'sucking up', Deborah buys into it and thinks Reg is a sensitive, nice guy – so unusual for a man in her department to like fine art.

2. Disclose obstacles to successful performance

A wise person once said 'success has many fathers but failure is an orphan'. From the ingratiator's perspective, the motivation to associate with success is powerful since everyone likes a winner and ingratiators want to be liked. But direct self-enhancement following success runs the risk of being perceived as haughty or boastful. Giacalone and Riordan (1990) found that by disclosing obstacles a person could gain credit for success without being perceived as overly pompous. They had respondents read a fictional account of a manager of a hospital research project who had discovered a cure for a fatal disease. The manager either disclosed obstacles to success – indicated at a press conference that the cure was found despite a fire in the lab and budget cuts – or was modest – said the discovery couldn't have been made without the support and help of colleagues. The results showed that the manager who disclosed obstacles to success was given more credit and recognition for the discovery than one who was modest.

3. Reduce salience of power differentials

Although differences in power increase the need for ingratiation, they also raise the likelihood of detection. Therefore, it is best to make ingratiation attempts when these power differentials are not salient. Complimenting the boss on what a fine family he has may work better at the annual company holiday party than the day before performance appraisals are conducted. Telling an interviewer during a job interview that she has nice taste in clothes may backfire, while the same statement during a chance encounter in a shopping mall may be viewed as sincere.

A Concluding Note

This chapter has reviewed different ways that people use ingratiation tactics to get others to like, reward, and view them favorably. Although many ingratiation tactics may seem simple or obvious, our review has found that they can be effective means of social influence among supervisors and subordinates, co-workers, and even strangers meeting for the first time. While targets of ingratiation may seem easily influenced by subordinate ingratiation, the ingratiator's dilemma limits the unfettered use of ingratiation and requires disguise and subterfuge to be effective. Ingratiation used by those high in organizational status is also effective (Gordon, 1996) however, by virtue of their greater social power, managers have other IM tactics available. As we shall see in Chapter 3, there are a number of other acquisitive IM tactics that are used in organizational settings to build and maintain reputations at work.

3 Beyond Ingratiation: Other Acquisitive IM Techniques

> Anyone logging hours to impress me – you are
> wasting your time
> Colin Powell describing work rules shortly after becoming
> US Secretary of State (Perlez, 2001, p. A3).

A Toast to Toastmasters

The name Ralph C. Smedley is probably not familiar to many serious trivia experts, or devoted viewers of *Who Wants to be a Millionaire*. Smedley was neither an IM researcher nor an organizational theorist. Yet his efforts over seven decades ago had a profound impact on the practice of managing impressions in organizational settings. Seventy-five years ago, in a basement of a YMCA building in Santa Ana, California, Smedley founded **Toastmasters International**, an organization dedicated to helping people make effective public presentations. Today, Toastmasters has over 8,300 chapters and more than 170,000 members worldwide in about 70 countries. It has also become very popular with businesses, many of which allow their employees to attend meetings on company time. Toastmasters still advocates the simple principles of public speaking proposed by Smedley: practice, plenty of feedback, and addressing a group just as one would address a single person (Hamashige, 1994).

Both employees who seek to improve their presentation skills at Toastmasters, and employers who support their involvement, realize that, in today's corporate world, effective presentations are important vehicles for building and enhancing reputations of the individual and the organization. A poor presentation may damage the employer's image in the community or with key customers, and limit an employee's chances for promotion to management or other executive positions.

In Chapter 2, we focused on ingratiation – a series of techniques that all share the common IM goal of making others like you. While ingratiation has been the most studied of acquisitive IM tactics, it is by no means the only one. The goal of members of Toastmasters, particularly those from the business world, is not just to be liked following a successful presentation, but to be viewed as competent and knowledgeable public speakers. This form of IM is known as **self-promotion**. Despite Colin Powell's admonition to State Department employees, engaging in self-promotion and other acquisitive IM tactics at work is often both diplomatic and effective.

In Chapter 3 we look at ways other than ingratiation that individuals and organizations use to manage impressions at work. We describe these other tactics, the impressions they seek to achieve, and their applications to organizational settings. We also consider how individuals utilize the principle of association while engaging in IM and how nonverbal behaviors may influence the impressions people make.

Self-Promotion

While at first glance, self-promotion may seem to be another form of ingratiation, it has a different goal. In contrast to the ingratiator who wants to be liked, the self-promoter wants to be seen as competent (Jones, 1990). According to Giacalone and Rosenfeld (1986, p. 321), 'The self-promoter tries to make others think he or she is competent on either general ability dimensions (e.g., intelligence) or specific skills (e.g., ability to play a musical instrument)'. Ingratiation is **attention giving** – it aims to build up a target so as to induce liking. Self-promotion is **attention getting** – it draws an audience's focus to someone's accomplishments so that they appear competent (Godfrey, Jones, & Lord, 1986; Harrell-Cook, Ferris, & Dulebohn, 1999).

Self-promotion tactics may work hand-in-hand with ingratiation attempts or conflict with them. Assume that Annette is being interviewed by Mark for a job as an aerobics instructor at the local health club. Upon first meeting Mark, she smiles and compliments him on his well-developed muscles (ingratiation). During the interview, Annette describes her extensive previous experience teaching aerobics in other clubs (self-promotion). Annette's behavior illustrates that in organizations it is often in a person's best interests to be both liked and seen as competent.

While individuals use self-promotion to make others think they are more competent, a related tactic described in Box 3.1, called **window dressing**, is used at the organization level to achieve similar ends.

Though self-promotion and ingratiation may go hand-in-hand, they are not always equally achievable. A study of conversation patterns (Godfrey et al., 1986) found that it was easier to be a successful ingratiator than a successful self-promoter. This may be because getting people to like you through ingratiation is usually a **reactive process**.

Box 3.1	**Window-Dressing on Wall Street**

Just as individuals engage in acquisitive IM tactics such as ingratiation and self-promotion to make themselves liked and viewed as competent, so do organizations or institutions attempt to enhance their images as being competent, fiscally reliable, and caring (Elsbach & Kramer, 1996; Mohamed, et al., 1999). One such tactic is called **window-dressing**. Individuals and organizations that use window-dressing engage in a form of superficial or expedient manipulation to make themselves look better publicly. One example, involves the New York Stock Market.

After a long and steady period of gains, the New York Stock Market experienced dramatic declines during 2000, especially in high-technology stocks that had done so well in previous years. Towards the end of 2000, many portfolio managers – individuals who manage large corporate investments (e.g., pension funds, insurance companies) in the stock market – engaged in window-dressing. Window dressing refers to the last-minute practice of purchasing stocks that have done well and selling stocks that have done poorly so that the overall portfolio presented to investors looks better than it would had these late adjustments not been made. While window-dressing may have helped the reputations of portfolio managers and the firms they represent, it had the impact of hurting the stock market even more. The increased sales of 'losers' resulted in the market falling dramatically during the latter half of December 2000.

The ingratiator can defer to the target, mumble agreement, and engage in positive nonverbals such as smiling. Self-promotion tends to be a **proactive process**. If Mona wants to convince the boss of her competence, she can't sit back and rest on her laurels – she has to actively say or do something.

There are times when self-promotion and ingratiation attempts are at cross-purposes. The ingratiator who acts modestly to curry favor, or passively agrees with his boss's opinions, may not be viewed as very smart, independent, or competent (Jones, 1990). Successful or aggressive self-promotion attempts also run the risk of making others feel jealous or resentful. If one of our work colleagues is viewed as smart, competent, and intelligent, what does that say about us? While many people acknowledge the computer savvy and brilliance of Bill Gates, the founder and former head of Microsoft, Gates is also widely disliked for the aggressive and highly competitive way he does business. It has been suggested that successful self-promotion may also be intimidating (Jones & Pittman, 1982). While we may like competent people up to a point, at some level they become scary and fear inducing. We may be afraid to publicly disagree with a Nobel prize winner in economics even when we have found an error in his calculations.

Research has shown that self-promotion is quite common, especially when the claims are for important audiences or occasions. In an early study, Gordon and Stapleton (1956) had high school students take a personality test either as part of a job application or for a guidance class. Higher scores were obtained when the test was to be for the more important job application. Hendricks and Brickman (1974) found that college students overestimated their expected course grade if their teacher was to see it but were more accurate if a peer was to see it.

Self-promotion also is more frequent when the claims are not likely to be challenged or discredited. In an organizational study, Goldstein (1971) compared the job applications of candidates for a nurse's aide job with their records of previous employment. It was found that over half of the applicants exaggerated their length of service and pay at their previous jobs. In Great Britain, one training organization indicated that $\frac{2}{3}$ of those 18–25 (and $\frac{1}{2}$ of those 56–65) admitted that they had lied on their resumés in order to appear more qualified. The bigger the job the greater the exaggerated self-promotion. Applicants for jobs paying about ST£100,000 were twice as likely to have used false qualifications as applicants for more junior positions (Welch, 1999). Self-promotion is common in politicians particularly those who are **charismatic leaders** (Gardner & Avolio, 1998). After Vicente Fox was elected president of Mexico in July 2000, it was reported that he hadn't attended Harvard University or received a graduate degree in management despite claims to the contrary on his official biography. In an effort to repair the damage, Fox's bio was changed to indicate that he actually had attended a six-week seminar taught by Harvard professors to business executives in Mexico ('Mexican president's resumé is erroneous', 2001). Thus, self-promotion claims can rarely be taken at face value and need to be verified. In Great Britain check the facts; in Mexico check the Fox!

We would expect that the occurrence of self-promotion would increase when people have the opportunity to publicly impress a higher status target about their competence. This was demonstrated in a field experiment using full-time New York state legislative interns (Giacalone & Rosenfeld, 1986). The interns were sent a survey that they were told to complete either anonymously or while identified and were to return it either to a fellow intern (low status) or to the director of the internship program (high status). The survey asked the interns to rate themselves on items related to their competence, abilities, and traits. It was found that the interns exhibited the most self-promotion (i.e., had the highest self-ratings of competence) when their surveys had identifying information and would be returned to the director.

The use and effectiveness of self-promotion depend on the situation. Individuals who score highly on a measure of 'dependency' are seen as having a strong need for getting along with their peers. They usually act modestly so that their peers will be evaluated more favorably. However, when dependent individuals are placed in situations where they need to please someone in authority, they will engage in self-promotion in order to be evaluated more positively than their peers (Bornstein, Riggs, Hill, & Calabrese, 1996).

In organizational settings, self-promotion has been found to be effective during job interviews (Howard & Ferris, 1996) but less effective during performance evaluations (Kacmar & Carlson, 1999). One reason is that a job interview is like a first date – the participants don't know each other – leaving the interviewer vulnerable to the candidate's self-promotion. Performance evaluations are more like long-term relationships – the participants usually know each other well so it is easier for the manager to detect last minute attempts at employee self-promotion. Research has found that subordinate self-promotion in performance evaluation situations may backfire resulting in more negative ratings (Ferris, Judge, Rowland, & Fitzgibbons, 1994).

Intimidation

While the ingratiator wants to be liked, and the self-promoter wants to be seen as competent, the goal of the intimidator is to be feared. The intimidator builds and enhances their reputation at work by creating an identity of being dangerous – one whose threats and warnings are to be obeyed, or negative consequences will occur (Arkin & Shepperd, 1990). As Jones and Pittman (1982, p. 238) note, 'the intimidator advertises his available power to create discomfort or all kinds of psychic pain'.

Intimidation is more likely to occur in nonvoluntary relationships such as the one between supervisors and subordinates. It occurs when one of the interactants feels superior to the other and is free to act as they wish (Schutz, 1997). One of us had a supervisor who would simply stare at subordinates during meetings and say very little. Some employees found this silent stare so intimidating that they would spill their guts far beyond what they intended to say when the meeting began. We would joke that employees would confess to crimes that they hadn't yet committed! As this anecdote illustrates, a supervisor's ability to influence or control a subordinate's salary, performance evaluations, and promotions often creates an atmosphere of intimidation – one where it is clear that noncompliance will have severe consequences.

Rather than being inherently good or bad, we think that intimidation, like ingratiation, is often a natural outgrowth of the social structure of organizations. Subordinates need to use ingratiation because they usually have little power; they have no better way of influencing others than by manipulating liking. Superiors (e.g., management), who by definition control power resources, have less reason to want to be liked. Indeed, to a person in power, being liked too much is risky business – it can reduce compliance by lessening respect and fear since bosses who are liked are often less respected (Stengel, 2000). Social psychologists have found that people who like each other are not as likely to use threats or other forms of coercive power. The library director who becomes overly 'chummy' with her staff may lose their respect and fear, undermining the effectiveness of her power base. As boss, she can't be one of the girls, or one of the boys. The intimidator who can't or doesn't back up threats may be viewed as weak and impotent. Although ingratiation is more effective when it flows from higher to lower status than vice versa (Gordon, 1996), it may not be advisable for the boss to go the ingratiation route too often with subordinates.

In many ways, intimidation is the opposite of ingratiation (Jones & Pittman, 1982). While the ingratiator dangles a carrot, the intimidator wields a big stick. To an ingratiator, every day is St Valentine's day; love and kisses for all. The intimidator is the tax collector arriving on income tax day, announcing 'pay up or face the music!' Successful intimidation often makes the intimidator less rather than more liked. While ingratiation may bring people together, intimidation drives them apart; if used indiscriminately or excessively it can reduce organizational cohesiveness.

Though intimidation is the opposite of ingratiation, successful intimidation often elicits ingratiation. The **intimidator's illusion** is that the intimidator may come to think that his or her behavior is liked and accepted when in fact it is loathed and detested. The liking and acceptance presented in response to intimidation is in reality strategic IM; an attempt to counter or neutralize the intimidator's influence attempts. While Heather 'gladly' agrees to work late to finish a presentation for her boss, Mr Grumps, she secretly despises him for constantly dumping work on her at the last minute. He takes her smiling agreement as both a sign of his successful management style and as a further reason to view Heather favorably. Mr Grumps later recommends that Heather receive a large bonus. Her smiling acceptance has influenced Mr Grumps's behavior more favorably in her direction than if she had frowned and complained; actions that would have been more reflective of her 'true self'.

In organizations, intimidation is typically a form of **downward influence**; flowing from higher to lower power individuals. There are cases, however, where those lower in status can intimidate those above them. Jones and Pittman (1982) refer to this use of intimidation by those low in status as **counterpower**. It has been suggested that inner-city, African-American males in the US may adopt an intimidating 'cool pose' – actions that advertise hypermasculinity, toughness and a willingness to use violence – as a way of gaining social power in the face of limited educational and employment opportunities (Freiberg, 1991).

In organizational settings, an incompetent handicapped worker who vows to sue if not promoted, or an elderly employee who lets it be known that he will file an age discrimination claim if disciplined for unauthorized absences, use intimidation even though they themselves are weak. A case of counterpower intimidation we witnessed involved a woman who had openly flirted with and willingly participated with her male colleagues in 'dirty joke' sessions. Later, when her work performance was criticized, she claimed to have been the victim of sexual harassment during those joke sessions. Her intimidating tactics successfully kept her supervisor from taking disciplinary action. Given the high personal costs associated with filing sexual harassment complaints, we suspect such blatantly false claims are uncommon (despite what many people think!). However, they do in some ways quickly shift the power to the 'victim' and therefore can be a potent source of counterpower.

Exemplification

Exemplification involves managing the impressions of integrity, self-sacrifice, and moral worthiness (Jones & Pittman, 1982). The exemplifier is the boss who shows up early and stays late, the co-worker who takes work home every day, and the colleague who never takes a vacation. Exemplifiers volunteer for the most difficult assignments. They willingly suffer to help others. They go beyond the call of duty.

From an IM perspective, exemplification involves **strategic self-sacrifice**. There is method to the exemplifier's martyrdom. The exemplifier attempts to influence and control through inducing guilt or attributions of virtue that may lead to imitation by others. The exemplifier wants others to know how hard she is working. Exemplifiers will let you know that they haven't had a day off in months, that they worked all weekend on the Annual Report, they were the only one at work during a blizzard, or that a killer migraine didn't keep them away from their desks.

Because exemplifiers need to advertise their behavior, they run the risk of being viewed by others as sanctimonious. Also, if their behavior doesn't live up to their lofty claims, they may be seen as hypocrites. Politicians who are more likely than others to use exemplification

(Schutz, 1997) often fail to live up to their own preaching. The nineteenth-century British prime minister, William Gladstone, was known for being a deeply religious moral crusader. He would venture into London's seedy areas at night and urge prostitutes to change their ways. When his diaries were published during the mid twentieth century the truth became known: Gladstone would 'partake' in the evils he preached against (Ehrenhalt, 2001). In the Fall of 1994, there were a number of media stories reporting that the well-known American football player, Barry Sanders (now retired), was the unmarried father of a 5½ month-old son. What made the item newsworthy was that Sanders was once a spokesperson against premarital sex and had said in interviews that he was celibate (talk about immaculate deceptions!). After being questioned about this apparent contradiction between his public statements and private actions, Sanders indicated that he no longer speaks about the premarital sex issue. Box 3.2 gives some additional examples of private behavior that didn't match public exemplification.

Supplication

Supplication is the acquisitive IM strategy of last resort. The supplicator exploits his own weakness to influence others. In graduate school one of our fellow students (let's call him Cal E.) always screwed up whatever tasks he was given and often 'played dumb'. We used to say that the only thing Cal was skilled at, was managing the impression of incompetence. But Cal was a nice guy, and despite his incompetence, someone always seemed to lend a hand. By advertising their incompetence, supplicators such as Cal attempt to activate a powerful social rule known as the **norm of social responsibility** that says we should help those who are in need. Supplicators gain strength from their weaknesses since their dependency makes others help them (Mohamed, Gardner, & Paolillo, 1999). When Betty lets Sam know that she can't sleep at night because she is intimidated by the firm's new computer system, Sam offers to teach her how to use it. When Robert, a new employee at the Kraft Day Care Center, tries unsuccessfully to change baby Josh's diaper, his supervisor Karen jumps in and does it for him. Negotiation expert Stephen M. Pollan claims this 'I-need-your-help' approach is an effective bargaining tactic in business negotiations for things such as increased severance pay

Box 3.2 | **Practicing What They Preach, NOT! Exemplification in Public and Private**

Throughout his tenure, former US President Bill Clinton made speeches advocating personal responsibility and the virtues of family-type values. At the same time, he was having an illicit affair with a young intern, Monica Lewinsky, that led to impeachment and nearly his removal from office. During the Lewinsky scandal, Clinton was counseled by civil rights leader the Reverend Jessie Jackson. In 2001, it was revealed that Jackson, who had often preached against illegitimacy, had fathered an illegitimate child with a former assistant (Ehrenhalt, 2001). Jackson had brought the child's mother to meet the president while she was pregnant and Jackson was counseling the president about the Lewinsky matter. Because the 'flesh is weak', the exemplifier's most difficult chore may be living up to the identity that he so carefully has crafted (Gilbert & Jones, 1986).

An organizational example of public exemplification that didn't match private behavior occurred in Dallas, Texas in 1981. Oak Communications surveyed members of the community to determine what sorts of cable television services the residents wanted. The survey results indicated that adult programming that involved sex and nudity came off very low. However, when cable subscribers could privately sign-up for the adult channel, 60 percent did.

Public exemplification not matching private behavior may be a cross-cultural phenomenon. In 1993, the British Broadcasting Corporation decided to air a documentary about Chairman Mao Tse-Tung, the former leader of Communist China (Tuohy, 1993). The documentary was aired over the objections of the Chinese government to the documentary's unflattering portrait of Chairman Mao as a leader who held markedly different views of sex and women in private than public. 'In public, Mao espoused the cause of women's rights... In private he collected, used, and discarded concubines by the hundreds. The image promoted by the Communist authorities of Mao as an ascetic, almost puritan figure, could not have been further from the truth'

(Tuohy, 1993, p. A4).

after being fired. It works, because 'Asking for help is like apple pie – nobody can say no' (Overstreet, 1994, p. 2B). In this way, successful supplication is the opposite of self-promotion; we get help from others if they believe we can't help ourselves.

There are limits, however, to how much people will help supplicators. If overused, the supplicator may gain a reputation as a malingerer, one who would rather feed at the public trough than do things for himself. Thus, it is best if the weakness is seen as temporary and used in the short run, rather than being a long-term characteristic (Mohamed et al., 1999). Supplication works best when it is associated with **compensatory exchanges** (Jones, 1990). For example, Neal may be a statistical and computer whiz but may lack presentation skills, while another member of his workgroup, Billy, may be 'Mr Slick' in public but lack quantitative abilities. Through compensatory exchanges, Neal helps Billy with the quantitative part of the quarterly report, while Billy expertly presents the results to their boss.

In organizations, people will sometimes deliberately try to **look bad**. Becker and Martin (1995) found over half of those they surveyed recalled occasions where they or others looked bad at work. With more and more organizations downsizing, reorganizing, being reinvented and reengineered, many employees are feeling increased stress and burnout as their workloads have increased (Fraser, 2001) Thus, rather than using IM to try to gain positive outcomes (which may mean even more work), employees may find it in their interests to use IM to look bad. Becker and Martin (1995) describe five ways people try to look bad at work.

Decreasing performance

Here an employee deliberately is less productive, they make more mistakes, and produce lesser quality work. Matt's company has instituted a Total Quality Management program where many processes are decided by employees on Performance Assessment Teams (PATs). Matt hates PATs, and thinks they are a waste of time. He shows up late for the 'Food in the Cafeteria' PAT, doesn't do a good job on the 'Ethnic Foods' PAT and ticks off most of his co-workers with his lousy cynical attitude on the 'Holiday Party' PAT. When its time for the next PAT to be tasked, he isn't asked to participate. The PAT's loss is Matt's gain.

Not working to potential

With workloads increasing as corporations downsize to maximize profits, its not always beneficial to know how to do too many different things well. To avoid being like one of our colleagues, a super competent assistant vice president who always gets news tasks dumped on him, a second form of looking bad is not working to potential. Here an employee knows how to do something but pretends not to. It was only years later when we heard that Cal, our incompetent friend from graduate school, was teaching statistics and computer science, that we realized that Cal was not as incompetent as he acted around us. Cal probably knew how to do statistical and computer analysis but kept that to himself. If Cal's advisor had known, he would have given him lots more work to do.

Withdrawal

Employees who use withdrawal never seem to be around when needed, often get sick when work is due, go on vacation to avoid new tasks, and disappear for long periods of time during lunch and other times. They may take breaks with the smokers even though they don't smoke. Our favorite example was Sal, a career civil servant. Sal never met a task he could do. When the going got tough, Sal's preferred withdrawal mode was to disappear to the nearest lavatory, usually taking a novel to read. Everyone knew what Sal was doing but not much could be done to get King Sal off of his throne! We used to joke that as a career civil servant, Sal could have read all of *War and Peace* with little fear of reprisal.

Displaying a bad attitude

Many popular management models, require employees to work together often in groups or teams. To avoid excessive 'teaming', those with a bad attitude may act strange, seem angry, or be generally hard to get along with. By being disliked, they also exert social power; others must conform to their behavior or they will get out of the tasks at hand. A colleague called these employees, 'toxic co-workers', whose very presence often poisons workplace relationships. Unlike chemical poisons, there rarely are effective antidotes when dealing with toxic co-workers and they often get their way. Your pain is their gain. When such an employee is denied a benefit such as a promotion or a raise, they may display a particularly bad attitude until the benefit is obtained. We know of one organization where there was a toxic manager, who both terrorized employees through intimidation and scared top management by threatening lawsuits. When one of her subordinates kept his door closed against her wishes, she called the maintenance department and had the door removed. When she was denied a promotion, she sued. Eventually, management settled just to get rid of her. However, they are still looking for the door!

Broadcasting limitations

Those who broadcast limitations are not shy about letting others know how incompetent or physically incapable they are, in fact they proudly advertise that they can't get the job done. While a supplicator seeks others' help to get tasks accomplished, the employee who broadcasts limitation doesn't seek help, they simply want to get out of the task. The rapid technological change in organizations is threatening to many employees who may be set in their old ways. Upgrading to a new type of software, or using a new business model may make sense to management concerned about the bottom line, but some employees find bliss in their ignorance.

Indirect IM

At the height of his wealth and success, the financier Baron de Rothschild was petitioned for a loan by an acquaintance. Reputedly, the great man replied, 'I won't give you a loan myself; but I will walk arm-in-arm with you across the floor of the Stock Exchange, and you soon shall have willing lenders to spare' (Cialdini, 1989, p. 45).

It is clear that IM has its risks; the best laid plans of mice and managers may backfire. Therefore, it often is prudent for the IMer to use indirect means. We owe much of our knowledge of indirect IM to the work of Robert Cialdini.

Cialdini and colleagues have found that individuals will utilize associations with positive others for IM purposes, even when the associations are due to chance or are trivial. Indirect IM is based on the simple premise that we can influence how others view us by managing information about things and people we are associated with (Cialdini, 1989). The indirect IMer lives by the slogan, 'you are judged by the company you keep'.

Indirect IM utilizes the **association principle**, which states that individuals will attempt to maximize their links to desirable things and minimize associations with that which is disfavored. People associate themselves with desirable things through behaviors or statements known as **claims** (Schlenker, 1980). By being attached to something positive, the person hopes that others will view him positively as well – even if the connection is casual. Indirect IM also capitalizes on the principle of **evaluative generalization** (Schlenker, 1980) which says that people linked to positive entities will themselves be rated positively. Politicians and advertisers are well aware of the power of positive associations and often hire celebrities (e.g., golfer Tiger Woods) to endorse their products.

Advertising is full of examples of indirect IM. For many years, pop star Michael Jackson appeared in advertisements for Pepsi, a relationship that was quickly terminated after Jackson was accused of sexually molesting a young boy. The *New York Times* reported that the late explorer Jacques Cousteau had sued a California dairy for 1.2 million dollars because the dairy had portrayed its mascot cow on a billboard wearing flippers and a wet suit as 'Jacques Cowsteau' ('For California cow, one caricature too many', 1993). Lawyers for Cousteau indicated that the explorer felt that people seeing the billboard would think that Cousteau was endorsing the dairy's milk when in fact he was not.

This notion of association with a positive other implying endorsement underlies much of indirect IM. After being hired as a junior partner in a law firm, Lloyd's colleagues noticed this sort of indirect IM. Lloyd always bought the best suits, ate in the best restaurants, drank the finest wine, drove an expensive sports car, lived in a posh neighborhood, and dated women from well-to-do families. Lloyd would likely subscribe to a cardinal principle of indirect IM, 'What we do is often less important than whom we do it with' (Cialdini, Finch, & De Nicolas, 1990).

In one of Cialdini's famous studies of indirect IM, he and his colleagues found that on the Monday following US college football games, students wore more school-related items (e.g., sweatshirts, buttons) when the school had won the previous Saturday than when they had lost (Cialdini, et al., 1986). They were also more likely to use the pronoun 'we' in describing the school's victory than defeat. This form of IM by association is called, **basking in reflected glory** (BIRG).

While the students in this BIRGing study had some connection to the victorious school, indirect IM occurs even when associations are accidental. This was demonstrated for a phenomenon called **boosting** (Finch & Cialdini, 1989). Boosting refers to the tendency for individuals who are somehow associated with a negative other to rate that person's character more positively. For example, although both former US President Jimmy Carter's brother Billy and former US President Clinton's half-brother Roger were widely portrayed as uncouth publicity-seekers by the press, their presidential siblings publicly boosted them, with Clinton pardoning his half-brother's drug-related offenses on his last day as President. In the Finch and Cialdini (1989) study, respondents were given an unflattering description of Rasputin, the Mad Monk of Russia. Half of the respondents learned that they had the same birthday as Rasputin, while the others were not given any birthday information. It was found that those who shared a birthday with Rasputin rated him less negatively. From an IM perspective, viewing Rasputin as less negative lessens the impact of being associated with a stigmatized other.

According to Cialdini (1989), a factor that increases indirect IM in organizations is **setbacks**, especially those that reflect on a person's self-esteem. Assume Earl is an up-and-coming salesman in a public relations firm. However, Earl's abrasiveness recently alienated one of his firm's clients and he lost a major account. While informing his boss that he has just lost this important advertising client, Earl makes sure to stress how prestigious the firms that he still has accounts with are, and how much better they are than the client that he lost. Earl is engaging in a form of indirect IM called **burnishing**, which involves stressing the favorable features of something we are positively linked to (Cialdini, 1989). That burnishing increases following failure was demonstrated by Cialdini and Richardson (1980). They found that students who thought they had failed a creativity test were more likely to describe the academic, cultural, and social environment of their school in glowing terms than those who thought they had done well on the test.

Acclaiming

The desire to engage in IM is especially strong following success. One application of the association principle is that people will try to stress, highlight, exaggerate, or distort their relationship to successful outcomes to bolster their public images (Schlenker, 1980). According to Schlenker (1980, p. 163), acclaiming tactics, 'are designed to explain a desirable event in a way that maximizes the desirable implications for the actor'.

There are two forms of acclaiming: **entitlements** and **enhancements**. Entitlements are attempts to maximize responsibility for positive events. They are especially likely to occur when responsibility for the positive outcome is either ambiguous or unclear (Schlenker, 1980). For example, when the present authors were all graduate students working in the same research laboratory we observed the following scenario: a graduate student would propose an idea for a research study at a meeting attended by other graduate students and our advisor. A year or two later, after the project was done and was about to be published, the graduate student who had come up with the idea (and done all the work) was surprised to find that he had three other people claiming that they merited co-authorship. 'I helped you come up with the idea' said one. 'You based your project on my past work' said another, 'I helped you with the stats' claimed a third. Success has many fathers (and mothers) and our journal articles often had many extra authors due to this entitlement phenomenon. Of course, all three authors of this book claim that they have done the lion's-share of the work, an entitlement that may change in intensity depending on how successful it turns out to be!

Enhancements try to maximize how desirable a positive occurrence is. When Peg claims that the award-winning advertising campaign was her own idea rather than giving credit to her campaign team, her claim is an entitlement. When Bob remarks that his son Farrell didn't just graduate from 'any business school' but got his degree from the best one in the country, Bob is offering an enhancement.

Research on acclaiming has typically focused on entitlements. A cross-cultural study (Rosenfeld, et al., 1983) found that entitlements, if challenged, can backfire. In that study, US and Hong Kong Chinese students read scenarios describing a medical research team that had discovered a cure for a serious disease. Some of the students read that the assistant project director called a news conference and claimed that he had the idea that led to the breakthrough. This entitlement claim was either confirmed or challenged by subsequent statements made by the project director. Respondents then evaluated the assistant director. Interestingly, while the ratings of the assistant director were somewhat more positive when he made an entitlement than when no entitlement was given, the differences between entitlement and no entitlement conditions for both American and Hong Kong Chinese students were not statistically significant even when the entitlement was confirmed. However, when the entitlement claim was disconfirmed, the ratings of the assistant director were significantly less positive for both Americans and Hong Kong Chinese. Apparently, using entitlements can backfire when they are not substantiated by accompanying evidence.

Giacalone (1985) applied this backfiring notion to organizational settings. He warned that employees who engage in **random entitlements** run the risk of 'slipping' when they thought they had put their best foot forward. How can entitlements be made more effective and less risky? Giacalone advises using the principle of **third-party IM** (also known as **self-presentation by proxy**) we noted to be effective for ingratiation attempts. In a study using a version of the medical discovery scenario described above, Giacalone (1985) had a hospital spokesperson announce at a news conference that the assistant director should be credited with the discovery. He found that the assistant director was seen as more intelligent, successful, competent, and moral when he was the beneficiary of this third-party entitlement. Third-party entitlements were more successful than no entitlements or entitlements that the assistant director made on his own behalf.

Nonverbal IM

The employment manager of a large New York department store
told me she would rather hire a sales clerk who hadn't finished
grade school, if he or she has a pleasant smile, than to hire a
doctor of philosophy with a somber face
(Dale Carnegie 1936, p. 67).

Dale Carnegie recognized the importance of smiling as a potent way of making people like us. Today we realize that many different types of **nonverbal behaviors** can be used to build and enhance reputations at work. Facial expressions, touching, body orientation, posture and interpersonal distance can strongly influence the impressions we form of others and they of us (DePaulo, 1992). Moreover, in order for communications to be effective, verbal and nonverbal cues need to be consistent with each other. In the case of IM, if a person says one thing, but communicates something very different with her body language, the effect of the verbal message will be undermined. Some have argued this is because there is a common perception that the tongue can lie more readily than the body (Gilbert & Krull, 1988).

Research indicates that audiences rely more on nonverbal behaviors than verbal ones when forming impressions (Bozeman & Kacmar, 1997). As might be expected, this is particularly true in hyper-IM occasions such as job interviews. Applicants who use positive nonverbals such as smiling, head nodding, and direct eye contact are seen as more competent than those who use negative nonverbals such as avoiding eye contact (Howard & Ferris, 1996; Stevens & Kristof 1995). These effects of nonverbals are also likely to be true in day-to-day interactions at work. Marie is encouraged when her boss Jerry nods and smiles during her presentation of a proposed new marketing strategy. Stephanie thinks her boss Rick looked bored and skeptical when she argues for a long-overdue raise and promotion. Her boss's 'nonverbals' make a clear impression; Stephanie doubts her plea will be successful. Table 3.1 provides six reasons why nonverbal behavior plays an important role in IM.

In addition to nonverbals such as facial expressions and body orientation, other types of nonverbal expression such as dress (Rafaeli & Pratt, 1993), office design (Ornstein, 1989), and seating arrangements (Riess & Rosenfeld, 1980) can be used in the service of organizational IM. Rafaeli and Pratt (1993) contend that the way individuals in an organization dress can convey powerful messages about the nature of the organization and the type of people who work there. Outsiders may use the way members of an organization dress as a cue to evoke **cognitive associations** that influence the impressions formed of the organization. When Nigel, a London executive, is sent to a business meeting in southern California, he is surprised at how casually the employees are dressed. Nigel would never dream of wearing jeans and

| Table 3.1 | **Six Reasons Why Nonverbal Behavior is Important for IM** |

1. Irrepressible

Explanation: It's hard to not make an impression nonverbally. Even if people don't move, their posture may send signals.

Example: Jim, a manager, tightens up when a female employee Nancy, who has charged him with sexual harassment, enters the office.

2. Linked to emotion

Explanation: Certain nonverbal behaviors such as facial expressions are automatically linked to emotions such as fear. These emotional reactions may more directly convey an impression than corresponding verbal statements which are under voluntary control.

Example: When Katie discovers that her co-worker Kurt has been promoted instead of her, she verbally congratulates Kurt. Her facial expressions, however, convey how disappointed and mad she really is.

3. Less accessible

Explanation: People know less about their own nonverbal behaviors than others do. Other people see our expressions but we don't. This less accessible feature of nonverbal behavior may constrain the use of intentional nonverbal IM since people can't control what they are unaware of.

Example: Paul passes his co-worker Jack at the company cafeteria several times a week. Paul is often preoccupied and rarely makes eye contact or acknowledges Jack's presence. Jack interprets these nonverbals as conveying dislike for him, while in actuality Paul doesn't realize the negative vibes he is giving off.

4. Off-the-record

Explanation: Nonverbal behavior is elusive. It is more difficult for people to describe what nonverbals occurred or to repeat them compared to verbal behaviors. Therefore, people may be more likely to risk expressing something nonverbally than verbally. If there are negative consequences they can deny that it happened or that they meant it.

Example: Bill is attracted to Hannah, one of the secretaries in the typing pool. When she walks by, he leers and stares at her. When Hannah later complains to Bill's boss, he denies that he has done anything wrong.

5. Communicates unique meanings

Explanation: There are some meanings that can't be easily expressed in words.

Example: Jules finds the negotiations with the union over a new contract to be very frustrating. When Stephanie asks for his impression of how things are going he looks upward and throws both his hands up as if to say, 'God only knows'. ▶

6. Occurs quickly and spontaneously

Explanation: Many nonverbal behaviors are quick and spontaneous reactions to events such as learning that you have won the lottery or someone has died. The quickness of nonverbal behavior increases its perceived sincerity since lack of time does not provide much opportunity for faking. Thus, nonverbal behaviors may convey more sincere impressions than words.

Example: After learning that she has cancer, Martha, an unpopular vice-president of a small manufacturing firm, calls a meeting to announce her retirement. Steve is in the back watching the audience's reactions. Although some people seemed shocked, Steve is surprised to see a number of expressions of relief and even some happy reactions. Later, of course, everyone verbally expresses how shocked and sorry they are at the news!

Source: DePaulo (1992)

sandals to work, let alone to an important business meeting. 'These people must not be very serious about their work', he concludes. At the same time, Paul, Nigel's California counterpart, is struck by how dressed up, Nigel is. 'Another of those uptight Brits,' Paul concludes. 'I'm glad I don't have to work with stuffed shirts like him every day.'

A Concluding Note

This chapter has reviewed ways, other than ingratiation, that people and organizations attempt to manage impressions. When used skillfully, sparingly, and properly, these acquisitive IM tactics often work – whether for an employee attempting to get a promotion or an organization trying to increase its profit margin. In addition to using acquisitive IM to build their reputations at work, people use a full-range of protective IM tactics to maintain those reputations. Protective IM is the focus of Chapters 4 and 5.

4 Protective IM I: Using Excuses and Justifications to Repair Spoiled Identities

> A stigmatized organizational identity can affect how members
> view themselves and their work, as well as how others view and
> interact with them ... Members of potentially stigmatized
> organizations often employ a range of interactional strategies to
> minimize the possible costs associated with their identity
> (Cain, 1994, p. 43).

> Offer quick and clear explanations, and, by all means,
> avoid any appearance of a cover-up
> (Hedges, Walsh, & Headden, 1994, p. 43).

Damage Control at Food Lion

Food Lion was the fastest-growing supermarket chain in the United States. That was until they were the targets of an exposé on the ABC television news-magazine show *Prime Time Live* in November, 1992. Long before anyone had heard of Mad Cow Disease, the show documented how Food Lion engaged in unsanitary food practices including selling cheese that had been gnawed by rats and doctored meat products. *Prime Time Live* reported that the supermarket chain used barbecue sauce to help sell old chickens and even dipped bad meat into bleach to remove the odor and make it seem fresh. Supermarket workers were shown in hidden videos to have removed and doctored 'sell by' tags that indicated the last day meat can be sold ('Food Lyin', 1997; Miller, Smith, & Mabry, 1992).

Surely, caught so red-handed, we would expect that Food Lion would be finished – their goose literally being cooked! Would anyone ever purchase meat from Food Lion again? The answer surprisingly was 'yes'. Food Lion quickly mobilized an all-out **damage control** campaign to restore their image. According to Miller et al. (1992), this campaign involved the following steps:

1. *A denial statement.* Tom E. Smith, the President and CEO of Food Lion, quickly issued a statement denying the charges. He said, 'these lies have got to stop'.
2. *Attacking the attackers.* The day after issuing the denial, Smith claimed, in a conference call to stock analysts, that *Prime Time's* sources lacked any credibility because they were union sympathizers.
3. *Admission of some blame.* Food Lion aired a television commercial that said although 'a problem can exist', their company had good procedures and policies.
4. *The best defense is a good offense.* Food Lion went on the offensive by putting their response to the charges on videotape and sending 60,000 copies to company employees. The employees were encouraged to watch the tape with family and friends. It was suggested that employees invite friends over for a party and serve them Food Lion food!

In addition to this short term strategy, Food Lion adopted a long-term approach where they continued to both attack the attackers and go on the offensive by suing ABC News. In order to uncover what Food Lion was doing, two ABC reporters had submitted false resumés, gotten jobs at Food Lion stores and taped the events wearing disguises containing hidden cameras. In their law suit, Food Lion did not challenge the accuracy of the *Prime Time Live* report but sued over the fraud its reporters engaged in to gain access to the Food Lion stores.

Food Lion eventually won the law suit, and while the amount of damages was eventually reduced on appeal from $5.5 million to just $2 they scored a huge IM victory. Although Food Lion never sued over the truthfulness of the story, the fact that they beat ABC in court signaled to many American viewers that the original ABC news story was inaccurate ('Food Lyin', 1997)

Faced with potentially fatal accusations, Food Lion's tactics were a very aggressive form of **protective IM** – steps aimed at repairing spoiled identities. Like many of the protective IM tactics we describe in this chapter and the next, they were remarkably effective. Though Food Lion's sales went down immediately after the *Prime Time* exposé, they showed consistent increases after the damage control campaign began. As we shall see in Chapters 4 and 5, defensive IM tactics, if applied correctly, can help snatch a semblance of victory from the jaws of apparent defeat.

Predicaments

No organization or individual is perfect. Mistakes, screw-ups and blunders characterize social and workplace life. Bill spills his coffee on the boss's new suit. Faith shows up late for an important meeting. Stacy erases accounting data from the company's Intranet.

In IM terms, Bill, Faith, and Stacy all face a **predicament**. According to Schlenker (1980, p. 125), a predicament is 'any event that casts aspersions on the lineage, character, conduct, skills, or motives of an actor'. Snyder, Higgins, and Stucky (1983) have identified four general categories of predicament-generating behaviors. They are presented in Table 4.1.

Table 4.1	**Categories of Predicament-Generating Behaviors**
	1. *Doing something that shouldn't be done.*
	Example: Though Stacy was unfamiliar with the company's new accounting system, she still tried to run some analyses on it to answer a question her boss had. The result was she erased some key data from the system.
	2. *Not doing something that should be done.*
	Example: Because Faith was late for a meeting, she had no time to prepare hard copies of her presentation for potential clients.
	3. *Doing things badly.*
	Example: Being late also resulted in Faith not having time to research her sales pitch adequately. It 'bombed': The clients found her sales pitch confusing and difficult to follow. And, they still were annoyed that she showed up late.
	4. *Being caught 'red-handed'.*
	Example: Stacy is so upset at losing the accounting data that she sneaks into the office on the weekend and tries to change the company's main accounting program to cover up her mistake. Unaware of the recently installed security system, her unauthorized attempt is detected soon after she logs-on to the system.

Source: Snyder, Higgins, & Stucky (1983)

Predicaments are **identity risk factors**; a person's reputation, image, and self-esteem may be tarnished. The offender finds himself in a **sticky situation** (Snyder et al., 1983). Unless dealt with, the offender may be viewed negatively by others, face sanctions, punishments, and be denied future benefits and rewards.

In real-world settings, there are often financial consequences to being blamed for predicaments including loss of profit, pay, and denial of bonuses (Crant & Bateman, 1993). Some companies who are represented by professional athletes have even gone as far as to purchase 'image insurance' to protect themselves. The policies, which can cost up to 2 percent of the total revenue involved, protect the firm if something negative happens to the athlete's reputation. If the athlete commits a crime, an indecent act, or does something degrading or offensive to the community, the company is paid off (Hiestand, 1991). Most individuals and organizations, however, cannot afford image insurance. Instead, they make use of a series of protective IM behaviors described below.

Remedial Tactics

In popular culture the protective forms of IM are called **damage control, rezoning**, **spin-doctoring** and **spin-control**. IM theorists often refer to these image-repair efforts as **remedial tactics**. They are attempts 'to deal with the predicament, offering the audience, real or imagined, an explanation of it or an apology for it that can place the actor and the event in a different perspective. By so doing, the actor attempts to minimize the negative repercussions of the predicament' (Schlenker, 1980, p. 135).

Remedial tactics that follow predicaments try to ward off a potentially negative impression in one of four ways: reducing the negative impression, negating it, neutralizing it, or redefining it as positive (Giacalone & Rosenfeld, 1984). Faced with the predicaments mentioned above, Bill, Faith, and Stacy quickly engage in **facework** – behaviors that attempt to restore order to damaged interactions (Hodgins, Liebeskind, & Schwartz, 1996) Bill apologizes profusely and offers to pay the dry cleaning bill. Faith complains about the monster traffic jam that caused her lateness. Stacy blames her faux-pas on a flaw in a newly installed software package.

There has been much attention to the types of remedial IM engaged in following predicaments. In the remainder of this chapter we describe **excuses** and **justifications** – protective IM tactics known jointly as **accounts**. In Chapter 5, we will consider the other protective forms of IM as well as their organizational implications.

Accounts

Predicaments give birth to remedial tactics that aim to reduce the negative impact of the event on the person's reputation. These remedial actions, typically verbal repair statements occurring after the predicament has occurred, are known as **accounts** (Scott & Lyman, 1968). Table 4.2 describes a number of other terms that have been used to describe these forms of verbal damage control.

Accounts have been defined as 'statements made to explain untoward behavior and bridge the gap between actions and expectation' (Scott & Lyman, 1968, p. 46). An offender uses accounts to try and obtain the best possible deal under the circumstances. In the absence of an account, significant audiences will likely reprimand, think less of, or in some way punish the transgressor. Accounts are attempts to avoid this worst case interpretation of the offending behavior and manage the best impression possible under the circumstances (Schlenker, 1980). According to Braaten, Cody, and DeTienne (1993, p. 220). 'An effective account is one that the receivers find credible, and through which the account-giver is forgiven or is exonerated of blame, avoids negative evaluation, avoids penalties, and avoids conflict.' The function of an account is not necessarily to make individuals look good as much as it is to avoid having them look bad. Consider the case of Geoff, a pharmacist who is caught pilfering medicine from the drug store that employs him. If he says nothing, he likely will lose his job, be demoted or, at best, be continuously monitored. However, Geoff offers an account: 'My wife is suffering from cancer and needs the medicine to help relieve her pain'. If the account is accepted, the consequences to Geoff (compared to saying nothing) will not be as bad.

As we saw with our opening Food Lion story, organizations as well as individuals offer accounts. According to Bies and Sitkin (1992), organizational accounts often follow on the heels of **failure events** – actions such as budget cuts and layoffs. Unexplained, these failure

Table 4.2	**Verbal Damage Control**

A number of different terms have been used to describe the types of verbal statements individuals give when faced with predicaments.

Term: *Motive Talk*

Source: Mills (1940)

Definition: Motives to Mills were not internal processes but were words that addressed the anticipated impact of questionable conduct. People use a 'vocabulary of motives' to justify their actions.

Term: *Neutralization*

Source: Sykes and Matza (1957)

Definition: According to Sykes and Matza, verbal statements can be used to 'neutralize' unacceptable behavior and make it appear as not too deviant from accepted norms and societal practices.

Term: *Accounts*

Source: Scott and Lyman (1968)

Definition: Accounts are verbal devices that explain unanticipated or untoward actions. They consist of excuses and justifications.

Term: *Quasi-Theories*

Source: Hewitt and Hall (1973)

Definition: These are explanations offered on an ad hoc basis in problematic situations to give these situations order and hope. For example, a corporate consultant unable to find work attributes his lack of success to 'market forces' resulting from a bad economy.

Term: *Aligning Actions*

Source: Stokes and Hewitt (1976)

Definition: When social interactions or verbal conversations prove problematic people use verbal strategies to 'align' or make the problematic actions seem consistent with or motivated by cultural expectations and societal standards. The person faced with a predicament tries to show that she is still part of the social order even though she may have acted in such a way as to violate it.

events can cause an organization great harm – trust and cooperation will be lowered and organizational performance and productivity decreased. Failure events can be made less organizationally harmful if acceptable explanations for bad outcomes are offered. No one likes a pay cut, but, as one study to be described later found, a good account for a pay cut resulted in less employee theft than a comparable situation where no account or a perfunctory account was offered (Greenberg, 1990).

While individuals typically use accounts to extricate themselves from predicaments, managers in work settings may need to use accounts as a necessary means of maintaining their authority. Although managers have formal authority over those who work for them, their success often depends on the degree of support and cooperation their employees give them. Since managers cannot endorse all requests for raises, promotions, or outstanding performance appraisals, the use of accounts to maintain order becomes a daily part of the successful manager's repertoire. Through accounts, a manager tries to make his or her tough decisions seem fair, justified, and necessary (Bies & Sitkin, 1992). It has been found that accounts help reduce employee resentment and anger following organizational procedures they may view to be unfair (Conlon & Murray, 1996). Accounts are a way of putting 'Happy Faces' on unfavorable organizational outcomes (Bleifuss, 1994).

If these organizational accounts are accepted, subordinates will continue to perform and produce. If accounts aren't offered, or lack in credibility, then negative outcomes such as lowered morale, turnover, theft, and sabotage may increase. One of our former bosses would regularly call three-hour meetings, not allow anyone to go to the bathroom, and yell at employees for the slightest shortcoming. He would never admit that he was partly to blame for what had gone wrong. This failure to ever offer an account resulted in the boss literally finding himself in a sticky situation: one morning he arrived at work to find that his door had been super-glued shut. The offender was never found, partly due to the fact that every employee in the department was a suspect! Thus, the strategic use of accounts – often thought to be a sign of weakness – can actually enhance the power and authority of managers just as ingratiation serves as a means of heightened social influence for the powerless (see Chapter 2). As organizations grow more diverse, accounts can also be a way to reduce conflict between competing groups and help organizations better manage their work-force (Tata, 2000).

It is not simply the offering of an account but whether it is accepted that determines its effectiveness. Rather than viewing accounts as stand-alone forms of protective IM, it is useful to think of them as a **reparative process** where people try to align their actions with socially, culturally, or organizationally acceptable standards (Orbuch, 1997).

Schonbach and Kleibaumhuter (1990) describe four phases that comprise a typical reparative account process: (1) **Failure event**: a predicament occurs where an individual may be held responsible by an observer. (2) **Reproach phase**: the observer reacts either with a look or statement that communicates some disapproval to the individual. (3) **Account phase**: the individual offers an account aimed at reducing the potential negative impression. (4) **Evaluation phase**: the observer evaluates and accepts or rejects the account. If accepted, the negative impression is lessened and the parties can continue positive future interactions. If rejected, a negative impression is formed and unpleasant consequences may follow.

For example, say that Ted, a white male fileclerk, is overheard telling anti-Black jokes by Shirley, his Black supervisor. Ted's overheard racial jokes qualify as a failure event – he faces a serious predicament. Shirley's facial scowl and angry departure signal reproach, and heighten the need for Ted to engage in damage control. He quickly seeks out Shirley and says he only was repeating something he heard at a local pub and didn't mean to offend anyone. Although still miffed, Ted's account strikes Shirley as sincere. She also admires Ted for coming to her directly rather than avoiding the issue. Since Ted has never been heard to make remarks like this before, Shirley accepts his account and takes no further action. Just as Shirley drew inferences about Ted based on his accounts, organizations can use accounts as rich sources for information that is often difficult to obtain in other ways. Box 4.1 describes the information potential of organizational accounts.

IM theorists have described two specific types of accounts: excuses and justifications. They are reviewed in detail below.

Excuses and Justifications

A public relations professional noted, 'It is easier and less costly to change the way people think about reality than it is to change reality' (Bleifuss, 1994, p. F–13). Excuses and justifications are verbal IM tactics commonly used following predicaments. The offender acts as his own public relations agent trying to change the way people think about bad events rather than changing the events themselves.

Excuses and justifications differ in the assignment of responsibility. An **excuse** admits an action was wrong but the person denies that he or she is responsible. A **justification** accepts responsibility for the action, but the person denies that the act was bad (McGraw, 1991).

| Box 4.1 | **Accounts as Sources of Organizational Information** |

Because employees' IM concerns at the time of the incident may bias accounts, they are often dismissed as not being good sources of information. However, accounts can be rich sources of information about incidents such as those involving unethical behaviors or industrial accidents. In those situations it is often difficult to obtain accurate information because people rarely feel free to openly discuss their own or other's actions and motivations (Szwajkowski, 1992).

By looking at individuals' accounts surrounding unethical acts, we can learn, for example, what conditions people think would excuse or justify certain actions. People may pick the accounts they use because they assume they would be accepted, i.e., they appeal to accepted norms for behavior in that situation. Even if the accounts are not the real reason for a behavior, they convey what the individual thinks would be an acceptable reason for the behavior. 'I'm not cleaning up the rubbish because it's not my job,' is more likely to be heard in an organization that has a powerful union presence because it would be a more acceptable reason for failing to act than it would be in a small family business.

Sometimes employee accounts identify things the organization is doing that employees feel excuse or justify unethical behavior. Accounts may signal the likelihood of future ethical lapses even though the reasons given were not the real reasons for the particular act in question. An enlightened organization would want to stop doing those things believed to be justifying or excusing unethical behavior. For example, it has been found that frustrated employees were more likely to commit acts of sabotage than individuals not frustrated (Spector, 1975; cited in Giacalone & Knouse, 1990). If, in listening to employees' accounts of recent problems, they are describing situations in which they feel they were trying to do the right thing but were frustrated by other employees, supervisors, policies, or procedures, trying to change those frustrating factors would be one way to reduce the possibility of future sabotage. Suppose Linda knows she has an excellent product but Arch the quality control supervisor keeps it tied up with endless testing. When asked why her product hasn't been marketed yet, Linda goes into a 'blaming frenzy' pointing to Arch and others in the firm as ▶

the reason for the delays. Dealing with Linda's accounts for the delays may ultimately keep Linda from realizing her fantasy of putting a lethal virus in the company's email system.

Accounts can also inform organizations about the potential causes of accidents. Employees involved in an accident are often more in touch than management or outside investigators with factors that did lead or could have led to the accident. Even though a negligent person trying to get off the hook might use the factors as excuses, those same factors may be potential sources of future accidents and therefore are worth checking out. Suppose a chemical spill was due to Phil's carelessness, but Phil claimed it was due to the faulty equipment that often breaks down. If Phil's accounts were listened to as a source of information, they could stimulate an investigation that reveals equipment badly in need of repair. Even though the equipment was not the actual cause of the spill in question, the account may serve to get the repairs made and thereby prevent future accidents.

Finally, listening to accounts can reveal individuals' understanding of company policies. In the United States there are laws and regulations that can hold organizations liable for violations even if the individuals involved did not intend or were unaware of the violations they produced. For example, supervisors are responsible for preventing sexual harassment even if they did not know, but should have known, it was happening. Similarly, the Environmental Protection Agency can file charges against someone who illegally disposed of waste, even if the individual did so without knowing that what she was doing was wrong. From the organization's perspective, if problems of sexual harassment or improper waste disposal arise, and employees or managers are attempting to excuse their behaviors by saying they weren't aware anything wrong was going on, it points to the need for additional training. They need to know lack of intent or ignorance will not protect them from legal responsibility.

Excuses are attempts to reduce responsibility for failure events. Schlenker (1980) views the excuse-maker as someone who tries to get the best deal obtainable under the circumstances. Excuse-makers seek an IM plea-bargain. The transgressor can't totally eliminate responsibility for the predicament but can reduce it, cushioning the blow so that the damage is minimized. Consider the following excuses. When Harvey drops an expensive office PC, he says it was the slippery floor that made him fall. When the company comptroller questions Gwen as to why she purchased expensive office furniture, she says her boss demanded she order the best stuff. When Lloyd is asked why he hired Ian, an incompetent intern, he says that Ian had good grades and related experience, but neither Ian nor his previous employees had shared his checkered employment history, so Lloyd had no way of knowing of his incompetence.

Justifications, in contrast, try to redefine the questionable action so that it doesn't appear to be as bad. When Sammy, an employee in an organizational consulting firm, is asked by his boss why he has been overcharging an oil company client, Sammy justifies his misdeed by claiming that the oil company underpaid him in the past and it has a reputation for trying to cheat consultants out of their full fees. In essence, Sammy is claiming that stealing from a thief is really not wrong.

A Typology of Excuses and Justifications

Scott and Lyman (1968) have proposed a typology of excuses and justifications that are useful both to organizational researchers and practitioners. We review the major categories.

Types of excuses

1. Appeal to accidents

An attempt is made to reduce responsibility by claiming that the predicament was an accident. Appealing to an accident is an effective excuse if the accident is rare and doesn't occur again often. If Darla spills coffee on her co-worker Danni once, it can be excused as an accident. If it happens a lot, Danni may not easily forgive Darla.

2. Appeal to defeasibility

This excuse maintains that the person wasn't fully informed about what occurred and so can't be held fully responsible. A supervisor confronted with evidence that his subordinates are playing solitaire, checking stock portfolios, and accessing porno on their work PCs may contend that he had no idea what was going on. If he knew, he surely would have acted.

Markman and Tetlock (2000) have described a related account called a **counterfactual excuse**. This excuse takes the form of 'I couldn't have known' and is common in situations where individuals are viewed as responsible for events that have unpredictable outcomes such as stock market investments. After Rita's investment broker Regis tells her to buy technology stocks, the stock market takes a sudden downturn following an unexpected energy crisis in California. 'Sorry' says Regis, 'I just couldn't have known that this was going to happen.' In this way, Regis both avoids responsibility for the bad advice and maintains his own self-image. In Regis' mind, there was really nothing he could have done. Despite losing all of Rita's life savings, he still considers himself a good broker.

3. Appeal to biological drives

To avoid responsibility, the excuse-maker claims an uncontrollable biological factor made them do it. In an interview study, Scully and Marolla (1984) found that convicted rapists made frequent use of excuses which claimed that uncontrollable outside forces made them 'do it'. Variations on this excuse are found in organizations. After making a pass at Cass at the company holiday party, Simon says that he was so turned on by her that he couldn't control himself.

4. Scapegoating

This type of excuse involves blaming others for causing the predicament. When caught cheating on a promotion exam, Marguerite says she had to cheat because the exam was poorly constructed by her incompetent professor, Bob, and therefore unfair.

Types of justifications

1. Denial of injury

The individual acknowledges doing the act, but justifies it because there was no harm or damage caused. Bennie admits he used the company car for a personal trip to Scotland, but claims it's no big deal since no one else needed the car and he didn't damage it.

2. Denial of the victim

The behavior is justified on the grounds that the victim deserved it. Some supporters of Paul Hill, a man who shot and killed a doctor who had been performing abortions in Pensacola, Florida, claimed that his action was justified because the doctor was, in their view, killing innocent babies and had to be stopped.

3. Condemnation of the condemners

The claim is made that others do the same thing or worse and get away with it. Meyer is accused of using company-earned frequent-flyer airplane tickets for personal use. Meyer the frequent flyer admits violating organization policy, but claims his actions are justified since many supervisors in the organization are doing the same thing and getting away with it.

4. Appeal to loyalties

The negative action is justified because it helped another to whom the person feels loyal. G. Gordon Liddy justified his role in the Watergate burglary as having been motivated out of loyalty to former US President Richard Nixon for whom he was working at the time. Liddy's loyalty has been rewarded. Though Nixon is dead, Liddy hosts a popular radio talk show in Washington, DC.

Excuses and Justifications: Research Evidence

The offering of accounts may very well be a universal human tendency – when faced with a predicament people tend to explain it. One study found that only 7 percent of individuals who were asked to recall 'things they wish they hadn't said' indicated that they did nothing after making the regrettable remark. And most of those who did nothing were hoping that their 'regrettable message' would not be noticed (Knapp, Stafford, & Daly, 1986).

It seems just because an account is ludicrous, it can still serve a damage control function. Some people seem to operate according to the principle that an absurd account is better than none at all. In 1998, when confronted with DNA evidence and asked whether he had lied when he said that there 'is no sexual relationship with Monica Lewinsky', former US President Bill Clinton told a grand jury, 'it depends what the meaning of "is" is'! Earlier, Bernstein's (1993) analysis of excuses offered by psychology students found that in one class, 14 of the 250 students claimed that their grandparent died before the final.

Researchers have noted that there are dangers in the overuse of excuses. The short-term gain provided by an excuse may result in long-term harm to the excuse-maker's reputation. While a single excuse can provide short-term relief from a specific predicament, excuses may result in long-term identity damage. Excuses 'are effective in exonerating the account-giver of blame for a specific act. However, the claim that one is not responsible for actions can adversely affect the excuse-maker's public image by creating (or maintaining) an image that he or she is not committed to or involved in the organization, and that he or she is not competent to plan and execute actions in such a way as to perform work successfully' (Braaten et al. 1993, p. 222). As our colleague Jerry Greenberg (1996) found, accounts in organizations can backfire. Greenberg's study indicated that the 'forgive me I'm new' excuse worked if a new employee's performance did not directly affect those receiving the excuse. However, if a new employee's performance negatively impacted the evaluator, then knowledge that the employee was new resulted in negative ratings.

Despite these dangers, research has shown that excuses and justifications are very common. Wood and Mitchell (1981) found that nurses who offered excuses for incorrect nursing procedures (e.g., claiming that the reason they had not checked patients' vital signs was due to factors beyond their control) were perceived by nursing managers as being less likely to fail in the future.

With workplace violence on the rise in many organizations, and increased concern over who will be the next employee to 'go postal', it is of interest to note that even individuals accused of the most heinous violent crimes use accounts to excuse and justify their actions. When Ray and Simons (1987) interviewed 25 convicted murderers they found that 18 offered excuses for their actions and 6 gave justifications. While few of the murderers thought their crime was okay, they offered excuses, such as being drunk and on drugs or stressful life events (e.g., unemployment, divorce), or justifications like claiming they killed in self-defense. Henderson and Hewstone (1984) also found accounts to be common among convicted felons incarcerated in a maximum security prison, but in contrast to the previous study, they found justifications were more common than excuses. The prisoners tended to accept responsibility for their crimes such as murder and assault and offered justifications for its occurrence. Thus, individuals will offer excuses and justifications for what may seem to an observer to be a senseless, violent act.

While it may be hard to relate to the accounts of convicted murderers, we all have missed a class or a day of work and have needed to explain our absence to a teacher, boss, or co-worker. When Kalab (1987) looked at the accounts offered by students for their absences, he found that excuses were more common than justifications. Illnesses were the most commonly offered excuses. While students also used accounts such as family responsibilities, other classwork, oversleep, and accidents, Kalab notes that claiming illness is a particularly good excuse in that it can be used repeatedly and is not immediately met with skepticism. This would also seem to be true of excuses and justifications for absence from work. While car trouble or a faulty alarm clock may work occasionally, such excuses quickly become old and ineffective if used repeatedly. Being sick, however, is viewed in many organizations as a legitimate excuse for missing work and, unless there is some reason for doubt (e.g., being sick on Mondays and Fridays exclusively), it usually will be effective. We know of one employee who changed a planned vacation day to sick leave after hearing that some of his co-workers had recently gotten the flu.

Another common breeding ground for accounts is exam time. Albas and Albas (1988) found that students who did poorly on an exam – they were called 'bombers' – tended to conceal their performance or avoid encounters with 'aces' – those who did well. However, when they encountered other bombers they typically engaged in a mutual account session that the authors called a 'pity party'. Once again, excuses were more common than justifications. Especially when the grade distribution was low, the bombers engaged in excuses in the form of scapegoating to reduce their responsibility for doing poorly. They blamed the teacher for being a sadist, slave driver, or incompetent. Of course, being talented instructors ourselves, we doubt that any of our students would ever offer such obviously 'lame' excuses!

The work of Riordan and her colleagues (e.g., Riordan, Marlin, & Kellogg, 1983) suggests that excuses may be more effective than justifications. In one study she and her colleagues looked at how accounts influenced psychologists' perceptions of unethical research practices. The psychologist respondents to this study read scenarios in which a psychologist was charged with faking data or plagiarizing part of a research publication. They found the unethical action was viewed less negatively following an excuse than a justification. Also, the act was seen as more likely to occur in the future following a justification. Why might justifications be less effective than excuses? Riordan and associates suggest that when acts are clearly bad, justifications may fail because they try to claim that the action was okay. The audience may disagree and view the person negatively as a result. Excuses, in contrast, implicitly commit organizational actors to better behavior in the future because the excusing conditions often are temporary (e.g., flat tires, sick children). Moreover, this occurs regardless of whether the audience accepts the contention of lessened responsibility or not. Indeed, future behavior was predicted to be more negative following a justification than excuse (Riordan et al., 1983).

If an act is clearly bad, it may be harder to justify it than to excuse the perpetrator's responsibility for committing it. This is because a person's responsibility is often more ambiguous than knowing whether an act is bad or good. Since it is often harder for audiences to determine the responsibility of the actor than to characterize the act, excuses tend to be believed, even when they are false. Bernard Weiner and his colleagues had college students recall instances where they offered excuses for predicaments such as showing up late to a party (Weiner, Amirkhan, Folkes, & Verette, 1987). They found that respondents perceived 88 percent of their excuses to be believed and only 12 percent to be disbelieved by their target audiences. Interestingly, of the 28 excuses that were disbelieved, 13 were actually true and 15 were false. The practical lesson may be that following clearly negative actions, an excuse is more likely to work than a justification.

Excuses and Justifications in Organizations

When identity-threatening or stigmatizing events befall an organization, leaders typically provide explanations for those

events that are intended to minimize damage to the
organization's image and their own reputations
(Ginzel, Kramer, & Sutton, 1993, p. 228).

Excuses and justifications are common features of everyday social interaction in organizations. Since many organizational decisions are made in private, and only then explained publicly, employees are left to evaluate how fair a decision was through the type of account used to explain it. If managers do not explain decisions or if their accounts are inadequate, their employees may draw 'worst-case' scenarios and conclude that decisions are unfair even when they are not. According to Bies and Sitkin (1992), accounts, particularly in the form of excuse-making, serve as a **legitimatization strategy** in organizations. That is, managers need to offer accounts to legitimize their actions in order to maintain authority. As mentioned earlier, since a manager can't possibly agree to all requests for raises, promotions, or transfers, she must explain her decisions (i.e., offer accounts) or risk losing the support and cooperation of those who work for her. Managers who successfully offer accounts for organizational predicaments, minimize the destructive aspects of these failure events.

That excuse-making is a 'normal' way of doing business can be seen through the results of a study by Bies conducted with middle managers in ten companies (discussed in Bies & Sitkin, 1992). The managers were asked to recall instances where bad news (e.g., financial losses, budget cuts) was given to subordinates or bosses. These managers reported giving an excuse every time they were the bearers of bad news – regardless of whether they were delivering it to their bosses or employees. In addition to telling those directly affected by the bad news, the managers offered excuses about the bad news to key powerful others in the organization to build a **coalition of supporters**. They also engaged in excuse-making as a public-relations activity to those that had witnessed or had heard about the bad events. These managers were 'hyper' excuse-makers, using this form of protective IM to legitimize their status and authority within the organization by offering multiple rather than single excuses following failure. One reason that excuses may be so common in organizations is that they are often remarkably effective in reducing the potential damage of failure events. Bies and Sitkin (1992) cite evidence indicating that excuses make: (a) employees more accepting of being underpaid; (b) budget cuts seem more justified; (c) individuals more accepting of rejection for a job; and (d) poor performance evaluations appear fairer. Giacalone (1988) found that accounts improved the perceived leadership ratings of a male library director who had misappropriated funds.

Characteristics of Effective Excuses

Not all excuses are equally effective. Factors that have been associated with successful excuse-making in organizations are **perceived adequacy**, **normativeness**, and **perceived sincerity**. Successful excuses also can reduce anger in the aggrieved party.

Perceived adequacy

To be effective, an organizational excuse must be seen as adequate. The perceived adequacy of an excuse refers to whether it is viewed as logical and reasonable under the circumstances. Adequate excuses fit the facts and are sufficiently detailed so as to be convincing (Greenberg, Bies, & Eskew, 1991). Excuses which lack in perceived adequacy may be seen as arbitrary and be counterproductive.

Greenberg (1990) looked at the effect of perceived adequacy of explanations on employee theft in manufacturing plants following a temporary 15 percent pay cut. In one plant, the pay cut was announced with no explanation, in a second plant a minimal explanation was offered, while in a third plant, a detailed 'thorough and sensitive' explanation of the reasons for the pay cut was given to employees. The results showed that a detailed, adequate explanation for the pay cut resulted in less theft than a minimal explanation. One reason individuals given adequate explanations for the pay cut stole less is that they perceived the pay cut as less unfair than individuals who received a minimal or no explanation for it.

Normativeness

The study just described points to an important aspect of accounts: their effectiveness often depends on people's expectations for how actions *should* be explained. This is what is meant by an account's **normativeness**. As the study above demonstrates, when an organization takes an action that has significant harmful effects on employees, a detailed account is expected. Anything less results in adverse reactions.

Certain accounts seem to seen as appropriate for certain actions and not for others. If Kate is late for work, saying her son had a cold is usually an acceptable account. If Hugh is late for an important job interview, trying to excuse his tardiness with his son's cold would not be as effective. People's impressions of the appropriateness of certain accounts stems from a common understanding of the situation and norms for behavior in those situations. In the case of a job interview, it would be expected that some back-up child care arrangements would have been made. Given this, the sick child excuse isn't as effective.

It turns out that giving accounts that are normative may be more important than whether the account is truthful. In a study of perceptions of US senators accounting for their illegal and unethical actions, it was the accounts 'that other people might offer for that behavior' that led to relieving responsibility for negative acts and in recharacterizing the actions in a less negative way (Riordan et al., 1983). This perceived normativeness was more important than whether the account was seen as being the 'real' reason for the predicament-causing behavior. Accounts believed to be ones most people would offer produced more positive perceptions than those that were seen as closer to the truth. We may get out of being perceived badly following predicaments by merely showing we know the acceptable way to explain our actions. Knowing the acceptable explanation may be more important than truthfully explaining those actions.

Perceived sincerity

Perceptions of an account's sincerity are also important. The role of perceived sincerity was demonstrated in a study by Bies, Shapiro, and Cummings (1988) that looked at reactions by employees to management's refusals of their budget requests. They found that the perceived sincerity of the manager in communicating the excuse was associated with less anger, less perceived injustice, fewer complaints, and less disapproval of the boss. Interestingly, the excuse alone – a claim of extenuating circumstances – was not independently associated with any of these positive outcomes. It had to be perceived as sincere. Thus, the way a manager offers an account may be as important or more important than the content of the explanation. In this vein, Giacalone and Rosenfeld (1984) recommended that managers should properly 'stage' their accounts. They found that accounts offered by a library director for an erroneous decision were more accepted if associated with decisions that were portrayed as well thought out and proper.

That sincere excuses were associated with less subordinate anger in the Bies et al. (1988) study supports an important emotional consequence of excuses noted by Weiner and his colleagues (e.g., Weiner, Amirkhan, Folkes, & Verette, 1987). They found excuses, in addition to managing impressions, can serve as effective means of emotion or anger management. In a field study with college students, they found excuses that were believed were associated with less anger even when they were not true, while excuses that were not believed were associated with increased anger even when true. Ross's boss will likely not be as angry if he believes Ross's excuse that he was late for an important sales meeting because he had to take his pregnant wife Susan to a doctor. This will be occur even if Ross's excuse was believed, but had actually been made up.

A Concluding Note

When faced with predicaments, individuals and organizations react with a variety of protective IM behaviors aimed at reducing the damage to their reputations. This chapter has focused on excuses and justifications – after-the-fact damage control tactics known as accounts. Though there is long-term danger in their overuse, excuses and justifications appear to be effective means of reducing negative fallout from image-threatening events.

In addition to accounts, individuals and organizations use other types of protective IM. Also, to enhance the credibility of protective IM, indirect means of damage control may be used. We consider these forms of protective IM in Chapter 5.

5

Protective IM II:
Disclaimers, Self-Handicapping, Apologies, and Indirect Tactics

Walking a Tightrope

> In the first 24 hours after the crash, USAir – like all airlines after a crash –
> had to walk a tightrope between damage control for the company's
> image and expressing complete compassion for the victims
> (Schmit & Jones, 1994, p. B–1).

On September 8, 1994, USAir Flight 427 was on approach to its landing in Pittsburgh, Pennsylvania. Suddenly the airplane lost control and crashed, killing all 132 people aboard. For USAir it was the fifth deadly crash of one of its airplanes within five years. There was immediate media focus on the safety of USAir's planes and speculation about the future viability of the company.

In response to this terrible disaster, USAir quickly and effectively implemented a well-rehearsed and executed crisis plan; one that simultaneously tried to protect the company's image while tending to the needs of the victims' families. Phone banks were set up to deal with the flood of calls, spokespersons appeared on television news shows to deflect criticisms, and two employees were assigned to each victim's family. While not denying the magnitude of the tragedy, USAir representatives insisted that the company's airplanes were safe. At a press conference the next day, USAir's CEO claimed that had he thought the airplane were unsafe he would have grounded the entire USAir fleet. Even in the midst of a great tragedy, USAir engaged in protective IM, an effort designed to help the company survive by maintaining its reputation. USAir's damage control was effective. Within a few days, media focus and the public's interest had lessened, and USAir's operations were back to normal. The company had walked an IM tightrope and survived (Schmit & Jones, 1994).

USAir acted quickly to try to control the damage to their corporate image *before* it spread. Individuals and organizations often don't wait until the flames of predicaments spread and consume them, but may ward off potential damage by acting quickly following crises or by engaging in 'preemptive strikes' in the face of anticipated problems. In Chapter 5 we describe two of these anticipatory IM tactics: disclaimers and self-handicapping. We also consider the protective tactic of last resort: an apology, and conclude with a review of indirect defensive IM.

Disclaimers

A **disclaimer** is a form of excuse-making that occurs before a predicament. Sociologists Hewitt and Stokes (1975, p. 3) defined a disclaimer as, 'a verbal device employed to ward off and defeat in advance doubts and negative typifications which may result from intended conduct'. As the disclaimer described in Box 5.1 shows, perceived sincerity is as important to disclaimers as it is to excuses.

Jung (1987) found that disclaimers increased in advance of probable failure and were more likely when individuals expected to do poorly on a test. Disclaimers involve IM by prognostication, anticipation, and premonition. A disclaimer is a predicament insurance policy purchased before the disaster. If the predicament does not occur, then people can claim they were being modest or cautious (Jung, 1987). Disclaimers nip predicaments in the bud, they put out image-threatening fires before they engulf us and they alter the meaning of future actions so as not to damage fragile reputations at work. 'Don't get me wrong, some of my best friends are Spaniards, but Juan is a lazy thief and should be fired', Miles tells his boss De. The hope is that De won't consider Miles a bigot, even though his comment could lead to that impression. During the Clinton administration, criticism of the US President was often so strong that his staff sometimes put out rebuttals to charges before they were actually made. These political disclaimers came to be known as 'prebuttals' (Riechmann, 2001).

Hospital charges in the United States are often quite high. Stays of just a few days can result in charges of tens of thousands of dollars. Anger and resentment often result when patients learn about these

Box 5.1	**Lame Disclaimers**

Although disclaimers are very common, they are not always believed. Consider the following example. According to Lee Iacocca, at one time high-level employees from Ford Motor Company were sent to solicit donations from executives at other larger companies connected with the auto industry. Ford was often a very big customer of these companies. The executives were asked to donate money to one of Henry Ford's pet projects, a huge office/shopping complex that was to revitalize downtown Detroit. The executives sent to solicit funds would say, 'Now, I'm not here in my capacity as head of purchasing' even though they were doing millions of dollars of business with these companies each year. 'I'm coming to you as the personal representative of Henry Ford … and my visit has nothing to do with Ford Motor Company.' Apparently some of the executives being solicited didn't buy this lame disclaimer and burst out laughing. One thought the symbol for the office complex should be a twisted arm because so much of the money came as a result of undue pressure by these Ford Executives.

(Iacocca, 1984, p. 107)

charges. One study looked at how hospitals used disclaimers to avoid negative reactions (Elsbach, Sutton, & Principe, 1998). They found disclaimers effectively diverted patients' attentions from their bills so that their initial reactions would be less negative and less likely to escalate.

As these examples illustrate, disclaimers are very useful forms of anticipatory IM. Hewitt and Stokes (1975) describe five major categories of disclaimers that help us to appreciate their breadth and functions.

Types of Disclaimers

1. Hedging

A hedge is verbal statement which signals minimal commitment to a future behavior. A hedge indicates that the future behavior is not very important to a person's identity. 'I'm not very good in math,' says Amy, 'but I'll take a job in the accounting department if it will get me a promotion.' In organizations, hedging occurs when leaders voice tentative support for a position counter to their own, to avoid losing the support of those who may react negatively to aggressive one-sided advocacy. 'Yes, I can see why some people would want to start a union here, they have done some good in the past', says Joe the CEO of a mid-size corporation, 'however, given our current economic situation a union would clearly hurt the bottom-line'.

2. Credentialing

In some instances, a person knows that something they are about to do or say will be viewed negatively. To avoid a negative impression, the person claims a special 'credential' that allows him to say or do something bad without being viewed negatively. 'I'm a Jew,' says Lou, 'so when I say that the Jews control the movie business in Hollywood, you know its true.' Lou is using 'Jewish credentials' to avoid being labeled a bigot by others.

3. Sin licenses

The person who uses a sin license is trying to be the exception that proves the rule. By paying homage to the rule, the taint of being viewed as a rule breaker is avoided. 'I know its against the company nepotism policy to hire relatives', says Bill, a corporate CEO, 'but my daughter Chelsea is such a super typist and we are really short of administrative help since Monica quit.'

4. Cognitive disclaimers

It's generally good IM to be viewed as cool, rational and sane, even when doing things that might be seen as bizarre. A cognitive disclaimer tries to accomplish this by statements that avoid the labels 'crazy' or 'irrational'. 'You may think I'm nuts', Kristin tells her boss Marie, 'but I found my productivity has improved since I began taking megadoses of bee pollen and antioxidant vitamins before my Tai-Chi class.'

5. Appeals to the suspension of judgment or affect

This form of disclaimer asks listeners to delay judgment and negative emotional reactions until the questionable action is put into context. Trent tells his boss Linda, 'Before you get mad about the lost advertising account, listen to why it won't hurt us in the long run'.

Self-Handicapping: Setting Up Obstacles to Successful Performance

I was struck by the strategic benefits that one could derive from 'tying one hand behind their back' prior to entering a contest they knew they would lose... I recalled a variety of occasions when, as a summer bartender at an affluent country club, I heard members excuse crude or inept actions by claiming, 'I didn't realize how much I had had to drink' (Steven Berglas, quoted in Rosenfeld & Garrison, 1991, p. 176).

There has been much attention given to a particular form of protective IM called **self-handicapping**. According to Tice and Baumeister (1990, p. 44) self-handicapping involves 'placing obstacles in the way of one's task performance so as to furnish oneself with an external attribution when future outcomes are uncertain'. Simply put, the self-handicapper places impediments or barriers in the face of success. In this way, self-handicappers provide themselves with a double IM payoff: if they succeed despite the barriers, the value of their success is heightened and their reputations bolstered; if they fail, the negative impact is weakened because of the barriers. Assume that Mary and her boss Meredith decide to play tennis during the company's annual off-site business meetings. Meredith has heard that Mary is a good tennis player and is somewhat unsure of her own tennis ability. As they begin to play, Meredith mentions that she strained a calf muscle last week and is having trouble running at full speed. While Mary may think that Meridith is just pulling her leg (so to speak), Meredith's statement is actually a classic self-handicap. If she beats Mary it will be in spite of her sore calf; if she loses she can blame it on the injury and not on her lack of ability.

Since self-handicapping is especially likely to occur in situations where success and failure are important and people feel that their competence or self-worth is on the line, it is not surprising that competitive athletes engage in self-handicapping. One study found golfers and swimmers who scored highly on a measure of self-handicapping practiced less before big tournaments than before lesser ones (Rhodewalt, Saltzman, & Witmmer, 1984). When the event was less important, high and low self-handicappers practiced about the same. In this way, if high self-handicappers won the important event, they could claim victory even though they hadn't practiced very hard; if they lost, they had the excuse of lack of practice. It has been found that withholding effort for events on which a person is to be evaluated is a common form of self-handicapping (Tice & Baumeister, 1990).

As the opening quote from Steven Berglas indicates, the self-handicapping construct can help us understand the strategic benefits of alcohol and drug use, both areas of concern for many large organizations. Say that Mario is sent by his company to an important two-week training course. Mario enjoys the course but is somewhat worried about how he will do on the final exam. While the other students stay in and study hard, Mario goes out, hits the town, and gets drunk. He takes the exam with a hangover and just barely passes. While Mario's behavior may seem on its surface to be self-destructive, it also is an effective form of self-handicapping. Mario can blame his mediocre test performance on excessive drinking and avoid the more threatening conclusion that he lacked ability. He can tell himself and others that had he not gone out and partied he would have done better. Also, the drinking has helped bolster his barely passing test performance. Since he was able to pass the exam even with a hangover, the implication is that had he been sober and studied more, he certainly would have done better. Of course, the possibility that Mario would have done as poorly had he been sober is not considered – we, the audience, just won't know – which is precisely what the self-handicapper seeks to accomplish.

The strategic benefits of 'shooting yourself in the foot' are not limited to drug and alcohol abuse, but may apply to other **acquired** or **claimed** impediments such as illnesses, bad mood, obesity (Baumeister, Kahn, & Tice, 1990), and traumatic life events (DeGree & Snyder, 1985), all of which may impede employee wellness and ultimately harm the organization's productivity. For example, individuals who scored high on a hypochondriasis measure reported more physical illness symptoms when faced with an evaluative task than those scoring low on the hypochondriasis measure (Smith, Snyder, & Perkins,

1983). Hypochondriacs, apparently, strategically used illness symptoms as a form of self-handicapping. When his company relocated, Al, one of the white-collar underperformers who could do little else, was put in charge of packing and moving boxes. Although he had worked for the company for 30 years with no physical problems, Al said he was happy to help but his bad back prevented him from doing much lifting!

It has also been suggested that **procrastination** – putting off things that are needed to reach goals – is a form of self-handicapping (Ferrari, 1991, 1992; Ferrari & Tice, 2000). Consider the case of Marilyn who writes software manuals for a large consulting company. Marilyn procrastinates by throwing herself feverishly into other tasks. She is the head of the employee recreation committee, spending hours, days, nights, and weekends planning for the company picnic or the annual holiday party. She is a devoted member of the company diversity committee; she volunteers to write a plan suggesting how the firm can attract more women and minority employees. Marilyn spends hours testing new software products, and is always available to help junior colleagues in need of a mentor. In short, she would be the perfect employee except that she isn't carrying out her primary responsibility for writing quality software manuals. From a self-handicapping perspective, Marilyn's procrastination makes sense. Worried that her writing will be evaluated negatively by her bosses, colleagues, and readers, she uses time as her IM ally. Eventually Marilyn's procrastination causes her to miss a deadline. 'But, I've been so busy, I haven't been able to work on those manuals,' she tells all who are interested and some who aren't. She finally gets the manual done, but it takes several all-night work sessions and a couple of weekends. But her dawdling has not been for naught. Her delaying has cushioned the blow and provided a defense ('I didn't have enough time to do a better job!') against criticism of her writing ability. And, Marilyn's bosses are so happy to finally have a product that they aren't very critical. That she could get it done in a last-second panic gets her brownie points for producing under pressure. Marilyn tells her co-workers that she did the best she could under the circumstances and given more time in the future, she'd surely do better. (We're planning to try this strategy with our editor, so please don't tip her off!)

Research on self-handicapping began with a laboratory study conducted by Steven Berglas and Edward E. Jones (1978). They had college students take a test that supposedly measured their intelligence. The students were told they would be given one of two drugs before they took an equivalent form of the same test to see if the drugs affected their test performance. Some of the students had solvable problems as part of the first test, while others were given problems that were unsolvable. Despite these differences in types of problems, all students were told they had done well on the first test. The students were then given a choice between one of two drugs: 'Actavil', a drug that was claimed to improve intellectual performance and 'Pandocrin', a drug that supposedly hampered intellectual performance. In support of the self-handicapping notion, male students who had unsolvable problems on the first test, tended to choose Pandocrin – the drug that hurt performance – while those who had solvable problems chose Actavil – the performance-enhancing drug. Taking a test containing unsolvable problems led students to be unsure about their ability and uncertain whether they would do as well on the second test even if they had done well on the first test. Rather than find out for sure how well they could do, they choose to protect their intellectual reputation from failure by choosing a drug that supposedly hurt performance. The drug provided IM insurance. If they failed the second test it could be blamed on the drug. If they aced it again, their interpersonal stock would further rise because they overcame the intellectually harmful drug.

Self-handicapping needs to be used sparingly to maintain its effectiveness. The athlete who constantly cites injuries may be viewed as a malingerer; the employee who drinks before big meetings may be seen as untrustworthy; the procrastinator who always misses deadlines may lose future choice assignments. In this vein, Smith and Strube (1991) found that self-handicappers were perceived more negatively by others than non-handicappers were. The short-term gains offered by self-handicapping need to be balanced by the long-term bad impressions a self-handicapping 'habit' may create. Mel's claim of a bad headache before a big corporate presentation may be an effective tactic once, however, his career may suffer if he repeatedly claims to have headaches in similar future situations.

Given how important success and failure are to the corporate bottom line, we would expect self-handicapping to be a common form of organizational IM. Surprisingly little research has looked at self-handicapping in organizational settings. One exception is a study conducted by Crant and Bateman (1993). Because receiving credit for success and avoiding blame for failure is often tied to tangible outcomes such as promotions and bonuses, the motivation to manage impressions of success and failure is usually high in organizations. In a field study conducted at a large accounting firm in New York City, accountants and supervisors read scenarios that described an audit by a staff accountant, Richard Emmitt, who used self-handicaps. One self-handicap involved telling the boss that the audit would be difficult because the client had a new computer system with bugs that needed to be worked out. Emmitt was portrayed as having conducted a successful audit – it took him fewer hours than had been budgeted – or an unsuccessful audit; he needed more hours than had been budgeted. Interestingly, Emmitt's self-handicapping was effective following failure but not after success. He was blamed less in the failure conditions, but received less credit for success. The principle that self-handicapping enhances success in addition to cushioning failure was not supported in this organizational application.

Apologies

There are some situations in which a person cannot use excuses, justifications, disclaimers, or self-handicapping to extricate himself from a predicament. The thief who is caught with his hand in the cookie-jar; the manager who forgets to attend the CEO's birthday party; the professor whose wife finds him in the arms of a voluptuous graduate assistant. In these cases, the protective IM tactic of last resort – an **apology** – is the offender's only hope. An apology is an admission of responsibility, blame, and regret that tries to obtain a pardon from the target audience (Schlenker, 1980). In late October 2000, Singapore Airlines Flight SQ006 crashed after the pilot took a wrong turn onto a closed runway during a rainstorm. The plane hit a concrete barrier killing 81 of the 179 passengers on board. The subsequent statement by the CEO of Singapore Airlines is an example of an effective organizational apology: 'They are our pilots. That was our aircraft. That aircraft should not be on that runway' (Pan, 2000, p. A20). What is noteworthy about the Singapore Airlines statement is that in Asian societies concerns for loss of face are paramount and apologies are more difficult than in many Western societies. Box 5.2 describes a company in China that apologizes to others for a fee.

Box 5.2	**An Apology Company**

There are cultural differences in how apologies and other forms of defensive IM are given and received. Asian cultures are highly concerned with maintaining face. The offering and receiving of apologies is a more formal and stressful process than in Western countries where, the comedian Steve Martin's 'WELL, EXCUSE ME!' routine is not that far from reality. In Chinese culture apologies are 'weighty acts that are rarely offered or accepted which must be delivered just so, with the proper gravity. To Chinese, apologies require a great loss of face' (Rosenthal, 2001, p. A1).

While the expression of apology is difficult in China, the need remains since interpersonal transgressions requiring repair are universal: families quarrel over forgotten birthdays; businesspersons are offended following bad deals and neighbors damage each other's property.

Rosenthal (2001) describes a number of **apology companies** that have sprung up in China. These companies offer to apologize to offended parties for a fee. One company charges the equivalent of US$2.50 per apology and takes its task quite seriously. The professional apologizers are middle-aged men and women who dress conservatively, have good verbal skills, and receive extra training in counseling. For some clients, letters of apology are written, for others, gifts are offered on their client's behalf, and for others, verbal statements of remorse are proferred face to face. Apologies are seen as more sincere if directly offered by the offender, but the Chinese hesitancy to say 'I'm sorry' can make this direct route too awkward, offering an opportunity for Chinese entrepreneurs to move into the apology market niche.

At their core, apologies try to separate the bad act from the good actor. By profusely apologizing for being late to a job interview, Beau hopes his prospective employer will not consider his tardiness as indicative of his 'real' nature as an employee. Beau is attempting to capitalize on a feature of an apology called **splitting**. A successful apology will split the individual into the 'bad Beau' – the one who was late for the job interview – and the 'good Beau'; the one who realizes his transgression and won't do it again in the future. A courtroom example of splitting was provided by Danny Rolling, a serial killer convicted of the mutilation murders of five college students in Gainsville, Florida. In an effort to avoid the death penalty Rolling said, 'I regret with all my heart what my hand has done' (Serial Killer, *USA Today*, 1994, p. 3A). In essence Rolling's 'good' heart was expressing remorse over what his 'bad' hand had done.

While we may think of apologies as single acts such as saying 'I'm sorry' after squirting ketchup on a co-worker during lunch, or 'oops, pardon me' after inadvertently bumping into another dancer at a company shindig, a more complex apology sequence is often used for serious predicaments. Schlenker and Darby (1981, p. 272) have described a five-component apology sequence. We illustrate the steps with the case of Tim; an employee who gets drunk at the company New Year's party, damages some expensive furniture, and tells loud, dirty jokes that many of the other people find offensive.

1. *Statement of apologetic intent.* After getting drunk at the party, Tim tells his boss's secretary that he's really sorry and would like to apologize to the boss for his behavior.
2. *Expression of remorse.* During a meeting with the boss, Tim indicates how ashamed of his behavior he is and how sorry he feels. Tim tells the boss that he has had trouble sleeping at night since making a fool of himself. In a recent study, Gold and Weiner (2000), found that confessing to a transgression resulted in a positive future expectation of a person's behavior when an expression of remorse was included. A good apology means always having to say you're sorry!

   Expressions of remorse can be both verbal and nonverbal. In December 1970, in one of the most famous and well-received expressions of remorse, the chancellor of West Germany, Willy Brandt, fell on his knees in front of the memorial to the victims of the Warsaw Ghetto. Brandt won the praise and respect of the entire world even though his expression of remorse was totally silent.
3. *Offer of restitution and redress.* Tim offers to pay in full the cost to the company of replacing the damaged furniture.
4. *Statement of self-castigation.* Tim says he feels worthless and understands if the boss needs to discipline him. 'No one feels worse about this than I do', says Tim.
5. *Request for forgiveness.* Lastly, Tim begs the boss to not fire him and to forgive him this one lapse. He promises never to let anything like this happen again.

Apologies have occasionally been studied in organizational settings (e.g., Eylon, Giacalone, & Pollard, 2000). One area where apologies are a way of doing business is during service encounters such as between flight attendants and airline passengers, and servers and restaurant customers. Goodwin and Ross (1992) had students read scenarios of several service encounters (e.g., dental office, airline, auto mechanic) that had an unexpected delay. In one of the scenarios a mechanic tells a customer that a car repair promised by 5:00 pm that day won't be ready till 4:00 pm the next day. The service provider either offered or did not offer an apology and then indicated either that the customer would get a 10 percent discount or said there was nothing that could be done about the delay. The results showed that an apology alone was not enough to increase ratings of fairness or satisfaction. However, when a 10 percent discount was offered, an apology resulted in greater ratings of fairness and satisfaction than no apology. It may be that in real world settings saying you are sorry is not enough unless it is accompanied by some tangible restitution. Apparently, apologetic words work best if accompanied by apologetic deeds.

In a study that looked at how an organization reacted to complaints from customers, Conlon and Murray (1996) found that when a company quickly accepted responsibility for a customer complaint, customers responded positively and remained committed to the company's products and services. However, this positive reaction was lessened when the company did not promptly respond to the complaint.

While many managers may hesitate to show remorse or admit that they have done wrong, the judicious use of apologies may actually be a characteristic of an effective supervisor. Ave (1994) described the winning entries in a 'best-worst boss' essay contest. While one of the characteristics of the best boss was an ability to admit mistakes, worst bosses tended to blame their mistakes on subordinates. Box 5.3 describes how apologies can also help managers lessen the impact of destructive feedback.

Indirect Protective IM Tactics

The nature of bad news infects the teller
(William Shakespeare).

| Box 5.3 | **Apologies and Accounts: Reducing the Negative Effects of Destructive Feedback** |

Most managers are taught that it is important to tell employees how they are doing through some form of regular feedback. **Constructive feedback**, according to Robert Baron (1990), can enhance worker motivation and performance. Telling employees that they are doing well and offering a few pointers for improvement is not very hard, but providing more negative feedback is difficult according to most managers. In fact, many managers avoid giving negative feedback because it may harm their future relations with employees or upset employees.

But avoidance doesn't make the problem go away. Instead the manager's annoyance may build until it explodes in a burst of **destructive criticism**, which 'is often biting, sarcastic, and harsh' (Baron, 1990, p. 235). As you might imagine, the manager's outburst results in anger and tension in employees. Employees' performance may suffer and they may refuse to change.

What can be done? In two studies, Baron (1990) looked at different ways of reducing the negative impact of destructive criticism. In the first study, undergraduate research participants were asked to prepare an advertising campaign for a new shampoo product. An accomplice of the experimenter then looked at their work and gave pre-planned criticism to the participants that was either constructive or destructive. In the key destructive criticism conditions, the accomplice was threatening and inconsiderate and said things like, 'I don't think you could be original if you tried' (p. 237).

After the destructive criticism, the research participants were exposed to four different conditions:

1. Incompatible responses: Participants rated humorous cartoons rather than focusing on the campaign or the criticism.
2. External attribution: Participants were given an account. They were told that most people do poorly on the task.
3. Apology: Participants were told by the experimenter that the accomplice regretted his harsh comments and was sorry.
4. Catharsis: Participants were given a chance to 'get even' by rating the accomplice. ▶

Baron (1990) found that the apology and external attribution (account) conditions were most effective in reducing the negative impact of destructive criticism. Respondents in these conditions were less angry with the accomplice, were happier, and were more likely to view the criticism as fair than respondents in the other groups receiving criticism.

Baron's second study used actual managers and non-managers in organizational settings such as banks and telecommunications companies. The respondents completed a survey that asked them to imagine that they had received destructive criticism from a colleague and they had to rate how effective the four countering actions used in Study 1 would be in reducing their negative reaction to the criticism. Baron found results similar to those obtained in Study 1: both managers and non-managers rated the apology and account as the most effective of the four interventions in insulating them from the criticism. Protective IM tactics (apology, account) proved more effective than traditional behavioral techniques (incompatible response, catharsis) in reducing the negative effects of destructive criticism.

In Chapter 3 we saw how individuals use the principle of association to claim positive impressions for themselves. This form of indirect IM can also be used as a defensive tactic. People will try to minimize their links to negative events or people. They will distance themselves from failure, and downgrade unsuccessful others with whom they might be associated. After Jody's subordinate Rich is caught stealing from the company safe, Jody says she never wanted Rich to work for her in the first place, had never trusted him, and was trying to get him fired. In this way, Jody is trying to minimize the natural tendency of other people to link Rich's stealing with her. Cialdini (1989) has called this tendency to 'advertise' one's negative links to an unfavorable other, **blaring**. In a laboratory experiment, Cooper and Jones (1969) found that people expressed attitudes that were dissimilar to another person when that person had been obnoxious to the experimenter. By proclaiming differences from an obnoxious other, the blarer is trying to be viewed more favorably.

While blaring works by minimizing the connections to a stigmatized other, Cialdini and associates also noted some indirect tactics to minimize or devalue the person with whom we are connected. They called the tendency to exaggerate the bad qualities of someone with whom there is a negative association, **blasting** (Cialdini & Richardson, 1980; Cialdini, 1989). 'You can promote Woody over me', Carol tells her boss, 'but I want you to be aware that most of the people in this department have said they would quit before they would work for an incompetent like him!'

As we saw in Chapter 3, IM techniques such as entitlements often work better if offered by third parties (Giacalone, 1985). Public relations firms have used third parties to argue against laws or regulations that they have been hired to defeat. This form of blasting is called **white hats** (Bleifuss, 1994). White hats involves enlisting the help of groups with no apparent association to an issue to argue against it. The lack of association makes the blast more credible. Bleifuss (1994) provides the following example. A public relations firm was hired by several auto-manufacturing companies to help defeat a proposed requirement for stricter anti-pollution devices on automobiles. The firm got assistance from some elderly and handicapped individuals by convincing them that the anti-pollution regulations would result in smaller cars being built that would be hard for them to get into. Further, they convinced parents that more fuel-efficient station wagons would be too small to accommodate their families. With the opposition of the elderly, handicapped, and many parents, the proposed legislation was defeated. The public relations firm had effectively used third party blasting. They blasted the legislation to the handicapped, elderly, and parents, who in turn blasted it to their elected representatives.

In addition to blasting others, individuals may try to distance themselves from failure, a tactic called **cutting off reflected failure** (CORF; Snyder, Lassegard, & Ford, 1986). In a study of this phenomenon, students were given success, failure, or no feedback on a problem-solving task they had worked on together. It was found that those who failed tended to engage in the most CORFing – they were less likely to take part in their group's presentation and less likely to wear group identifiers that were students in the other groups (Snyder, et al., 1986).

Another way to distance oneself from failure caused by a negative association is to highlight other positive aspects of the relationship. Elsbach and Kramer (1996) found that business school students faced with a less than positive evaluation of their program in the magazine

Business Week tended to emphasize positive dimensions of their schools that we not included in the ratings.

Giacalone (Giacalone, 1987; Giacalone & Knouse, 1988) applied these notions of protective indirect IM to perceptions of women managers in organizations. Giacalone reasoned that because female managers often are viewed as having less potential than men or otherwise negatively stereotyped in organizations, male managers would be more likely to blast a female manager, especially if she fails. In one of several related studies, Giacalone (1987) had undergraduate business students read short fictitious descriptions of a corporate vice-president who was blamed for a decision that led to a huge financial loss for a company. The manager was portrayed as being either a male or female. Giacalone found that female students' ratings of the manager did not differ as a function of the manager's gender, whereas males' ratings did. Males rated themselves less similar to a failing female manager than to a failing male manager. In a second study, Giacalone found that this tendency of males to disassociate from a failing female manager occurred primarily in male respondents who had negative attitudes toward women. In this study, the males whose connections to females were already the weakest, seemed to be first to blast the failing female manager. It suggests when things get tough in organizations, prejudicial attitudes may have more negative effects on organizational functioning (Giacalone & Knouse, 1988).

A Concluding Note

In this chapter we have described disclaimers, self-handicapping, and apologies, three types of protective IM that individuals and organizations use in addition to accounts. As with acquisitive IM, the danger exists that overly aggressive or obvious tactics may be ineffective or backfire. Thus, indirect means are also used in the service of damage control and image repair.

All IMers are not created equally. While the full repertoire of both acquisitive and protective IM behaviors are available to all, not everyone engages in IM in the same way or with equal proficiency. There are a number of different IM behavior patterns or personality traits based on the type and frequency of IM used and the skill or lack of skill in engaging in it. How these differences in IM styles are measured, and their implications for organizations, are the focus of Chapter 6.

6

Measuring IM

In a personnel selection situation, for example, a correlation between self-reported motivation and a measure of IM has a number of plausible interpretations. A stylistic interpretation would suggest that chronic impression managers are faking high motivation. Alternatively, the nature of the position (e.g., public relations) may be such that chronic impression managers would continue to be motivated and are, therefore ideal candidates
(Paulhus, 1991, pp. 23–4).

Different Strokes from Different Folks

In the previous chapters we learned of the many ways that individuals and organizations engage in IM to build and enhance their reputations. While everyone manages impressions, they don't all do it in the same way. Researchers refer to these individual variations in IM tendencies and behaviors as differences in **style** (Arkin, 1981). Styles are characteristic ways people manage impressions. Styles are one way to capture the idea of **individual differences** in IM. Different folks use different IM strokes. Consider the following examples. They may remind you of people you know and work with.

James is a consultant who speaks his mind, and is confrontational in his approach. When a company hires him to help solve organizational problems, he tells them what he thinks, despite how they might feel about it. He disregards how the people in the organization tend to act toward each other. This was particularly true of his interaction with the Happy Camper Company. Happy had a culture with one rather implicit rule that James knew about: 'Never directly challenge Happy employees'. One day when James was at a meeting, Jeff, a Happy executive, made a statement with which James disagreed. James looked at him, stood up and pointingly said, 'Jeff, prove it!' The executives had never seen such confrontation in their organization before. The executives weren't feeling too Happy, and they decided to make James a very unHappy Camper. Their contract with James was soon terminated. As one Happy executive noted, 'James apparently thinks that he can say anything he wants. He's wrong. He may be able to act that way elsewhere, but not at Happy.'

Dawn is an executive who is constantly trying to put her best foot forward. She is quick to tell about her expertise in business process re-engineering and information technology, although she privately tells her husband that 'It is all an act. I know very little about those areas, but they are hot topics now, so I learned the buzzwords and BS my way through the rest.' Her assistant, Leigh, has the same level of inexperience as Dawn, but also claims the same degree of expertise. Yet Leigh is different: She really believes that she is an expert in these areas. As her colleague Vince notes, 'I think that if you hooked Leigh up to a lie-detector, you would see that she isn't lying. She believes that she has the expertise. Unfortunately, she cannot do the work.'

In what was to become a highly publicized dismissal, Gerry's fur-company, 'Pelts are Us' was about to lay off Gerry and his entire group of formerly hot shot mid-level managers who used to be known in corporate circles as the 'Eager Beavers'. Now the 'Eager Beavers' were being dismissed for what Pelts called 'corporate incompatibility'. When Glenn, Gerry's friend in public relations, came by to ask him what he intended to do, Gerry said he was planning how he could market himself to prospective employers after all the bad publicity. 'There aren't many choices,' Gerry finally concluded, 'It's all a sales job. These days you've got to make it seem like you've got every skill a company would ever want or you're dead meat.'

Harold is an engineer at a major manufacturing company. Harold's a rising star. He becomes known as an employee who is quickly climbing the organizational ladder. What is his secret? Harold is an ingratiator par excellence. He is quick to do favors for the executives, and doesn't need to read Dale Carnegie or Chapter 2 to know when to agree with his boss on appropriate topics. Harold is well-liked and that gives him an edge over colleagues even those who are as competent as he is. When promotions are on the line, his 'friends' (the executives he has helped) are quick to remember and reward him.

James, Dawn, Gerry, and Harold are all engaging in organizational IM, but in very different ways. As we shall see in Chapter 6, James is a low self-monitor, someone whose deeds correspond closely to his beliefs. Dawn is high in the trait of IM: She deceives others to make herself look good. Gerry's style is one of high attributive IM – he tends to use IM to ascribe positive characteristics to himself. Finally, Harold is a hyper-ingratiator. He tries to succeed by 'kissing up' to anything and anyone. Ifs, ands, and especially buts!

In this chapter, we present four measures of IM that correspond to the styles of James, Dawn, Gerry, and Harold. These measures illustrate the ways that IM might be assessed, how assessment provides us with an understanding of the varied nature of IM, and how such assessment could be utilized by organizations.

Measures of IM

The measures we have chosen differ in their focus. The *Self-Monitoring Scale* (Snyder, 1974) is the most popular measure of IM behaviors, focusing on the extent to which individuals differ in their attentiveness and responsiveness to social cues. The focus is on both the choice to engage in IM and how skilled the person is at it. The *Balanced Inventory of Desirable Responding* (BIDR) (Paulhus, 1991) is a measure that conceptualizes IM as a process driven by two different tendencies. One is the tendency to deliberately convey a distorted image of self to others (what some have cynically viewed as describing all IM). The BIDR also measures the extent to which individuals give overly positive statements about themselves that they actually believe. The *Self-Presentation Scale* (Roth, Snyder, & Pace, 1986) is a measure of whether individuals tend to use IM that focuses on the positive characteristics they hold, or on the denial of negative characteristics. Lastly, the *Measure of Ingratiatory Behaviors in Organizations Settings Scale* (MIBOS) (Kumar & Beyerlein, 1991) focuses on the extent to which individuals use various ingratiation tactics (see Chapter 2) in supervisor–subordinate relationships.

Self-Monitoring Scale

> From the early stages of deciding where to work and in what
> capacity through the ending of one's association with an
> organization, self-monitoring may influence the types and qualities
> of interactions between individuals in an organization
> (Snyder & Copeland, 1989, pp. 17–18).

Some people, both inside and outside of organizations, appear to be **social chameleons**: Individuals who change their attitudes, perspectives, and behaviors so as to fit into the social situations at hand. Others, as the story of James shows, do not adapt to the constraints of the social environment.

The Self-Monitoring Scale (Snyder, 1974) most directly assesses the degree to which people act like social chameleons. It measures the extent to which individuals in social situations actively monitor, manage, and control their public behaviors and appearances (Gangestad & Snyder, 2000; Snyder & Copeland, 1989). In an organizational setting, when a manager asks the opinions of employees about a new performance appraisal system, high self-monitoring employees may carefully control what they say and adjust their response to fit what the manager wants to hear. Others who are low self-monitors may offer their opinions and beliefs in a manner that is close to what they actually feel irrespective of what they think the manager's position is. What they feel is what you get!

The Self-Monitoring Scale is presented in Table 6.1.

Gabrenya and Arkin (1980) have described the high self-monitor as having five key tendencies. First, high self-monitors have a strong concern for the social appropriateness of behavior. Second, they show a greater attentiveness to behavior of others as cues for their own IM. Third, high self-monitors possess a greater skill at modifying and controlling their own IM. Fourth, they use IM skill in more circumstances. Finally, the high self-monitor exhibits different behaviors in different situations. As summarized by Gangestad and Snyder (2000), high self-monitors are both skilled actors and **social pragmatists** – ready, willing, and able to use IM to strategically control the impressions they make on others. It has been found that high self-monitors use IM tactics such as ingratiation and self-promotion more skilfully than do low self-monitors (Turnley & Bolino, 2001).

Table 6.1	**The Self-Monitoring Scale**

1. I find it is hard to imitate the behavior of other people.
2. My behavior is usually an expression of my true inner feelings, attitudes, and beliefs.
3. At parties and social gatherings, I do not attempt to do or say things that others will like.
4. I can only argue for ideas which I already believe.
5. I can make impromptu speeches even on topics about which I have almost no information.
6. I guess I put on a show to impress or entertain people.
7. When I am uncertain how to act in a social situation, I look to the behavior of others for cues.
8. I would probably make a good actor.
9. I rarely need the advice of my friends to choose movies, books or music.
10. I sometimes appear to others to be experiencing deeper emotions than I actually am.
11. I laugh more when I watch a comedy with others than when alone.
12. In a group of people I am rarely the center of attention.
13. In different situations and with different people, I often act like very different persons.
14. I am not particularly good at making other people like me.
15. Even if I am not enjoying myself, I often pretend to be having a good time.
16. I'm not always the person I appear to be.
17. I would not change my opinions (or the way I do things) in order to please someone else or win their favor.
18. I have considered being an entertainer.
19. In order to get along and be liked I tend to be what people expect me to be rather than anything else.
20. I have never been good at games like charades or improvisational acting.
21. I have trouble changing my behavior to suit different people and different situations.
22. At a party I let others keep the jokes and stories going.
23. I feel a bit awkward in company and do not show up quite so well as I should.
24. I can look anyone in the eye and tell a lie with a straight face (if for a right end).
25. I may deceive people by being friendly when I really dislike them.

Source: Reprinted by kind permission of the author, from Snyder, M. (1974) Self-monitoring of expressive behavior, *Journal of Personality and Social Psychology, 30*, 531. Copyright 1974 by the American Psychological Association.

Low self-monitors act in ways that coincide with how they feel. Their behaviors are determined more by their actual attitudes, beliefs, and feelings, rather than the particular situation at hand. Low self-monitors are far less attentive to the social appropriateness of their self-presentations, perhaps because they lack the necessary skills to be effective IMers. As such, they are more cross-situationally consistent in attitudes, beliefs, feelings, and behaviors (Snyder, 1987). James, the formerly Happy consultant, is a low self-monitor. He stated his beliefs as he felt them, regardless of the sentiments against open confrontation of the Happy corporate culture.

In Chapter 1 we described an expansive view that maintains that everyone engages in IM but to different degrees. Thus, rather than being someone who does not engage in IM, the expansive view sees the low self-monitor as being an IMer concerned with maintaining different kinds of identities from that of the high self-monitor – those that project sincerity, independence, honesty, and integrity (Gangestad & Snyder, 2000) The low self-monitor's style might be expressed as: 'IM what IM!'

Dr Mark Snyder, who developed the Self-Monitoring Scale, provides a personal 'Behind the Scenes' look at his work.

Self-monitoring has been linked with a variety of organizationally-related processes including job choice (Snyder & Gangestad, 1982), personnel selections tasks (Smith & Davidson, 1983; Snyder, Berscheid, & Matwychuk, 1988), job performance (Caldwell & O'Reilly, 1982; Giacalone & Falvo, 1985), and leader emergence (Garland & Beard, 1979). The results indicate that high self-monitors usually prefer jobs where they can use their superior IM skills while low self-monitors show a preference for jobs that allow them to act as they truly feel. Similarly, high self-monitors usually do well in jobs that require adaptability and flexibility while low self-monitors succeed where these factors are less important (Gangestad & Snyder, 2000). For example, Latham (1985) found that high and low self-monitors differed in how they looked for jobs. While high self-monitors tended to use social connections (e.g., friends) to find jobs, low self-monitors used more formal means such as employment agencies. These results have implications for organizational recruitment. In order to attract the full range of potential employees, Snyder and Copeland (1989) suggest that organizations should use both formal and informal means. Job advertisements and agencies that would tend to attract low self-monitors, and informal means such as friends and acquaintances of current and former employees would attract high self-monitors.

Job selection is not only affected by the self-monitoring orientation of the applicant but is influenced by the self-monitoring level of the job

Behind the Scenes
Mark Snyder

Twenty-some years ago, as a graduate student in psychology, I discovered this quotation from the works of W. H. Auden: 'The image of myself which I try to create in my own mind in order that I may love myself is very different from the image which I try to create in the minds of others in order that they may love me'. Why, I asked myself then, and continue to ask myself today, do some people have so much in common with the state of affairs described by Auden? Why do some people seem to be living lives of public illusion, forever striving to create images, always trying to control the impressions they convey? My attempts to answer these questions have grown out of a long-standing fascination with the differences between reality and illusion – the contrast between the way things appear to be and the reality that often lurks beneath the surface. As a psychologist, I wanted to understand this world of appearances, to discover how and why people deliberately choose their words and deeds to create images appropriate to particular circumstances, to appear to be the right person in the right place at the right time.

This creating of images in the minds of others, this acting to control the impressions conveyed to others, is no doubt practiced to some extent by just about everyone. But for some people, it is almost a way of life. These people are particularly sensitive to the ways they present themselves in social situations. Indeed, they carefully observe their own performances and skillfully adjust these performances to convey just the right image of themselves. I call these people **high self-monitors** because of the great extent to which they are engaged in monitoring or controlling the images of self they project in social interaction. In contrast, other people, known as **low self-monitors**, think of themselves as consistent beings who value congruence between 'who they are' and 'what they do'. They are not so concerned with constantly assessing the social climate around them. Instead, they can be expected to speak their minds, vent their feelings, and bare their souls, even if doing so means sailing against the prevailing winds of their social environments.

To identify people high and low in self-monitoring, I have developed the Self-Monitoring Scale, an inventory of true–false statements. ▶

Over the years, studies of self-monitoring have taught us that self-monitoring meaningfully influences people's views of themselves and the world around them, their behavior in social situations, and the dynamics of their relationships with other people. Among the life domains where the self-monitoring orientations are evident are the activities of people in organizations, particularly those in which people find employment and in which they pursue their careers. Researchers have examined how people choose occupations compatible with their self-monitoring orientations, how self-monitoring reveals itself in personnel selection interviews, and how high and low self-monitors fare when it comes to matters of job performance and job promotion. With the insights gleaned from such research comes the potential for more informed decision-making and planning, both on the part of individuals and organizations.

interviewer. Snyder et al. (1988) had college students act as evaluators in a job selection task. They found that evaluators tended to make hiring decisions that matched their own self-monitoring styles. The decisions of high self-monitoring evaluators favored appearance over the applicant's personality while low self-monitoring evaluators tended to make their decisions based on the applicant's personality and temperament rather than appearance.

Self-monitoring has also been applied to the area of leadership. Dobbins, Long, Dedrick, and Clemons (1990) investigated the role that self-monitoring plays in leader emergence. Groups consisting of a female high self-monitor, female low self-monitor, male high self-monitor, and male low self-monitor were asked to work on a salary allocation task. Respondents then completed questionnaires that asked them to choose a leader from the group. They found that high self-monitors were more likely to emerge as leaders than were low self-monitors. However, other studies have found the relationship between self-monitoring and leadership to be inconsistent (Anderson & Tolson, 1989).

Although self-monitoring impacts a number of work-related processes, neither high nor low self-monitors are at a distinct organizational advantage. Success depends on the nature of the work and the demands of the job. As Snyder and Copeland (1989, p. 13) write, one may be led to believe that when it comes to performance on the job high self-monitors have better chances for success than low self-monitors. However, this is not necessarily the case. Low self-monitors may be more effective in job performance than high self-monitors in those occupations that call for their characteristic interpersonal style. For example, an occupation that requires an employee to be relatively self-motivated and capable of performing duties without a great deal of supervision or interpersonal contact may find better employees in low self-monitors than in high self-monitors.

Table 6.2 summarizes the results of some representative studies in which self-monitoring plays a role in the organization.

Although the self-monitoring construct helps us understand a great many organizational phenomena, the Self-Monitoring Scale has not been immune from criticism. Briggs, Cheek, and Buss (1980) and Briggs and Cheek (1988) found that the scale was multi-dimensional and did not assess a single unitary construct. Lennox and Wolfe (1984) developed another scale to assess ability to modify self-presentation and to determine sensitivity to the expressive behavior of others. While acknowledging the various controversies over the validity of the original scale, Gangestad and Snyder (2000) make a strong case for the continued usefulness of the self-monitoring construct. Though critics have questioned the validity of subscales that comprise the self-monitoring scale, the full scale has been a reliable measure of self-monitoring even if the subscales have not. In their view and ours, self-monitoring has stood the test of time and remains the predominant IM instrument.

The Balanced Inventory of Desirable Responding

The *Balanced Inventory of Desirable Responding* (BIDR) consists of 40 items designed to measure two very different aspects of the spectrum: impression management (IM) and self-deceptive enhancement (SDE) (Paulhus, 1991). On this scale, IM is the tendency to deliberately over-report desirable behaviors and under-report behaviors that are undesirable. SDE is the tendency to give overly positive reports. SDE differs from IM in that respondents actually believe their positive SDE self-reports. Selected items from the BIDR are presented in

Table 6.2	**Organizationally-Related Studies Using Self-Monitoring**	
Authors	Focus	Major Findings
Anderson & Thacker (1985)	Assessment center ratings	• Significant relationship between self-monitoring and overall assessment rating for women • Self-monitoring scores predicted job retention as well as assessment center ratings for both men and women
Eppler, Honeycutt, & Ford (1998)	Sales Professionals	• Among male sales professionals, there was a significant positive relationship between current income and self-monitoring
Fandt & Ferris (1990)	Management of information	• High self-monitors were more likely to engage in information manipulation under conditions where high accountability existed
Harrison, Chadwick, & Scales (1996)	Cross-cultural adjustment	• High self-monitors expressed greater degrees of general and interaction adjustment as compared to low self-monitors
Jenkins (1993)	Turnover	• Organizational commitment was a better indicator of intent to leave for low self-monitors, while job satisfaction was a better predictor for high self-monitors
Kilduff & Day (1994)	Careers	• High self-monitors were more likely to achieve cross-company promotions, to change employers and make geographical moves that were low self-monitors • Among employees who did not change employers, high self-monitors achieved more internal promotions than did low self-monitors
Levine & Feldman (1997)	Emotional displays	• High self-monitors and women expressed less negative and more positive emotion than men and low self-monitors did
Miller & Cardy (2000)	Performance appraisal	• High self-monitors produced self-ratings that were comparatively higher than those self-ratings done by low self-monitors
Smith, Berry, & Whitely (1997)	Interviews	• High self-monitors scored significantly higher on femininity when the interviewer used a feminine guise, but lower when the interviewer guise was androgynous
Snyder, Berscheid, & Matwychuk (1988)	Personnel selection	• High self-monitoring individuals placed more emphasis on information about applicant physical appearance than did low self-monitors • Low self-monitoring individuals placed more emphasis on information about personal dispositions than did high self-monitors
Turban & Dougherty (1994)	Mentoring	• Individuals with internal loci, emotional stability, and high self-monitoring were more likely to initiate and receive mentoring

Table 6.3. The BIDR has recently been revised and its name changed to the Paulhus Deception Scale (PDS).

The distinctions between IM and SDE can be seen in the following example. Let us look at Steve, an employee with a mediocre work record who is seeking employment. Steve responds to a question by an interviewer in which he is asked to 'describe the credentials you possess that make you most qualified to do this job.' Steve proceeds to provide a lengthy answer about his education at Oxford, his ten years of experience with his previous organization, the accomplishments he has achieved in his time with the company, and the enormous respect he receives for doing a similar job with his present organization. In fact, while Steve did go to Oxford, it was Oxford, Mississippi (home of University of Mississippi) not Oxford, England (home of Oxford University). Furthermore, his grades were barely passing. Rather than graduating 'Magna Cum Laude' as he claimed, the truth was closer to 'Don't Cum Back!' Steve's experience and accomplishments are hardly noteworthy, and his co-workers and supervisors find him acceptable at best. An objective observer would listen to Steve's response and conclude that it was not entirely accurate. The question is why? One interpretation, that of IM, is that Steve is intentionally distorting his responses for the sake of creating a positive impression and getting the job. Another interpretation, that of SDE, is that Steve is a self-enhancer (Robins & Paulhus, 2001) and may actually believe what he said, perhaps because he has little insight, and is very self-centered and egotistical. It could also be that both processes are at work in

Table 6.3	**Selected Items from the Balanced Inventory of Desirable Responding (BIDR)**
	1. My first impressions of people usually turn out to be right.
	2. It would be hard for me to break any of my bad habits.
	3. I never regret my decisions.
	4. I sometimes tell lies if I have to.
	5. There have been occasions when I have taken advantage of someone.
	6. I have done things that I don't tell other people about.

Source: Reprinted with kind permission of Multi-Health Systems, 65 Overlea Blvd., Suite 210, Toronto, Ontario, M4H 1P1, Canada, (800) 268–6011 from Paulhus, D. L. (1998) *Manual for the Balanced Inventory of Desirable Responding* (BIDR-7). The BIDR is currently known as the Paulhus Deception Scale (PDS). Copyright 1998, Multi-Health Systems Inc. All rights reserved.

Steve's case, perhaps a bit of other-deception mixed in with a dash of self-deception. The BIDR was therefore designed to measure the extent to which each of these dimensions – deception of others, deception of oneself – is driving the socially desirable responses Steve is giving.

Responses to the BIDR are categorized along these two dimensions: SDE and IM. The first 20 items of the BIDR measure SDE, the remaining 20 items measure IM. Going back to our opening scenario, it seems that Dawn, the executive using buzzwords to feign expertise would score highly on IM, while her assistant, Leigh, who falsely believes she is an expert, would likely have a high SDE score. A person who scores high in SDE is likely to endorse an item on the BIDR such as 'My first impressions of people usually turn out to be right'. Conversely, a person who scores high on IM is likely to endorse an item such as 'I have never dropped litter on the street'.

In a 'Behind the Scenes' look, Dr. Delroy Paulhus gives us a more personal view of his work related to the BIDR.

An organizational application has been in the area of computer surveys. A number of studies have used the scale to look at the implications of utilizing computers to administer organizational surveys (Booth-Kewley, Edwards, & Rosenfeld, 1992; Lautenschlager & Flaherty, 1990). These studies have addressed an issue that has both important theoretical and practical implications: to what degree are responses on computer surveys similar or different from those obtained on standard paper surveys? Some published studies (see Rosenfeld, Booth-Kewley & Edwards, 1993, for a review) have reported that computer survey responses are more candid, less biased, and less influenced by IM motives than responses given on paper surveys. These studies have, however, been difficult to replicate. Comparisons between paper-and-pencil and computer surveys have frequently yielded virtually identical responses (Dwight & Feigelson, 2000).

The findings of studies that claimed computers either reduced the tendency to engage in IM and those reporting no computer–paper differences were both challenged by Lautenschlager and Flaherty's (1990) findings. They compared responses of undergraduates on the BIDR completed in either computer or paper-and-pencil conditions. They found that students in the computer condition gave more socially desirable responses on the BIDR than their counterparts in the paper-and-pencil condition. Also, respondents who were identified had

Behind the Scenes

Delroy Paulhus

A researcher interested in IM and self-deception faces a special hurdle in composing a background profile. That hurdle involves overcoming the skepticism of the reader who assumes that I, like many researchers, conduct research on my own most prominent tendencies. Whatever the reason, I have long been fascinated by individuals who seem consistently to self-promote and wondered whether such individuals actually believe their self-promotion. This interest in IM was piqued in graduate school at Columbia University – a program notable for its combined training in personality and social psychology. Because of this dual training, I was exposed to the IM literature from both the situational and individual differences perspectives. Indeed, my dissertation examined both sources of variance in the phenomenon of cognitive dissonance. Strongly influenced by my graduate advisor, Harold Sackeim, I focused on separating the unconscious component from the conscious component of IM. Several of my early publications argued that traditional measures of socially desirable responding actually confounded the two components. This distinction evolved over the years along with my new test instrument, the *Balanced Inventory of Desirable Responding* (BIDR). Ultimately, I settled on the labels, Self-Deception (sometimes also called Self-Deceptive Enhancement) and IM, for the response styles measured by the BIDR.

I believe that this distinction is central to a number of issues in organizational behavior. These include personnel selection, workers' compensation, malingering, as well as control of desirable responding in research contexts. In personnel selection for example, few interviewers accept at face value the self-descriptions of job applicants. Often, however, interviewers fail to differentiate the applicant who knowingly dissembles from the one who exaggerates his/her qualifications because of over-confidence and optimism. The BIDR has proved to be an ideal tool for making such discriminations. In simulated job interviews, for example, my colleagues and I showed that the IM scale, but not the Self-Deception scale, was sensitive to attempted faking. In actual personnel selection studies, the BIDR scales have been used to evaluate the ideal test conditions for ▶

minimizing desirable responding in US Navy recruits. More and more organizations are now incorporating the BIDR as a standard feature of their personnel selection batteries. Another common application of the BIDR scales is in evaluating self-report instruments used in organizational research: some instruments correlate significantly with self-deception and some with IM (Moorman & Podsakoff, 1992). Nonetheless, statistical control methods should not be applied hastily. Often response styles such as IM and self-deception are an essential component of the organizational concept being measured (Zerbe & Paulhus, 1987). In short, content and style are sometimes one and the same.

Finally, in looking back at this summary, I must admit that my own tendency to manage impressions played some part in the presentation. I'll leave it to the reader to judge whether self-deception also played a role – after all, I'd be the last to know!

significantly higher scores on both scales than students in the anonymous condition. These results led the authors to conclude that individuals may be *more* likely to distort their responses on the computer and that 'the administration of . . . attitude questionnaires in organizational research may be adversely affected when converted from paper-and-pencil format. Increases due to IM on such diagnostic measures may produce inaccurate and potentially misleading results' (Lautenschlager and Flaherty, 1990, p. 314).

Given the potential implications of this finding, Booth-Kewley et al. (1992) attempted to replicate the study in a non-college environment. Male US Navy recruits completed surveys in either a computer or paper-and-pencil condition, and their responses were either identified or anonymous. The results supported the finding discussed above that identified respondents had higher IM and SDE scores than anonymous respondents did. Contrary to those findings, however, whether responses were made on the computer or on paper had no effect on either IM or SDE scores. Booth-Kewley et al. (1992) concluded that computer vs paper administration does not appear to alter scores on organizational scales in any consistent way. They argued that, where financial and logistical considerations allow, organizations are justified in using computer-based surveys instead of paper-and-pencil administration.

Rosenfeld, Booth-Kewley, Thomas, and Edwards (1996) again attempted to directly address these inconsistencies found in computer versus paper-and-pencil survey administration. Their study used paper and two computer conditions, linked and unlinked. The linked-computer condition was included to simulate the **Big Brother Syndrome** – an increasing fear individuals have that their computer responses are being monitored or will be checked. Rosenfeld and friends predicted that responses in the linked-computer (Big Brother) condition would be more socially desirable than those in the unlinked-computer and paper conditions. It was expected that this effect would be enhanced when respondents were identified rather than anonymous. Male Navy recruits completed the BIDR. Scores on the IM subscale of the BIDR were higher in the identified than in the anonymous conditions. More importantly, in identified conditions, IM scores were significantly higher in the Big Brother condition than in the other two conditions. It was concluded that perceiving one's responses are linked to a larger database might activate the Big Brother Syndrome leading to greater IM on computer surveys.

Rosenfeld et al. (1996) suggested that these differing results might be due to increasing fears of privacy and monitoring on computers compared to in the past when they were viewed as being more anonymous. Support for this contention comes from a meta-analysis (Dwight & Feigelson, 2000) that tried to statistically summarize the studies that have looked at whether computer surveys result in more or less IM than paper. In their meta-analysis of over 30 studies, Dwight and Feigelson (2000) found a small but statistically significant effect indicating that less IM occurs on computer surveys. However, this effect has gotten smaller over time and most current studies have found little or no effect. As people have gotten increasingly knowledgeable about computers, computers have lost whatever lie-detecting capabilities they once had. The good news is that while computers no longer seem to consistently reduce IM on surveys, they nonetheless are equally good measurement devices as paper surveys are.

Self-Presentation Scale

Gerry's reply to Glenn in one of the scenarios opening this chapter points to yet another facet of IM. While the BIDR distinguishes between IM driven by conscious deception of others or self-deception, there is yet another way of conceptualizing differences in how individuals manage impressions. C. R. Snyder and associates (Roth, Harris, & Snyder, 1988; Roth, Snyder, & Pace, 1986) have created an instrument that measures the tendency toward **attributive** versus **repudiative** IM. The contrast between attributive versus repudiative tactics of IM represents a basic distinction in the general **style** in which impressions are managed rather than in the underlying motivation to manage impressions. The essence of this style is that individuals will tend toward favorable IM by either attempting to ascribe positive traits to themselves via the use of attributive tactics or deny the existence of negative characteristics through the use of repudiative tactics.

The Self-Presentation Scale (SPS) is a 60-item measure of the tendency to use either attributive or repudiative tactics. For each of the items, respondents indicate whether the statements made are true or false regarding themselves. The attributive measure has 30 items containing unrealistically positive statements. Because all of the statements are highly unlikely to be true, those responding 'true' to these statements are seen as engaging in attributive IM. The repudiative measure also has 30 items that describe undesirable characteristics that are likely to be true of almost anyone. Those responding 'false' to these measures would also be engaging in IM, but of a repudiative type. The scale can be found in Table 6.4.

Although the SPS has been around since the late 1980s, organizational studies have yet to utilize it. Still, the potential for diagnostic information from the SPS is clear. The ability to categorize individual styles of IM could aid understanding of communication. For example, knowing whether an employee will tend to use repudiative or attributive self-presentation can help a manager anticipate and better understand the employee's behaviors and responses to success and failure feedback. Similarly, employment interviewers might be able to ask better questions (and follow-ups) if they were alerted, in advance, that the interviewee tended to self-present in either an attributive or repudiative manner. Also, the types of responses regarding employee turnover or other organizational phenomena given during an exit interview may vary depending on whether the interviewee tends to be an ascriber of positive traits or a denier of negative ones.

Table 6.4	**The Self-Presentation Scale**

1. My childhood was always happy.
2. I would lie to get out of trouble.
3. I contribute all I can to charity.
4. All of my successes can be explained by my abilities.
5. I sometime think about attacking others physically.
6. Everyone thinks I am a calm person.
7. At times I feel like swearing.
8. I voice opinions on issues that I know little about.
9. I obey all laws.
10. I worry about things over which I have little control.
11. Before voting, I thoroughly investigate the issues and candidates.
12. My solutions to problems are original and effective.
13. I evaluate the physical attractiveness of people the same sex as myself.
14. I am loyal to my friends at all times.
15. Money is an important motivator for me.
16. I have thought of suicide as one way I could get back at those who have hurt me.
17. My shyness prevents me from meeting new people.
18. I argue only when I know I'm right.
19. I am always on time for appointments.
20. Pornography arouses me.
21. I am completely happy with the way my life is going.
22. My behavior is influenced by the expectations of others.
23. When angry, I sometimes feel like smashing things.
24. If I find something that is not mine, I make every effort to return it to the real owner.
25. I sometimes avoid people I do not wish to speak to.
26. When I was a child my parents were mean to me on occasion.
27. I always enjoy accepting new responsibilities.
28. When wronged, I sometimes want revenge.
29. I always practice what I preach.
30. I understand all of the problems of the disadvantaged.
31. My family life is totally happy and peaceful.
32. I have cheated on schoolwork in the past.
33. The success of others sometimes makes me jealous.
34. My friends and acquaintances are all exceptional people.
35. In my private thoughts, I laugh at the incompetencies of others.
36. I will always go out of my way to help others.
37. My parents always did what was best for me.
38. I have doubted my sexual adequacy.
39. I always help people who feel lonely.
40. My peers should follow in my footsteps.
41. I try to figure out what others think of me.
42. I am always courteous, even to disagreeable people.
43. I am willing to admit all of my mistakes.
44. I am completely honest.

▶

45. I am sometimes rude to other people.
46. I am responsible for some of my failures.
47. I live by the highest moral standards.
48. Some of my thoughts are too bad to talk about.
49. I have deliberately hurt other people's feelings.
50. I am always kind to animals.
51. I feel sad sometimes.
52. I have felt hatred toward others.
53. I feel sexually attracted to many people.
54. Everyone thinks I am important and knowledgeable.
55. I worry about my own death.
56. Everyone likes me.
57. I am always trying to improve myself.
58. I feel resentful when I don't get my way.
59. I sometimes quarrel with family members.
60. I completely control my own destiny.

Source: Reprinted with kind permission of the authors, from Roth, D., Harris, R., and Snyder, C. R. (1988) An individual differences measure of attributive and repudiative tactics of favorable self-presentation, *Journal of Social and Clinical Psychology*, 6, 164–5. Copyright 1988 by the Guilford Press.

The Measure of Ingratiatory Behaviors in Organizational Settings (MIBOS)

Understanding the ability of employees like Harold the engineer described in our opening case study to ingratiate themselves to others is the focus of the *Measure of Ingratiatory Behaviors in Organizational Settings* (MIBOS). The MIBOS (Kumar & Beyerlein, 1991) aims at a rather different aspect of IM measurement than did the previous three measures. The MIBOS is a measure of 'the frequency with which ingratiatory tactics are used by subordinates in superior–subordinate relationships' (Kumar & Beyerlein, 1991, p. 620). The measure can be broken down into four factors representing the ingratiation tactics of other-enhancement, opinion conformity, self-presentation (what we call self-enhancement), and favor rendering discussed in Chapter 2. The MIBOS, therefore, differs from the previously discussed measures in two distinct ways. First, the MIBOS is focused on particular IM tactics rather than the more global concepts of IM response style or orientation. Second, the MIBOS is the only one of the three measures that specifically focuses on organizationally related IM. The MIBOS measure can be found in Table 6.5.

| Table 6.5 | **Measure of Ingratiatory Behavior in Organizational Settings (MIBOS)** |

1. Impress upon your supervisor that only he/she can help you in a given situation mainly to make him/her feel good about himself/herself.
2. Show him/her that you share his/her enthusiasm about his/her new idea even when you may not actually like it.
3. Try to let him/her know that you have a reputation for being liked.
4. Try to make sure that he/she is aware of your successes.
5. Highlight the achievements made under his/her leadership in a meeting not being attended by him/her.
6. Give frequent smiles to express enthusiasm/interest about something he/she is interested in even if you do not like it.
7. Express work attitudes that are similar to your supervisor's as a way of letting him/her know that the two of you are alike.
8. Tell him/her that you can learn a lot from his/her experience.
9. Exaggerate his/her admirable qualities to convey the impression that you think highly of him/her.
10. Disagree on trivial or unimportant issues but agree on those issues in which he/she expects support from you.
11. Try to imitate such work behaviors of your supervisor as working late or occasionally working on weekends.
12. Look for opportunities to let the supervisor know your virtues/strengths.
13. Ask your supervisor for advice in areas in which he/she thinks he/she is smart to let him/her feel that you admire your supervisor.
14. Try to do things for your supervisor that show your selfless generosity.
15. Look out for opportunities to admire your supervisor.
16. Let your supervisor know the attitudes you share with him/her.
17. Compliment your supervisor on his/her achievement, however trivial it may actually be to you personally.
18. Laugh heartily at your supervisor's jokes even when they are not really funny.
19. Go out of your way to run an errand for your supervisor.
20. Offer to help your supervisor by using your personal contacts.
21. Try to persuasively present your own qualities when attempting to convince your supervisor about your abilities.
22. Volunteer to be of help to your supervisor in matters like locating a good apartment, finding a good insurance agent, etc.
23. Spend time listening to your supervisor's personal problems even if you have no interest in them.
24. Volunteer to help your supervisor in his/her work even if it means extra work for you.

Source: Reprinted by kind permission of the authors, from Kumar, K. and Beyerlein, M. (1991) Construction and validation of an instrument for measuring ingratiatory behaviors in organizational settings, *Journal of Personality and Social Psychology*, *76*, 622. Copyright 1991 by the American Psychological Association.

Watt (1993) did a study using the MIBOS in a bank setting. He asked subordinates to complete the scale, and their supervisors to evaluate them on a performance evaluation instrument. Results showed that employees who engaged in more ingratiating behaviors (according to the MIBOS) were judged significantly higher in motivation, competence, cooperation, promotion potential, and overall performance by their supervisors. Strutton, Pelton, and Lumpkin (1995) used a modified version of the MIBOS to assess the degree of ingratiation in salespeople. As noted in Chapter 2, males were more likely to use ingratiation tactics than women were, particularly the more assertive tactics such as favor doing and self-enhancement.

Although the MIBOS appears to show some usefulness in predicting whether ingratiation impacts outcomes such as performance appraisal, a number of studies have shown it to have measurement shortcomings. In a study using data from state government employees, Kacmar and Valle (1997) failed to find statistical support for the four factor version of the MIBOS. Similarly, Harrison, Hochwarter, Perrewe, and Ralston (1998) could not validate Kumar and Beyerlein's four-factor model. Together, these findings suggest caution in using the MIBOS until the validity of the instrument is better established. One way organizational researchers have addressed these shortcomings is to use modified versions of the MIBOS that contain a subset of the MIBOS scale items (Aryee, Wyatt, & Stone, 1996; Strutton et al., 1995)

Utilizing IM Measures

How might organizational practitioners and researchers use IM measures? In trying to illustrate the utility of IM measures, the differing perspectives of these two groups is important to consider. On one hand, business practitioners might be very interested in using IM measures as part of their overall set of assessments. Practitioners would be interested in these measures from the general perspective of how to change organizational processes. However, researchers would be interested in using these measures to study the impact of IM on processes and effects in organizations. Their interest would not be from a hands-on applied perspective, but from the standpoint of scientific inquiry. Thus, we address the issues of practitioner and scholarly utility separately.

How Organizational Practitioners Might Use IM Measures

While the measures we have discussed are both interesting and potentially useful, relatively little has been done with them in actual organizations. In our view, there is yet much untapped potential for using measures such as these in organizations, both as measures of actual performance, and as moderators/mediators of self-report organizational measures. The distinction between these two types of measures is an important one. **Hard measures** gauge actual performance, including such things as measures of performance appraisal, productivity, and training effectiveness, as well as measures of events such as absenteeism, tardiness, and medical claims filed. **Self-reports** involve perceptual or attitudinal concepts measured by surveys or interviews: included in this would be measures of morale, job satisfaction, ethical climate, and organizational commitment. While IM has been used extensively with self-report measures, very little has been done in response to hard measures explaining performance or other organizationally relevant outcome measures.

Individual differences in IM and hard measures

There are a number of ways the scales reviewed above might be used to understand how IM impacts hard measures in organizations. Table 6.6 provides some specific examples.

IM measures could be used to predict those positions in which different abilities and motivations can promote job success (Riordan, 1989). For example, in **boundary-spanner** positions – those that require an employee to work in a position requiring multiple roles (e.g., acting as a liaison between a union and management) self-monitoring ability may have an impact, since such positions require closer scrutiny of situational variables. Indeed, high self-monitors are more effective in boundary spanning tasks than low self-monitors are (Caldwell & O'Reilly, 1982). Snyder and Copeland (1989, p. 17) suggest that an employer can use knowledge of differences in self-monitoring to gain different types of information from an exiting employee that can assist with future selection decisions.

Table 6.6	**Potential Applications of IM Scales to Hard Performance Measures in Organizations**

Self-Monitoring (SM)

Interviewing: High SM interviewers could be used to help detect candidate IM as well as create an 'appropriate' organizational image on the candidate.

Recruitment: High SM recruiters could be used in realistic job previews so as to promote the most realistic/accurate view of the organization.

Behavioral Inventory of Desirable Responding

High Visibility Positions: In high visibility positions, individuals who have been assessed to have the requisite abilities can be screened for IM. Those low in this can be remedially trained. Alternatively, those high in SDE can be trained to be more aware of self-deception.

Self-Presentation Scale

Employee Feedback Interviews: Management awareness of the candidates' tendency to use repudiative or attributive self-presentational strategies can help to redirect the feedback toward realistic concerns and improve the efficiency of feedback.

Measure of Ingratiatory Behaviors in Organizational Settings (MIBOS)

Defensive Management: Knowledge of the degree of ingratiation in the organization can help in the training of managers to overcome dysfunctional and/or excessive IM.

From a low self-monitoring employee, an employer may be able to determine what personality or behavioral characteristics of that employee did not mesh well with the particular job's requirements and use this information for future personnel decisions. From a high self-monitor, on the other hand, an exit interview might provide the employer with information about how an employee in a given occupation views the occupation's necessary vocational prerequisites.

Second, IM measures could be used within work units and organizations to better understand the culture and/or facilitate organizational development and change. The simple assessment techniques we described earlier can help identify individuals who are particularly proficient or deficient in IM ability. Proficient IMers can be monitored for excesses and overt deceptions, while deficient IMers can be trained to present themselves more honestly and effectively. Imagine an organization in which certain departments are thought to be deficient on a particular criterion such as work productivity and believed to have employees who are more interested in image construction than substantive effort. They are better actors than workers, as one employee we knew put it, getting bonuses, raises, and promotions instead of Academy Awards! Administering the MIBOS could tell us about the tactics employees use to manage images for themselves and their departments and, by comparing them to scale norms, whether they were being used excessively. After having assessed an entire department, an **IM profile** for the department could be developed – high in self-presentation, low in opinion conformity, etc. If in a particular department the strategy of opinion conformity was rarely used, but self-enhancement was used frequently, we would be able to help managers better identify what tactics they should lock their IM sensors on and which they should put off their detection screens. This profile could then help increase management awareness so that the organization could more effectively exploit IM to its benefit and minimize its abuse. If it could lead to a better effort to reward actual output over superficial image, we would expect productivity to increase in the long run as the sizzle is better separated from the steak.

Also, IM measures could help identify those employees who are deficient in their IM skills and in need of training. For example, if we found that an employee had a profile which showed he was probably engaging in very little acquisitive IM (e.g. a low self-monitor, low on the BIDR, a low attributer of positive qualities on the SPS), we might want to take a look at helping this individual learn to put his best foot forward to represent the company positively (see Martinko, 1991). Training such individuals would not be intended to help them exploit others, but to present themselves, their work and the organization more realistically and effectively. This is in line with our view that IM is a useful and necessary organizational skill. In this vein, Giacalone has suggested that being good at IM may be related to adapting well to working in a different culture. A study conducted by Montagliani and Giacalone (1998) found that self-monitoring and BIDR scores were significantly associated with measures of cross-cultural adaptability. These results led to the suggestion that good IM skills may be required for expatriate employees to successfully adapt to their new host culture. Even strangers in a strange land need to be good IMers.

Individual differences and self-reports

Measures of IM may also help explain the responses that individuals give to attitudinal, perceptual, and personality measures.

First, IM measures may help us understand *whose* responses to self-reports will be biased. If we knew that employees high in IM and employees low in IM were being given a morale measure, we would predict that high-IMers would be better able and more motivated to distort the responses given to the employee morale measure than would low-IMers. Thus, some statistical adjustments could be made to the responses of individuals who score high in IM if it was determined that they gave inflated responses to particular questions or overall measures.

Second, IM measures may help us to better interpret the responses given in employee self-reports. If we found that employees tended toward an attributive rather than a repudiative style on the SPS, we might interpret agreement with positively worded self-report questions more conservatively, since such agreement would more likely be expected among those with an attributive style.

Third, IM measures may help explain why some individuals will give biased responses on self-report measures even when they are anonymous. The BIDR, for example, can help us determine whether biased responding exists because of a deliberate attempt to control one's image, or as a result of self-deception. One of the authors of this text used the BIDR to understand why a group of 'at risk' youths with few job-related skills report that they expect to get 'very good jobs' when they receive their Graduate Equivalency Degrees. Are they trying to impress the interviewer? Are they deceiving themselves? The distinction may be important, since it has been traditionally assumed that a reduction in IM bias can be achieved by increasing the anonymity of responses (Giacalone & Rosenfeld, 1986). Unfortunately, employees who are high in SDE will not necessarily give less biased responses when anonymous since they really believe what they are saying (Rosenfeld, et al., 1994).

How Organizational Researchers Might Use IM Measures

In addition to being used as simple assessment/diagnostic tools for individual workers, IM measures can also help researchers determine the role that IM plays in the way employees in organizations work and interact.

Except in some specific areas of organizational research (e.g., job interviews, performance evaluations, exit interviews), the role of IM has often been overlooked. These measures can help researchers understand more about organizations by providing insight into the extent to which IM processes play a role in various organizational areas. In a very general way, the measures themselves raise some very interesting questions about how employee differences in IM may result in different reactions to organizational processes and events. For example, would individuals who have high scores on the MIBOS have quicker or smoother career paths? Are high self-monitors more likely to adapt to new environments after transfers to new jobs? Do those who score high on IM more often get selected for the jobs they apply for? Support for this last contention was provided in research that used the BIDR with college students and US Border Patrol agents (Vasilopoulos, Reilly, & Leaman, 2000). In two studies it was found that those with high IM scores also had scores on other diagnostic instruments that were associated with getting subsequent job offers.

Why would researchers wish to use IM measures? Researchers focusing on IM realize that there are basically two strategies to investigate its organizational impact. As the Appendix indicates, one strategy is to manipulate variables such as identifiability (anonymity or identification of one's responses) or the source of an evaluation (one's manager or co-worker). The manipulation of variables in organizational settings, however, can be disruptive or ethically questionable. For example, if we asked some employees to put their names on surveys, while asking others to remain anonymous, we might arouse suspicion, fear, or mistrust. Employees might ask how it was decided who would be identified and who would be anonymous. Similarly, if we attempted to show that interpersonal behaviors would change, based on whether one's own or another manager was the evaluator of those behaviors, we would be inconveniencing outside parties and perhaps causing still more suspicion about the 'true' purposes behind the intervention.

A less intrusive strategy is to use the IM measures we have described. Measures of IM allow an organizational researcher to administer questionnaires and see how groups of individuals who are high or low in these traits perform in various tasks and settings. Utilizing this approach can provide us with a great deal of information about when

IM impacts organizational phenomena, when it does not, and when it actually hinders performance. Today employees are used to being assessed; few get testy when being tested. Therefore, using IM measures as part of a larger organizational assessment can be done without overly disrupting organizational functioning or arousing undue suspicion and ill-will.

Using IM Measures in Organizations: Advantages and Disadvantages

Although many organizational practitioners and researchers have underutilized IM measures, we believe it is important to look carefully at the advantages and disadvantages before using these measures in work settings. Summarized in Table 6.7, are a number of advantages of measuring differences in IM in organizations.

An organizational researcher we know had a sign on his door, 'In God we trust, all others bring data!' This researcher knew the dangers of drawing conclusions about organizational behavior based solely on anecdote, insight, or intuition. This researcher would surely see an important advantage of using IM measures: they may help managers make decisions that are supported by empirical data. For example, knowledge that an individual is a high self-monitor might lend support to a manager's decision to give him a boundary-spanning job or one that involves lots of interaction with the public. Conversely, for an employee in a boundary-spanning position who is a low self-monitor, such knowledge may justify further training in interpersonal sensitivity

Table 6.7	**Advantages of IM Measures**

- Provide quantitative information on which individuals can be compared
- Are unbiased indicators of IM, especially when managers perceive such behavior as nefarious or dysfunctional
- Provide an empirical basis for evaluating IM in individuals or groups, rather than the more political characterizations motivated by self-interest
- Provide empirical data to justify managerial decisions
- Provide respondents significant insight into their own behaviors

The issues addressed herein are based on categories from Furnham, A. (1992). *Personality at Work: The Role of Individual Differences in the Workplace.* London: Routledge, p. 38–9.

and communication or transfer to a job that requires an ability to successfully work alone.

In organizations as elsewhere, knowledge is power. Measuring IM can provide testers and respondents with some knowledge into their own behaviors. Using this as part of an overall communication skills training package, for example, may help to direct both the tester and respondent toward greater self-understanding and career development. We've found that one of the best ways to explain IM measures to our students or clients is to have them complete the scales, score them, and then tell us whether their IM profile really fits their personality. Interestingly, most of the time it does!

Disadvantages can also be encountered when using these measures. These are summarized in Table 6.8.

Any testing process involving self-ratings assumes that respondents are capable of providing insight into themselves. In fact, some individuals may lack an understanding of themselves sufficient to provide such insights. Their version of Hamlet reads, 'To thine own self be false!' The SDE component on the BIDR is, in itself, a measure of this phenomenon.

Conversely, some individuals may have the insight to provide accurate responding, but may be *unwilling* to do so and distort their responses. While an individual who has self-monitoring tendencies may recognize these in himself, he may be unwilling to respond truthfully when completing the scale, fearing that his responses would adversely impact the perception that his boss has of him.

Table 6.8	**Disadvantages of IM Measures**

- Some respondents may be incapable of providing insight into themselves
- Measures may be fakable
- As knowledge of IM testing becomes common, potential respondents can 'practice' their responses in advance
- The measures may have limited organizational validity. They may provide interesting but not significant insights into key organizational processes
- Sample norms generated with non-working populations may provide misleading comparisons
- Use of the measures may result in legal challenges

The issues addressed herein are based on categories from Furnham, A. (1992). *Personality at Work: The Role of Individual Differences in the Workplace*. London: Routledge, p. 39–40.

In the future, with the potential for increased use of such measures by organizations, another problem may emerge. Individuals may go beyond unwillingness to tell the truth, and move more toward a manipulation of their responses so as to conform to organizational 'criteria' of how they should respond on IM measures.

A more serious concern is that the measures herein, as well as others related to IM (e.g., Lee, Quigley, Nesler, Corbett, & Tedeschi, 1999), have not been subjected to the rigorous validity studies required for many organizational purposes. When such tests are used to make critical personnel decisions, it is essential that we be able to show that tests measure, in a consistent and unbiased way, factors important to job performance and other key organizational outcomes such as job satisfaction and turnover.

Additionally, the current environment of legalistic responses to various business practices, both from individuals (as lawsuits) and from government (in the form of legal restraints) may be problematic for organizations testing for IM. The reaction to these measures will depend on whether these tests discriminate or show adverse impact against particular groups, and can adequately predict job-related performance. At present, tests for differential or predictive validity have not been made. Using these scales in certain applications without prior validation on organizational populations is legally risky and ethically questionable.

Measuring Concepts Related to IM

Those interested in measuring IM behaviors might also want to measure related traits which may impact a person's willingness, desire, or motivation to use IM behaviors. Table 6.9 summarizes some of these related measures.

These measures provide additional insights into what motivates and fosters IM usage. For example, Machiavellians may be more inclined to use IM tactics for manipulative reasons, while those who are interactionally anxious might be poorer at managing the right impression.

Whether these measures are useful components of organizational IM will require much more basic and applied research. In fact, these measures, like the earlier discussed IM measures, suffer from many of

Table 6.9	Measures of Importance to IM*			
Measure	Sources	Characterization of measure	How characteristics could be related to IM	Process impacting IM
Bases of Power	Hinkin and Schriesheim, 1989	Measures designed to ascertain bases of power	• Various bases of power, by their presence or absence, may facilitate particular forms of IM • IM and various bases of power form a reciprocal relationship; IM facilitates the base of power (e.g., expert), which, once gained, brings with it IM potential	Power bases
Fear of Appearing Incompetent Scale	Good and Good (1973)	Measures the extent to which individuals are concerned with the maintenance of face	• Level of concern may impact the extent to which an individual will try to control activities and behaviors so as to maximize perceived level of competence	Self-esteem
Interaction Anxiousness Scale	Leary, 1983a; Leary and Kowalski, 1993	Measures the extent to which individuals exhibit the tendency to be nervous in social encounters	• Greater concern with how people perceive them may motivate IM attempts • Lower confidence in the effectiveness of their IM • Greater motivation to make impressions	Social anxiety (Leary and Kowalski, 1993) (Maddux, Norton, and Leary, 1988)
Machiavellianism	Christie and Geis, 1970	Measures the extent to which individuals behave in manipulative ways, have a cynical view of human nature, and disregard the parameters of conventional morality	• Machiavellians may tend to use IM strategies with a distorted focus on self (Ickes, Reidhead, and Patterson, 1986) • Machiavellians will tend toward unethical IM usage	Unethical decision-making strategies

Measure	Sources	Characterization of measure	How characteristics could be related to IM	Process impacting IM
Marlowe-Crowne Social Desirability Scale	Crowne and Marlowe, 1960	Originally designated as a measure of need for social approval; current thinking (Crowne, 1979; Millham and Jacobson, 1978) is that it is a measure of avoiding disapproval	• The desire to avoid disapproval may foster IM behavior, both to avoid disapproval and/or garner approval	Social desirability
Self-Handicapping Scale	Jones and Rhodewalt, 1982; Strube, 1986	Measures the tendency of an individual to engage in behaviors designed to protect self-esteem via the creation of appropriate barriers to performance	• Self-handicapping individuals will use various forms of IM to emphasize impediments that inhibit performance	Self-esteem
Willingness to Communicate Scale	McCroskey, 1992	Measures the respondent's predisposition to approach or avoid communication	• A willingness to communicate positive information may facilitate IM, while an unwillingness may deter observers from perceiving the communicator positively. Similarly, a willingness to communicate negative information may allow for some IM flexibility, while an unwillingness virtually ensures a negative conclusion	Communication

Note: *These measures should by no means be construed as representing an exhaustive list of measures which could impact or be impacted by IM in organizations. The measures listed herein are intended as a representative sample of the many possible measures which could impact IM.

the same deficits that preclude organizational implementation. However, there are ways to deal with these deficits.

Some Suggestions for Successful Implementation

In order to utilize IM measures successfully, a number of steps need to be taken.

1. Validate measures on large organizational samples and develop adult-worker norms

A major issue that managers must address prior to implementing IM measures is the question of appropriate validation and development of adult-worker norms. With the exception of self-monitoring, the other measures we have discussed represent relatively new attempts at measurement. As such, much more development work is needed. Second, because many of the measures have used undergraduates and MBA students in their research samples, questions about the validity of the test for employed adult populations are a serious consideration. It is essential that the validity of the measures be established for organizational populations using large samples. As these populations are sampled, norms can be developed which both increase the justification for the measures and protect against the potential legal liability of questionable norms and validity.

2. Assess and determine differences within and between organizations/industries

An important question remains regarding differences within and among organizations, as well as within and among industries: will individuals in particular organizations and/or industries differ in the need, type, degree, and distribution of IM traits in order to be successful? For example, does a company that focuses on cleaning services have any great need to employ individuals with certain IM abilities? Would a retail store clerk require the same type or intensity of IM as an advertising executive? Should a group of retail store employees have the same distribution of IM traits as a public relations firm? The answer to these questions intuitively would appear to be no. Research needs to be conducted to make this determination.

3. Assess impact

The question for the practicing manager always remains the same: is it worth it? In order to justify the expense and resources of measuring IM-related phenomena, managers will need to show that there is utility in the measures themselves. It will be important to show *how* these measures are useful to managers. For example, do these measures affect the bottom line in any way? Do they predict which salespeople are more likely to be effective? Do they influence training evaluations? Studies are needed which show a direct relationship between the measures themselves and the desired performance.

4. Market IM as a positive organizational force

As Rosenfeld and Giacalone (1991) have noted, the IM perspective has gone from being viewed as extreme to being seen as organizationally mainstream. Still, there are detractors who associate IM with nefarious and malevolent manipulation attempts. In order for organizations to fully use IM measures, it will be important to market these measures as ethically and practically acceptable and positively contributing to the organization's bottom line. Indeed, the field of organizational IM needs to practice what it preaches: it could benefit from a good dose of positive IM to disassociate from extreme and dysfunctional stereotypes and associate with positive organizational outcomes. While this may appear to be a simple suggestion, the negative ethical insinuations cast upon IM still make association with it controversial in some circles.

A Concluding Note

The measurement of IM differences for the purposes of organizational applications is an area yet in its infancy. Much remains to be done both from a theoretical and an applied standpoint before measurement of individual differences in IM can take its proper place within organizational IM. Still, we cannot help but see the enormous, untapped potential that lies before tomorrow's managers and organizational researchers. Hopefully this chapter has provided a starting point.

7 IM and Human Resource Management (HRM)

> It is not enough to have great qualities; we should
> also have the management of them
> (La Rochefoucauld).

Managing Desirable Qualities

La Rochefoucauld's statement has two basic premises – an assumption that great qualities are desirable, and that their management is essential. It raises a number of intriguing questions. For example, what are 'great' qualities? Is La Rochefoucauld talking of physical qualities (like a well-conditioned body) or of psychological attributes such as motivation and ability? Is the concept of greatness a subjective one, determined by the perceptions of those who have witnessed it? Who defines such greatness? Are the qualities self-defined, defined by a management hierarchy, by consensus, or by some long-held social traditions? If an individual who has these qualities does not produce great achievements, who is to blame? The manager? The employee? The authors of this book?

Those are some of the questions that human resource (HR) managers, implicitly and explicitly, ask themselves daily. The questions pervade the basic functions of the HR department – recruitment, selection, training, and appraisal – and are a source of confusion and frustration to the HR manager. Why? We would argue that these questions involve **judgment calls**. These judgment calls are based on the perceptions that HR managers have of their employees. Perceptions often based not on first-hand knowledge of the employee's objectively measured performance and ability, but on the impression that the HR manager has of that employee; an impression that the employee has contributed to by means of his skillful or not so skillful IM.

For HR managers, IM is a powerful force that must be understood. Employees are not passive observers of their organizational destinies, they are players in the drama that pervades organizational life. As such, employees' attempts to create images of themselves and their performance must be a part of the overall process that assists or thwarts the HR manager. For example, HR managers must consider that it is probably incorrect to see performance evaluations as true indicators of actual performance. Rather, performance evaluations represent a more complicated matrix of actual performance, moderated by the IM of the ratee (who has a stake in being seen positively), the IM of the rater (whose stake may be a positive impression based on a perception of fairness, equity, etc.), as well as many other factors (Villanova & Bernardin, 1989; 1991). Thus, HR managers need to understand how and why IM affects their decision making.

Why Human Resource Managers Need to Understand IM

Aside from personal and intellectual interest that they may have in IM, HR managers should be interested in IM for a number of practical reasons. These reasons are based on the pivotal role that IM plays in much of the organization, specifically in terms of its impact, its potential to contribute positively and negatively to organizational functioning, fairness, functionality, cues, and stakeholders.

Impact

HR functions impact directly and forcefully on employee lives and careers. HR managers make decisions on a daily basis which impact salaries, benefits, promotions, layoffs, and other factors that have long-term repercussions in employees' lives. What is defined as 'excellent performance' or 'good customer relations' is a matter of **social reality** – a reality defined, by consensus among people rather than an **objective reality** (Halle, 1965). For example, all employees present at the meeting in the boss's office would agree that the boss's desk is in her office; it can be physically verified. While the **function** of the boss's desk may be disputed, its existence is not. In contrast, the existence of excellent performance is subjective in nature; it must be interpreted and gauged against some standard. For example, Hillary may distort information, provide a 'best case' view of her mediocre performance, or supply evidence to help define her performance to benefit her career. Hillary's motivation to do so depends in part on the impact that managing the right impression may have on her. As such, IM tactics are vital to Hillary's ability to define how she is perceived at work.

The new competence

It has been argued that IM ability is a **new competence** (Wexler, 1986). In previous centuries, workers produced a tangible product that could be evaluated in and of itself. But, as Wexler (1986, pp. 253–4) notes,

> While fewer and fewer people today are engaged in the production of foodstuffs and even fewer in manufacturing, more and more ... are engaged in generating nothing that is tangible at all, indeed, in generating services, resulting in an entirely new game – one in which man no longer sutures his notion of competence in his struggle with things, but now and in the near future in his ability to impress upon people his or her worth.

HR managers are entrusted with validating skills, abilities, and potential that are not tangible, clearly defined and subject to the employee's ability to create the impression she has those skills and they are useful, scarce, and excellent. For example, one of the authors viewed two talks by scholars from two universities in the United States. The first, from a non-Ivy league school, provided a thought-provoking presentation based on some rather creative scholarship. The second, a scholar from a prestigious Ivy League school gave a lackluster performance, was often boring, and meandered in and out of various topics. Still, he repeatedly referred to his Ivy-league lineage, his Ivy League colleagues, and the 'great minds' of the discipline, which he subtly reminded us were also at Ivy League schools. Can you guess what transpired after the talk? As you may have surmised, the scholar from the non-Ivy league school received good reviews from the audience. But the scholar from the Ivy League school was even more impressive to some, even though they admitted that they understood little of what he said. Why? Members of the audience were impressed with his 'credentials' – teaching at an Ivy League school. 'If he is at a place like that,' remarked one person, 'he must be onto something good.' The use of indirect IM (being associated with Ivy League schools) overwhelmed the talk, leading to a positive evaluation of the talk and the scholar.

Fairness at work

HR managers also need to understand IM in order to perform their duties fairly. Fairness is a goal to be achieved from an ethical standpoint, which says that it's the right thing to do (Arvey & Renz, 1992). However, fairness is desirable for more than ethical reasons. One of these is unfairness that may serve to reduce employee motivation or otherwise neutralize it. Rewards that are unfairly distributed, or otherwise allocated without performance in mind will not motivate employees (Luthans & Kreitner, 1985). IM is of interest to HR managers because knowledge of how it works can help them distinguish quality performance from image, so that resources are more fairly allocated on substance rather than style. Also, because the suspicion of unfairness can be harmful to the ethical climate and employee motivation, HR managers and others making HR decisions need to skillfully use IM to package their decisions as being fair (Feldman & Klich, 1991). For example, Ariel is accused of playing favorites with a few of his subordinates. Employees claim that the 'Ariel clones' get most of the rewards in the department. When a promotion within the department opens up, Ariel recommends Sharon, an employee that the department agrees is the most qualified for the job. Although Ariel personally dislikes Sharon, he believes that she is best for the job. In order to have himself perceived as a fair decision-maker, Ariel leaks his recommendation so as to portray himself as a fair manager.

Functionality

IM may be beneficial or detrimental to the organization. When IM is beneficial, it is thought to be functional to achieving organizational goals. IM is beneficial when it: (1) facilitates positive interpersonal relationships and increases harmony within and outside the company;

(2) accurately portrays positive persons, events, or products to those in or out of the organization; and (3) facilitates decision-making regarding persons, events, or products, and leads management and/or consumers to successful decisions. To reap these benefits, organizations may wish to train employees in good IM techniques.

Sometimes, however, IM is detrimental to the organization and is **dysfunctional**. We believe that the use of IM may adversely affect the company when: (1) it inhibits or obstructs positive interpersonal relationships either within or outside of the company; (2) its use fails, thereby incorrectly casting persons, events, or products within the company in a negative light in the eyes of insiders or outsiders; and (3) it distorts information about persons, events, or products, and leads management and/or consumers to erroneous conclusions and/or decisions.

HR managers should not confuse functionality with truth. Functional strategies are those that effectively accomplish an intended objective. IM strategies may be functional but deceptive, or may be dysfunctional but truthful. Ultimately, managers may need to decide between making **ethical judgments** – choosing paths because they are the right and truthful thing to do – or **Machiavellian judgments** – choosing the functional courses even if they mean being deceptive or unethical. In the long run, the ethical approach seems to us the best way to proceed.

Cues to appropriate behavior

HR managers need to recognize that IM is a reciprocal and continuous process. While aware of the IM strategies of others, HR managers often do not recognize that their own IM provides cues to employees as to what they consider appropriate behavior. Such cues will impact the strategies and images that employees choose to create.

Individuals will elicit cues regarding what they are expected to do, either passively or actively (Ferris & Mitchell, 1987). These cues can serve to enhance or diminish the content of an employee's performance. When cues from managers result from the manager's poor IM, employees may fail to grasp the appropriate strategy to use. Instead, in order to alleviate a potential problem, they may choose to 'go with the manager', never fully realizing that the manager may have managed his impression improperly. An employee who sees his manager shaking his head at a suggestion for restructuring the department may oppose the restructuring attempt in order to be seen as a team player. His manager, on the other hand, may not have intended to signal opposition to the restructuring, but may have shaken his head while thinking about other things.

Stakeholder management

IM is an important competence in dealing with **external stakeholders** – individuals or groups outside the organization who feel that they have an interest in the decisions the organization makes. As HR managers realize, the processes of recruiting and interviewing, are not just one-time interactions with the candidate, but are often complex public relations exercises. The contact with external stakeholders offers the organization the opportunity to impress these stakeholders with their competence, fairness, and community mindedness on the one hand, and to increase the potential for lawsuits, bad publicity, and boycotts on the other. If in an interview, a job candidate is given the impression that the company is treating him fairly and with respect, his overall impression of the organization will likely be positive even if he does not get the job. On the other hand, if the job candidate is treated with contempt, made to feel uncomfortable, or otherwise disrespected, his overall impression of the company will be negative. One of our friends applied for a job as an assistant VP in a large state university. During the interview our friend was asked to give a presentation outlining his vision and academic philosophy. The president, who was to make the ultimate decision, didn't show up for the presentation, claiming a scheduling conflict. When they had dinner, the president seemed remote and asked some rude and confrontational questions. It seemed to our friend as if he had already made up his mind. Although the others were cordial to our friend, the president's behavior made him feel like trash. Several weeks later, our friend got an email telling him he hadn't been selected. He was so angry that he took all the materials the school had sent him, ripped them up, and burnt them in a pyre. In retrospect, a little better IM by the arrogant president could have defused our friend's anger even if the hiring decision turned out to be the same. In this case, the president's poor IM resulted in some trickle-down image damage. Our friend told this story to many others who likely have transmitted it to the community at large, further compounding the damage.

IM and HRM Processes

Although the HRM department usually has much control over the areas of recruitment, selection, placement, and training, IM can also influence these processes. The remainder of this chapter will focus on examples of HRM processes that have been shown to be influenced by IM. Our perspective is that IM can play a positive role in improving many HR management functions but excessive IM can act as an obstacle to organizational effectiveness. The focus in this chapter will also shift somewhat to include the management position, because much of the earlier chapters have focused on how employees use IM to build and enhance their reputations at work. For example, in considering the area of employment interviews, there is much that can be said about which IM tactics a candidate *should* use. However, the concerns of the HR manager in defending against employee IM that could negatively influence the fairness of the selection process, need also to be considered.

Employment Interviews

Hal Melbourne knew that this interview was the opportunity of a lifetime. He had the possibility of getting an executive job with one of the most prestigious banks in the country. Hal imagined what the interviewer would ask; he rehearsed what he would say and how he would say it. Hal talked to five of his closest executive friends and asked what he should wear. He even rode down to the hotel where he would be interviewed in order to become familiar with the surroundings. As Hal kept telling himself, this was too important an opportunity to leave things to chance.

While we have seen that IM phenomena occur in many organizational situations, the 'high stakes' nature of the employment interview makes it a setting particularly ripe for IM. In a typical job interview, both the candidate (who wants to get hired) and interviewer (who wants to attract the best candidates) generally engage in a reciprocal IM process with both attempting to manage positive impressions to achieve desired outcomes. At times, IM in the selection interview may be deceptive. Our colleague Clive Fletcher (1989) describes survey results indicating that 25 per cent of respondents admitted that they had lied during a job interview.

Although the employment interview has been conceptualized as a form of cognitive information processing, and as a selection technique having legal and civil rights implications (Eder & Ferris, 1989), it can also be viewed as a type of social interaction (Liden, Martin, & Parson, 1993) where both the applicant and interviewer try to influence each other through the use of IM. The near universality of the employment interview and the importance ascribed to it by managers has made it fertile territory for the occurrence of IM.

Both conceptual analyses and empirical studies have focused more on the IM behaviors of applicants than those of interviewers. Because the applicant is relatively powerless and the interviewer may be aware that much of the applicant's behavior represents style more than substance, the IM task of the applicant is far from easy. To be successful, the applicant must balance being 'confident but not brash, polite but not sycophantic, lively and interested but not voluble or manic, sufficiently nervous to show an appreciation of the importance of the occasion but not visibly anxious throughout' (Fletcher 1989, p. 273). While IM may positively influence interviewer perceptions of the applicant, its overuse might be seen as intentional manipulation and can backfire (see Chapter 2). Dr Clive Fletcher, a pioneer in the area of selection interviews and IM, presents a 'Behind the Scenes' view of his work.

Much of the research on IM in the employment interview has focused on the behavior of the applicant. Von Baeyer, Sherk, and Zanna (1981) found that female job applicants tailored their nonverbal and verbal behaviors to align themselves more closely with the views of women that were held by their interviewer. When the male interviewer was known to hold views in-line with the traditional female stereotype, female applicants gave more traditional responses to questions about family and relationships, spent more time on their physical appearance. and were less assertive in their verbal and nonverbal behaviors than when the interviewer held less traditional attitudes.

Baron (1989) found that IM behaviors in interview situations can be counterproductive if overused. In his study, male and female students conducted employment interviews with a female applicant who was an

Behind the Scenes

Clive Fletcher

I first became interested in IM when I was training people in selection interviewing skills in the 1970s. It was clear to me as I watched them doing practice interviews that they were influenced by differing candidate self-presentation strategies. Subsequently, I talked to my own undergraduate students about their ideas on how to behave in interviews, and it became clear that they varied widely in what they thought was appropriate or effective in this rather peculiar social encounter. Some felt it best to be very open and honest, some felt it wiser to be much more guarded; some felt that you had to sell yourself in a fairly direct manner, while others did not; and so on. Looking at the extensive research literature on the interview, I was amazed to find that this, the candidate's perspective, was almost completely missing. Much of the research done up until then seemed to treat the candidate as an entirely passive element in the situation – to the extent that many studies did not have real candidates at all, and simply presented interviewers with written descriptions of the people they were assessing. So I started doing some basic research myself. Since then, there has been more work in this area, though still not a great deal.

Why would it be helpful to know more about IM in this context? Well, first it would be useful to find out what are the determinants of IM tactics; do they vary with experience of interviews, do they arise from candidate training, to what extent are they personality-linked? From an interviewer's perspective, more knowledge of this would help interpret and assess the implications of different candidate interview behaviors, and perhaps throw some light on whether they had any relationship to future job performance. It would also be valuable to know just how much different aspects of IM do impact on interviewer assessments, so that some account of this could be taken in the training of interviewers; their awareness of the behaviors concerned could be raised, which would enable the interviewers to detect and evaluate the behaviors appropriately.

The need for this information is growing, as it is increasingly common for school and college graduates to be given some training in how to cope with interviews, and there are many books on the ▶

market addressing the same issue. All this serves to enhance the likelihood of IM tactics being adopted, perhaps in a quite deliberate way. The result may be a decrease in the already rather low validity of the interview as a selection tool. One of the possible strategies organizations could adopt to offset differences in candidate IM tactics is to specify the 'rules of the interview game'; in other words, spell out to candidates what they felt was appropriate behavior in the interview, and what was expected of them. This would provide a level playing field for all, and such differences that were observed between candidates could be evaluated against that background.

experimental accomplice. The female applicant was seeking an entry-level position and she responded in a standard fashion to questions asked by the interviewers. The applicant either used a number of positive nonverbal behaviors such as smiling and leaning forward or emitted few positive nonverbal cues. She also either wore or did not wear perfume. Baron's results supported the notion that too much IM in an employment interview can have a negative impact. Male interviewers rated the female applicant as being more intelligent and viewed her as having greater potential for success if she emitted positive nonverbals or wore perfume, but rated her lower if she used both sets of IM behaviors. Interestingly, this effect was not found when the interviewers were female.

Gilmore and Ferris (1989a) showed that an IM tactic, if skillfully executed, could influence interviewer perceptions more than information about the applicant's actual qualifications. Interviewers viewed a videotape in which a female applicant either engaged in IM (e.g., complemented interviewer, smiled) or did not. She was also portrayed as being highly qualified for a customer representative job or less qualified. The results indicated that evaluations of the applicant were influenced by IM but not applicant credentials. The applicant was perceived as doing better in the interview and was slightly more likely to be recommended for hiring when she used IM than when she did not. However, her credentials had little impact on interviewer ratings.

While Stevens (1997) showed that job applicants who expected to receive job offers engaged in more IM than those who didn't, an implication of the Baron (1989) and other studies is that not all IM tactics work or are equally effective in employment interviews. Kacmar,

Delery, and Ferris (1992) demonstrated this more directly. They distinguished applicant IM tactics in the employment interview as those that were **self-focused** (e.g., self-promotion) or **other-focused** (e.g., complementing the interviewer). They found that job applicants who used IM tactics that focused on themselves were rated higher than applicants whose IM tactics focused on the interviewer. Consistent with this, Stevens and Kristof (1995) showed that the use by job applicants of self-focused IM tactics such as self-promotion was positively related to interviewer evaluations of the applicant and other outcomes such as a job offer or site visit. However, Howard and Ferris (1996) also found that excessive IM doesn't always work to the advantage of the interviewee. They found that when interviewers were exposed to applicants using a high level of self-promotion, they perceived applicants to be less competent than when lower levels of self-promotion were used. Why would this occur? It may be that the tactics were ineffective because in a job interview situation they were easily perceived as being IM and backfired.

Coping with IM in Selection Interviews

Given that applicants are likely to continue to use IM, what should HR managers strive to accomplish in regard to controlling IM in the interview?

1. Be cognizant of fairness

At first glance, applicant IM tactics, such as those described in the studies reviewed above, would appear to be unfair (Rosenfeld, 1997). Arvey and Renz (1992) note that one criterion of fairness is that the processes and procedures used are objective and consistent across all applicants. Subjective manipulative behaviors in which interviewees are able to 'fake good' by distorting responses given to the interviewer are considered less fair. Given that some researchers view IM as a form of deception with significant impact on interviewer judgment (Anderson, 1991), it appears that one could easily argue that IM tactics are unfair. Fletcher (1992, p. 364), however, notes that while IM occurs in employment interviews, not all of it is inherently deceptive or manipulative. 'In relation to interview behavior, it may be more useful to think of it as a continuum of strategic IM behaviors, the most extreme of which involve conscious deception.' We believe that forms of IM that involve honestly and accurately presenting and highlighting one's attributes are both fair and desirable applicant behaviors. Candidate IM which is authentic and involves a legitimate portrayal of positive traits would seem to be fair, particularly since failing to attempt to create such an image may be seen as a sign of disinterest or a lack of interpersonal skills necessary for success in the workplace.

This changes the task for interviewers from elimination of IM to the systematic creation of interview situations in which interviewees are understood to be putting their best foot forward, but where deceptive, manipulative, insincere IM is detected, minimized, and discounted.

2. Train interviewers to recognize various kinds of applicant IM

Some of the previous interview literature has viewed applicant IM as 'noise' which should be detected and discounted. In our view, IM is far more complex and not inherently bad or nefarious. Thus, some knowledge of the nature of the positive and negative aspects of IM could be added to training to help interviewers recognize and defend against various IM techniques. As Fletcher (1990, p. 747) writes, 'it might be possible to sensitize interviewers to the different kinds of IM strategies that candidates use and the effects they have, so that they can identify them more readily and take account of them in their decision-making process'. Indeed, trained interviewers were better at detecting applicant IM in an employment interview and were less affected by it than untrained interviewers were (Howard & Ferris, 1996).

3. View IM as a skill, not a deficit

There is little doubt that IM is very common in employment interviews. Instead of maligning or discounting this behavior, Fletcher (1989) recommends using the employment interview to assess how good candidates are at IM. Rather than viewing IM in the employment interview as an obstacle, it might be better seen as a potential source of valuable information about an applicant's ability to do the job. We believe, as do others (e.g., Stevens & Kristof, 1995) that a good IMer in an interview, often turns out to be a good employee at work. Regarding IM as a valuable work skill rather than as inherently dysfunctional recognizes that much of organizational success depends on the ability to master organizational politics (Gilmore & Ferris, 1989b). The skilled use of authentic IM displayed in an interview context might be a useful indicator that the candidate will be able to successfully utilize IM when needed in future job settings. As Lautenschlager and Flaherty (1990, p. 313) note, 'the ability to manage one's impression may be quite valuable as a variable in its own right, especially in contexts where either social influence or conformity is important, such as in sales settings'.

4. Reduce ambiguity and uncertainty of the employment interview situation

Ambiguous uncertain environments increase the frequency of IM behaviors (Bozeman & Kacmar, 1997). As such, the issue is how one might reduce such ambiguity and uncertainty. Herb Baker suggests using more structured interview procedures, since the unstructured employment interview situation 'plays into the hands of those interviewees bent on obfuscating or diverting attention from their qualifications' (Baker & Spier, 1990, p. 86). Fletcher (1989) advocates using board or panel interviews and assessment centers to reduce manipulative IM by applicants. A more novel way of reducing ambiguity and uncertainty, Fletcher (1990, p. 747) suggests, is 'by giving all candidates for a post a briefing on how they were expected to present themselves in the interview. This would help to establish a common set of expectations about what behavior is appropriate.'

5. Train interviewers to focus on verifiable information

In order to increase the usefulness of interview responses, candidates should be steered toward more sincere forms of IM. A way to encourage more sincere IM is to increase the verifiability of the information sought. IM research (Schlenker 1980) has found that individuals will often act in excessively self-enhancing ways to please significant audiences in the absence of a 'reality check'. However, when information exists that could repudiate an overly positive claim, individuals will present themselves in a more accurate fashion, one that is closer to what they really believe. As Schlenker (1980, p. 188) writes, 'The more difficult it is for the audience to check the veracity of a self-presentation the more likely people are to self-aggrandize.' Fletcher (1989, p. 275) concurs, noting that, 'individuals moderate their self-assessments when they know they will be subject to subsequent external checking'.

In this vein, Gilmore and Ferris (1989b) point out that an interviewer often has a great deal of information relevant to an applicant's long-term identity, usually in the form of an application or resumé data. Furthermore, the applicant knows that the interviewer has this information and is aware that much of this information is verifiable (i.e., can be checked for accuracy). It would seem that focusing the employment interview on aspects of a candidate's competence, credibility, and long-term achievements that are closely related to material that can be verified would ultimately result in less distorting IM (Rosenfeld, 1997).

Exit Interviews and Surveys (EIS)

Vernal Sanders was sitting across from the HR manager on her last day of work at Bartlett Bagel Company. Vernal was leaving the organization in order to get away from the unfriendly work environment at Bartlett. Vernal and her spouse agreed that the pay cut that she had to take in order to get a new job was worth it. 'Less money', her husband noted, 'is acceptable if there is also less stress.' But when the HR manager asked why she was leaving, Vernal looked at him, 'chickened out' and said, 'Oh, it's simple: Better pay.'

The exit interview and survey (EIS) process was developed as a means of gathering data from people such as Vernal whose employment with an organization has been voluntarily or involuntarily terminated (Goodale, 1982). They are very popular in many large organizations particularly those such as the US military that face problems retaining key personnel. Because the specification of what topics should be included in EIS is not well defined, the issues on which an EIS focuses may vary according to short- and long-term organizational purposes and the manner in which those goals are conceptualized.

Diagnostic purposes

Organizations use the data gathered from EIS for diagnostic and strategic purposes: determining the reasons for company turnover; helping to identify training and development needs; creating strategic planning goals; and identifying necessary organizational changes. Exiting employees are interviewed for two reasons. First, it is believed that they may have important information about what might have gone wrong in the organization that caused them to leave. Relatedly, it is assumed that they may be more willing to share such information at the time of separation, since they no longer fear the repercussions of transmitting negative information.

Measurement properties

There has been little systematic research on the reliability or validity of EIS; what has been done suggests that responses within the EIS process may be tainted by response distortion even though the underlying assumption is that they provide more candid responses. Sometimes there is little consistency between original EIS information and responses given months later (Lefkowitz & Katz, 1969). For example, Zarandona and Camuso (1985) compared exit interviews given at the time of separation with an independent telephone survey administered a year-and-a-half later. It was found that responses had changed over the 18-month period. On the second survey, salary and benefits were cited significantly less as the reason for leaving, while supervision was cited significantly more frequently. It was concluded that because respondents had little reason to be deceptive on the second survey that they likely distorted their answers in the original exit interview.

Because of studies such as these, some have challenged the view that employees are more honest on the way out the door, and have concluded that respondents are probably not especially truthful at the time of separation (e.g., Giacalone & Duhon, 1991; Giacalone, Knouse, & Ashworth, 1991). Various explanations have been offered for the response distortion. For example, the exiting employee may not want to discuss uncomfortable material, might anticipate needing a letter of recommendation from management (Hinrichs, 1975), may fear retribution from management (Jablonsky, 1975), or may not want negative information to reach the new employer. Additionally, the exiting employee may perceive the questions as too personal (Drost, O'Brien, & Marsh, 1987), that there may be little to gain from the process (Garretson & Teel, 1982), or that management may bring about retribution on remaining employees based on information from the EIS process.

Employees' impression management

IM offers a comprehensive explanation for employees' tendencies to distort information in EIS processes: Employees distort information during the EIS process so as to create or manage an image of themselves or of others in the organization. The distortion may represent an intentional attempt to act maliciously and deceptively in retaliation for perceived offenses on the part of management or fellow employees, but it is more likely an attempt to hide controversial, personal, or inside information which could endanger future options for themselves or friends left behind. Good IMers don't burn their bridges! The separating employee may seek to provide feedback that creates, at worst, a neutral image of herself. This attempt may be moderated by other factors. One study found that willingness to discuss EIS issues was based both on feelings toward the topic (e.g. value of supervision, salary) and the status of the person receiving the information (Giacalone & Duhon, 1991). Similarly, another study found that feelings toward the interviewer and organization moderated the willingness to discuss issues during the EIS process (Knouse & Giacalone, 1992). These studies by Giacalone are consistent with the view that separating employees will create their impressions contextually, considering who will hear the information, the information itself, and its ultimate impact on the separating employee and those remaining (Giacalone, Elig, Ginexi, & Bright, 1995).

Reducing Insincere IM in EIS

What changes could be implemented so as to reduce separating employees' desire to insincerely manage impressions?

1. Reduce the identifiability of responses

Employees are apt to consider identifiability of their responses, especially when it could have negative repercussions for them. Identifiability is associated with increased self-enhancing IM (Giacalone & Rosenfeld, 1986), and is therefore likely to be a concern within the EIS process. Instruments which request identification in the hope of validating EIS responses against actual work records or other employee databases may be hurting the statistical quality of data due to heightened respondent IM concerns.

In both the practitioner and scholarly literatures, the discussion of the negative impact of identifiability and the resulting lack of confidentiality have been common themes (e.g., Giacalone & Knouse, 1989; Woods & Macaulay, 1987). The practitioner literature on EIS also leads us to conclude that the identifiability of responses and the subsequent lack of confidentiality may be powerful motivators of biased responding within the EIS process (Jablonski, 1975). In fact, in an exit survey administered by the US Army, responses given under conditions of anonymity resulted in generally more critical comments about military service as compared to those given under conditions of identifiability (Giacalone, et al., 1993).

As the Army study shows, to avoid 'shooting oneself in the foot', anonymity of responses should be maintained on EIS. Although this is difficult in the exit interview, it can be achieved in the exit survey process by not asking for identifying information (e.g. name, social security number) and/or using a third party outside of the organization to administer the survey. In our example, one could see how Vernal would react differently if she was not identified or was interviewed by an individual to whom she would not feel uncomfortable telling the truth.

2. Change the measurement time period

While the EIS process is generally thought of as part of the final week (or final day) procedures, this may not be the best time for organizations to request this information. Inasmuch as there is much the organization still controls at this time (e.g. recommendations to new employer, final payment, etc.), the employee may remain highly motivated to create the 'proper' impression.

It is advantageous to the organization to engage the employee in the EIS process at a later date, when all the loose ends have been tied up, and the employee is established in a new job. The organization may consider paying the employee for EIS information at a later date, where the former employee is less interested in managing a good impression and may provide unbiased responding.

3. Eliminate data from involuntary separations

Employees who separate involuntarily (i.e., are fired, terminated, laid-off, or 'rightsized') place the information they are giving management within a very different context than those employees who quit voluntarily. While the voluntarily separating employee usually leaves with greater choice, the involuntarily separating employee typically departs with no choice, and may view the separation and the entire experience in a more negative context. The resulting responses may be distorted by either the desire to manage a positive impression (so as to reduce the implied impression of incompetence or relative lack of value to the organization), or to retaliate by saying many negative things about the organization. The latter strategy was noted by Giacalone, et al. (1991) who observed that involuntarily separating employees may be taking on **negativistic roles** (Weber & Cook, 1972), that may result in unduly severe appraisals of the organization. Evidence of this 'screw the organization' attitude was found in involuntarily separating Army personnel. They were more negative about their military experiences than were personnel who volunteered to separate (Giacalone, et al., 1993).

It is common for organizations to collect data from voluntary and involuntary separation. Woods and Macaulay (1987) report that 83 percent of companies surveyed gathered and used data from involuntary separations. Involuntary separations increase the potential for responses that may be highly distorted by the need to manage an impression that helps the separating employee save face. Indeed some researchers have advocated not gathering data from those who are involuntarily separated (e.g., Garrison & Ferguson, 1977; Sherwood, 1983), and found greater divergence between responses at separation and later follow-up among those involuntary separations than among voluntary ones (Lefkowitz & Katz, 1969).

It is best to deal with the responses of involuntarily separating personnel in a different way than responses gathered from voluntary separations. Information gained from involuntary separations may be of use – especially in determining what factors lead to such separations – and should be collected and critically evaluated. However, the data on involuntary separations can contaminate data collected on voluntary separations because it involves different and more varied IM motivations. As such, we advocate that to minimize contamination by heightened IM concerns, the two groups of responses should be kept separately.

Labor Arbitration

The arbitration of labor grievances involves the voluntary, final, and binding resolution of disputes between unions and employers by mutually acceptable third parties (St Antoine, 1984; Zack, 1989). The arbitrator serves as the interpreter of that part of the collective bargaining agreement that management is allegedly violating. The expectation is that the interpretation will be done in an equitable and fair manner to both management and the **grievant** (the individual who has filed the grievance).

The objectivity of the arbitrator is particularly important, since the award he or she makes involves the appropriate interpretation of ambiguous contract language and an intention to make sense from confusing and contradictory evidence (Hill & Sinicropi, 1987; Rehmus, 1984). The arbitrator does so by reviewing the issues, the facts, the testimony, and the evidence, as well as cited arbitration decisions.

Assuming the positive intentions of the participants, the process of arbitration is only as good as the integrity and fairness of its procedures. While research has shown that factors outside the merits of the case also impact arbitration decisions, such as biographical data (Heneman & Sandver, 1983) and arbitration experience (Nelson & Curry, 1981), these factors account for only a small portion of the arbitration decision.

Giacalone and colleagues (Giacalone & Pollard, 1989; Giacalone, Pollard, & Brannen, 1989; Giacalone, Reiner, & Goodwin, 1992), have suggested an IM interpretation of the labor arbitration process. They have argued that the award made by the arbitrator is subject to the IM strategies and abilities of the grievant and his representatives. While the discussion in this section focuses on the IM of the grievant, it does so because of the research that has focused on the grievant as IMer. However, we recognize that management representatives also engage in IM and impact the arbitrator. Arbitrators may have their judgment influenced by impressions made; such impressions may, in fact, be made at a level beyond their conscious understanding, since much of IM is controlled by scripts that guide behavior automatically (Bozeman & Kacmar, 1997; Schlenker & Pontari, 2000).

This idea is supported by research on forensic studies. It has been found that the defendant's actions within the courtroom can create impressions, which directly impact the jury decision. These impressions can be inadvertently drawn from actions within the process such as a refusal to testify (Shaffer & Sadowsky, 1979), or testimony that is impertinent or self-aggrandizing (Kalven & Zeisel, 1966). Similarly, impressions can be created (intentionally or unintentionally) by a defendant's explanations (e.g., via remorse, regret, or emotional conveyance) which may affect the subsequent sentence or disposition (Rumsey, 1976; Savitsky & Sim, 1974).

Arbitrators are subject to what forensic specialists call **extralegal factors**. According to Austin and Utne (1977, p. 170), an extralegal factor is one which

> can be defined as information not directly bearing on the individual's guilt or innocence, nor on the nature of a convicted offender's crime or the situational context within which the offense was committed. . . . Extralegal factors can be either positive or negative, mitigating or incriminating, consequently they can either help or hurt a defendant.

To manage the proper impression in front of the arbitrator, the grievant needs to control the impression made, as well as the impressions extralegal factors may leave, in order to create a more favorable overall impression of herself or of the questioned behavior. IM can then be an extralegal variable in itself (e.g., as in the use of an excuse or apology), or can be used to present extralegal variables in a way that creates the desired impression for the grievant.

The forensic literature provides ample evidence that the impressions created by an offender have a marked impact on punishment received for an offense. These impressions may involve the demeanor of the offender (Parkinson, 1979) as arrogant or humble, courteous and deferent, or able to control anxiety (Pryor & Buchanan, 1984).

In the case of arbitration, the grievant's record, either as a work record, or record of offenses, provides an extralegal factor that can be controlled by either side to make a particular impression. For example, raising the previous record of offenses (or lack thereof) can significantly impact the ultimate decisions made in the case (Kalven & Zeisel, 1966). If management's representatives raise a previous record of improper behavior on the part of the grievant, this may create an impression of the grievant as a troublemaker and may contribute to an award made against him or her (Hatton, Snortum, & Oskamp, 1971).

A study by Giacalone and Pollard (1989) found the degree to which arbitrators felt punishment for the grievant was appropriate was differentially influenced by the grievant's previous record and type of IM strategy (account or apology) used. Mock arbitrators, who read of an employee infraction that led to a grievance, recommended less punishment when the grievant gave an account on the third offense as compared to an account on the first offense. When an apology was given, no significant differences between first and third offense recommendations occurred. In a later study, Giacalone, Pollard, and Eylon (2000) included information for practicing arbitrators regarding the consequences of the infraction by the grievant, as well as manipulations of IM strategy and previous record. Results showed that all three variables independently affected the severity of the arbitrator's ruling. Creating the impression that an infraction was severe, that a grievant had a history of similar infractions, as well as using a particular IM strategy resulted in differential perceptions of the grievant and awards by an arbitrator. What was supposed to be simple 'interpretation' of a contract quickly appears to become a case of managing the impressions caused by extralegal variables.

Reducing Excessive IM in Arbitration

The potential that IM may bias the judgment of an arbitrator leaves HRM practitioners with the issue of how to deal with these concerns. The following suggestions can help address these issues.

1. Require justifications based on strict contractual interpretation

The extent to which arbitrators are capable of using extralegal factors in their awards depends largely on how much latitude they are allowed and what consequences exist for doing so. Because arbitrators are typically given considerable latitude, the likelihood of impact by IM is high. Contractual ambiguity, along with the amount of discretion afforded the arbitrator, creates a vague situation in which either side may capitalize on the opportunity to redefine the data for the arbitrator through the use of IM tactics. As noted previously, IM increases under ambiguous, uncertain conditions (Ferris, King, Judge, & Kacmar, 1991).

It is also important that labor arbitrators who take non-contractual factors into account when making their decisions suffer sanctions. Such sanctioning need not be formal, but may be as simple as deciding never to use an arbitrator again. Management and labor leaders need to work together on such sanctions, since the biases do not necessarily always favor the grievant, but may favor the organization when their case is presented by company lawyers or management representatives who are skilled IMers.

2. Train arbitrators to recognize IM strategies

Recognition of IM strategies is certainly not an expected ability of arbitrators. Still, the ability to recognize deceptive IM, and ignore its biasing of contractual interpretation, remains an important factor in the equitable resolution of labor-related disputes.

Training arbitrators to recognize and discount IM must go beyond simple recognition of tactics used by grievants and management; it must focus on a variety of biases (of which IM is but one) that can influence decision-makers. Training must increase the arbitrator's ability to critically evaluate contractually relevant data to discount irrelevant data, and to render decisions that focus only on contractual interpretation. Understanding the impact of IM can lead to the implementation of techniques that minimize its influence.

Careers

> You will find it a distinct help ... if you know and look as if you know
> what you are doing
> (From US Internal Revenue manual for tax auditors, quoted in
> Petras and Petras, 1994, p. 108).

It was his first day on the job as executive vice-president, but Dick Kesler knew the questions he was asking himself all too well. It was his habit to list for himself the traits and accomplishments that he would need to have to have in order to get to the next level – in this case, president. Dick knew that it was not a list he could develop in a day or a week. It would require listening to what others said about the job, reading the records of his predecessors, and carefully trying to understand the environment. Eventually, Dick knew, he would find out what it was they were looking to have in the president's office, and he would give it to them.

As Dick Kesler's story illustrates, a new and often effective work ethic has come into vogue in organizational life. This ethic stresses superficial, image-building and manipulative IM rather than hard work, accomplishment, and performance (Riordan, 1989). Feldman and Weitz (1990) have called this ethic the **careerist orientation to work** (see also Feldman, 1985; 1990). Careerists go beyond competence and seek to advance through non-performance means that include IM (Aryee, Wyatt, & Stone, 1996).

The careerist orientation is characterized by six primary beliefs listed in Table 7.1. While these beliefs all have some IM components, four appear to be most relevant to IM use.

First, high caliber performance is not necessarily enough for advancement in organizations. What is more important, is that one 'appears' to be promotable, and is seen as worthy of advancement. Such appearances are founded in the effective use of IM career strategies. According to Feldman and Klich (1991), this can be attained by using symbols of power and influence (e.g. dress, office design) (Ornstein, 1989), generating outside offers that attest to a more absolute measure of worth, varying techniques in resumés (Knouse, Giacalone, & Pollard, 1988) and interviews, politically finessing moral dilemmas at work, and creating artificial relationships at work which offer more opportunities

Table 7.1	**Six Central Beliefs of a Careerist Orientation**

1. Merit alone is not enough to move up the organizational ladder
2. Social relationships provide critical assistance in career advancement
3. The appearance of team play affords one help in career advancement
4. Significant amounts of work cannot be assessed tangibly, either in an absolute sense or a relative (comparative) sense
5. An individual's long term goals are generally not compatible with those of any one organization
6. Career advancement sometimes requires that one use unethical behaviors

Adapted from Feldman and Klich (1991)

to get ahead. Dick Kesler would probably be attempting to figure out exactly who the powerful people in the organization were and ingratiating himself with them. Dick would try to understand what power symbols he needed to have in his office, and how he should react if faced with a variety of moral dilemmas.

Second, climbing the organization ladder requires interpersonal relationships with co-workers and supervisors that appear to be social in nature. In fact, these 'social' relations are used calculatingly to ingratiate oneself with formal and informal organizational gatekeepers of information in gathering inside information and job contacts to promote one's own best interest. As we have seen, the creation of a likable organizational identity provides one such political influence. Dick Kesler would no doubt make the rounds at organizational parties, maintaining friendly relations so that he could get needed information when he needed it.

Third, the image of being a 'team player' offers career opportunities through the appearance of cooperation while still searching for more information that will strengthen one's personal image and market value. This appearance of cooperation is important, since it seems to offer potential competitors for promotion security at a surface level, while one inwardly scrutinizes information that will aid in the toppling of the competition. In his attempts to get upward mobility, Dick Kesler would not only identify his competition for the presidency of the company, but would appear to cooperate with the competition so as to avoid alerting potential competitors to any threat.

Finally, much of what is actually done cannot be accurately measured, nor can the person doing the work be objectively assessed relative to others. The issue is once again one of social reality rather than of physical reality. This problem can be understood in the work on performance appraisal and IM showing that variables appraised in performance may be highly subject to IM influences. Box 7.1 describes how the IM motives of raters can also influence the objectivity of the performance appraisal process.

How does this careerist orientation affect organizations? Gould and Penley (1984) investigated the role that career strategies play in organizational life. After surveying over 400 employees in a large municipality, they found that salary progression was related to the strategies of creating career opportunities (developing and seeking particular skills and experiences), extended involvement (working

| Box 7.1 | **IM in Performance Appraisal: It's Not for Subordinates Alone** |

When one of the authors was young, he worked in a department store where managers would discuss the 'performance appraisal (PA) blip'. The PA blip was a surge in performance (be it quality or quantity) right before management engaged in the predictable yearly review. Just as US major league baseball players pad their statistics during the end-of-season 'salary drive', employees would try to manage the impression of being 'good workers' by engaging in higher quality or quantity performance right before PA time. Their objective was to get better PAs from managers. The 'blip' was a source of many funny stories about the various employee strategies that would be used to manage the right impression.

Research has found that the influence of employee IM on performance evaluations is much greater than a mere blip. The general finding is that better IMers get better performance evaluations, especially in those professions (e.g., service industries) where performance doesn't have an objective outcome measure (Abdullah, 1997). Frink and Ferris (1998) found that evaluation systems where employees set performance goals are particularly prone to the effects of IM. Their study varied the degree that employees would be held accountable (i.e., potentially being evaluated by someone or being answerable for one's actions) for performance goals they set. They found that when ▶

accountability was low, the goals were used for performance-related reasons, however, when accountability was high, goal setting was more influenced by IM.

There is some evidence that management also uses PA to manage impressions. Villanova and Bernardin (1989; 1991), have provided us with the other side: management use of PA to create certain impressions on subordinates and superiors. PA, they argue, can provide managers (as performance raters) with the *means* to engage in social influence by manipulating PA ratings for IM purposes. These means, consisting of inadequacies in the PA systems itself (e.g., criteria used are irrelevant, rater is untrained, rater is left unaccountable for ratings), when intertwined with the rater's **motivation** to create particular impressions (e.g., when the PA has a personal impact on the rater) provide for the opportunity to use ratings as IM tools in PA, and can distort this supposedly objective process.

Let's take the example of one department manager in a clothing retail chain who insisted on selecting his own staff. When PA time came along each year, he would give everyone in his department incredible appraisals, with glowing commentary on everything each person did. This created the impression that he had an excellent staff which he was responsible for assembling. So what happened? In fact, the manager worked within a PA system in which the criteria were largely unverifiable Employees were evaluated on issues such as friendliness, appearance, punctuality (there were no time clocks), and enthusiasm. They were never judged on the one criterion related to their job: number of sales! Perhaps, more importantly, because the company highly valued the evaluation that staff gave the manager, the manager was placed in a position of giving good evaluations so that there would be some **reciprocal leniency** (Villanova & Bernardin, 1989) on the part of staff. In other words, you scratch my blip and I'll scratch yours! PA ratings were a way of creating the impression that the manager supported his staff, thereby insuring that they, too, would help him maintain and enhance his position in the organization. Inadvertently, the company had created a PA process in which the ratings could be manipulated via IM; it was the easiest way to prosper within the organization. ▶

So how can an organization stop IM from having a major influence on PA? Villanova and Bernardin (1991) offer eight strategies:

- Make the criteria used in PA relevant to the job: develop and utilize criteria which are essential or important to job performance.
- Clearly define those criteria used in PA: provide raters with a clear understanding of what the criteria mean, rather than providing terms which can be interpreted in a variety of ways.
- Provide training for raters which focuses both on the appraisal process as well as IM. Good training which focuses on the intricacies of the rating process and offers periodic refreshers can avoid falling into IM pitfalls.
- Increase the frequency of PA. Help the rater do his or her job by providing smaller time periods so that memory or generic impressions do not have to be relied on.
- Aggregate individual performance ratings to a group level when individual level performance is too interdependent. In some jobs, the interdependence of performance in a group does not allow for individual evaluations. Group performance situations increase uncertainty and ambiguity that heighten the potential for IM if individual level performance must be evaluated.
- Evaluate performance on specific dimensions and combine statistically to create an overall index of performance. Asking raters to provide overall indices of performance facilitates IM behaviors; focusing on individual items and making a statistical judgment for aggregate data reduces the IM impact.
- Increase the number of raters used. As the number of raters increases, more perspectives on performance are brought forth, and a more accurate evaluation will likely be obtained.
- Hold raters accountable for their behaviors/judgments. Including accountability as part of the rating process forces raters to consider their IM driven distortions and may help them to reconsider non-performance related criteria. Interestingly, this is opposite from the Frink and Ferris (1998) finding that greater accountability in those being evaluated *increases* IM distortions. Apparently, what's good for the rater is not always good for the ratee.

beyond the traditional 40-hour week), and opinion conformity and other enhancement (i.e., ingratiation). Self-nomination (i.e., self-enhancement) and networking (creating a group of contacts in and out of the organization) were also related to the salary progression of managers.

Judge and Bretz (1994) gave a survey assessing careers, influence behaviors, and factors impacting career success, to a sample of past college graduates. Their findings clarify and lend further credibility to the idea that careerist IM strategies *may* work, depending on the strategy used. Judge and Bretz found that job-focused strategies (i.e., self-promotion) negatively predicted career success, while supervisor-focused tactics (i.e., ingratiation) were positively associated with career success.

Strategies of a careerist orientation

In trying to understand the effectiveness of a careerist orientation, it is clear that the primary interest from a management standpoint is to gauge how these strategies impact the long-term career. To understand this long-term impact, we must first be able to identify basic IM strategies that careerists use to better identify and differentiate among them. Table 7.2 summarizes some IM strategies, adapted from the sociological, organizational and psychological literatures that are potentially related to advancing the careerist's goals.

A few issues are worth noting regarding these strategies. First, the careerist may use other strategies that are of a more political nature in gaining whatever he or she might wish to gain. As such, some political tactics (such as **coalition-building**) will involve activities like social exchange that go beyond simple attempts to control impressions. Second, the IM strategies listed are by no means exhaustive. For example, many of the strategies listed in Chapters 2 and 3 might also serve careerist goals and achieve similar ends.

We know little about whether these strategies are differentially effective at various career stages, or which of these strategies predominate in particular organizational settings. While identification of these strategies has been relatively easy, specifying when and where the strategies are used and whether they are effective needs further investigation.

Table 7.2	IM Career Strategies		
Strategy	Definition	IM goal	Source
Altercasting	Strategies which seek to cast another person into a different role	To create a different image of another which brings about one's own goals	Weinstein and Deutschberger (1963)
Disclosing obstacles	The process by which an individual reveals those obstacles, real, imagined, or fabricated, which impeded an already successful performance	The impression that the individual has overcome great hurdles in achieving success and is therefore very competent and/or motivated	Schlenker (1980)
Scapegoating	Putting the blame for failure on an external source who is minimally or not at all blameworthy	The appearance that one is not to blame for an apparent failure	Ashforth and Lee (1990)
Window-dressing	The use of physical changes in one's environment or appearance which makes a person appear more desirable	The impression of greater prestige, wealth, competence, or other socially desirable characteristics	Ornstein (1989); Riordan (1989)
Playing dumb	Giving others the impression that one is ignorant of, or unable to do, the work associated with a given job	Allows employee to help define his/her career by working only on those tasks which have the greatest social desirability and career pay-off	Ashforth and Lee (1990); Becker and Martin (1995)
Depersonalizing	The avoidance of the unwanted demands of others by treating them as objects or numbers	The appearance of detachment, objectivity and professionalism which signals to others that no 'personal', discretionary decisions will be made	Ashforth and Lee (1990)
Smoothing	The hiding of fluctuations in one's effort or output in performance	The appearance of a steady, productive rate of performance	Ashforth and Lee (1990)
Stalling	The overt appearance of activity while doing little or nothing	The impression is made that one is a supportive team player while actually undermining the activity	Ashforth and Lee (1990)
Buffing	The use of rigorous documentation and/or creation of documents designed to manage the impression of competence or motivation	The appearance of competence or motivation is enhanced by producing proof of work activity	Ashforth and Lee (1990); Shem (1978)

Strategy	Definition	IM goal	Source
Playing safe	The evasion of those situations and decisions which may give an unfavorable impression of the employee	A pre-emptive attempt at minimizing or eliminating any unfavorable image	Ashforth and Lee (1990)
Misrepresenting	The avoidance of blame by manipulating information via distortion, embellishment, deception, selective presentation or withholding	To create an image of oneself that is consistent with career goals	Ashforth and Lee (1990)
Escalating commitment	The continued and enhanced commitment to a series of decisions in an attempt to make the initial decision appear to be a good one	An impression that one's decision or decision-making strategy was correct	Ashforth and Lee (1990)
Stretching	The prolonging of a given task so that one appears to be occupied	The impression given to observers is that one is busy and has little 'down' time	Ashforth and Lee (1990)
Expert-citing	The use of outside status references or people to support one's decision-making	The impression that significant people respect or otherwise value your contributions	Pfeffer (1981)
Association/ disassociation	The use of symbolic association with positive events and people and disassociation from negative events and people	Impression that one is a part of good things and apart from negative things	Giacalone (1987); Giacalone and Knouse (1988)
Overconforming	Strict adherence to one's defined responsibilities and the associated guidelines, procedures and precedents associated with those responsibilities	Impression that one 'plays by the rules' and/or that one is not to blame for problems associated with such strict adherence	Ashforth and Lee (1990); Lipsky (1980); Morgan (1987)
Passing the buck	The passing of one's responsibility for the completion of a task onto another person	A preventive strategy designed to avoid a negative impression of one's ability, especially when the task is not one that the person is particularly strong on	Ashforth and Lee (1990)

Countering Careerist IM

With the likelihood of a careerist approach becoming increasingly popular in organizations, we offer several practical suggestions for the HR manager to address the issue.

1. Go beyond punishment

As noted previously, some prior IM theorists and researchers tended to view IM as manipulative and consciously deceptive. Such a view of IM might lead to more readily disciplining the IMing employee who is viewed as using it. We would argue, however, that this approach is often shortsighted and incorrect.

In the previous chapter, we saw that the BIDR scale suggests that there are *two* types of IM-related phenomena – one deceitful, and the other, self-deceptive enhancement, that is sincere but exaggerated. It may be that the careerist is assumed to be using deceitful IM, but may, in fact, be engaging in self-deceptive enhancement. It would be ethically questionable to discipline individuals for things they believed to be honest. Also, even if the careerist behaviors are conscious and deceitful, they may be employed as self-protective survival strategies. An employee may enter an organizational environment without a careerist orientation, but may develop such an orientation in response to an organization that rewards the careerist approach, in order that he or she can survive. Harrell-Cook, Ferris, and Dulebohn (1999) suggested that one way employees cope with organizations that are overly political is by themselves acting more political as a means of exerting greater control. Dealing with the careerist orientation, therefore, must go beyond indiscriminately punishing the careerist to determining if the organizational culture fosters and rewards careerist behaviors.

2. Use objective standards and measures

IM flourishes in ambiguous environments where employees may redefine their behaviors or the standards expected. Management may wish to use career-related measures that involve more precisely defined behaviors and outcomes, rather than measures which focus on interpretation. Management needs to establish clear goals and expectations so as to prevent the careerist from retrofitting his accomplishments and behaviors to a vaguely established series of organizational goals.

3. Link fates

With the increased focus on teamwork, management will need to consider evaluations that link the fates of many on a team, rather than the conventional practice of singling out individuals for evaluation. Linking the fates of many people on a team fosters cooperation in order to achieve a goal. It makes self-serving IM difficult by focusing more on team outputs than on perceptions of individual worker accomplishments. Under such conditions, careerists will need to either abandon the careerist ethic, or engage in group IM as a team. The latter will not only be more difficult to execute, but also harder to conceal from management.

4. Disempower dysfunctional IM

Because manipulative IM has long been relegated to back-room discussion, its use has been limited to employees who know how and choose to use it. We wrote this book because we believe that *everyone* in the organization should know about the various techniques that IM encompasses. Much as we have argued that interviewers and arbitrators should be made aware of these strategies, all employees and managers would be well-served to learn the strategies and know that others know and recognize them. Training all employees in IM strategies levels the playing field to where everyone is at least aware of the practices. More importantly, it raises the risks for IM usage, because recognition of dysfunctional strategies is more likely to occur when IM comes out of the closet.

What We Know and Beyond

The impact of IM on HRM decisions goes well beyond the four areas of employment interviews, exit interviews and surveys, arbitration, and careers that we have focused upon in this chapter. HRM practitioners know intuitively that IM can influence many other organizational areas and concerns. Table 7.3 summarizes several of these other areas.

While space limitations have prevented us from focusing on all the areas, we believe that these organizational issues and processes are also susceptible to IM. Although research has been conducted to explore the impact of IM in some of these areas, others remain to be investigated. There have been theoretical pieces written on issues such as IM motivation, and goal-setting (e.g., Huber, Latham, & Locke, 1989), but little work has been done in terms of actual empirical research. Still other areas have seen some preliminary research (e.g., resumés), but have done little in terms of theoretical development. A third group of areas such as organization development and employee assistance programs are potentially impacted by IM, but research and theory have yet to appear.

Much needs to be considered about the *positive* contributions that IM can offer the organization and the HR manager. For example, training employees to monitor their own behavior and its impact may facilitate interpersonal communication. Acknowledging and discussing the existence of IM tactics may limit their excessive use for fear of being caught. We believe that proper use of IM may facilitate helping behaviors among friends and co-workers (Schlenker & Britt, 1999), improve workplace relationships, increase group cohesiveness, and create a more pleasant organizational climate. In short, a 'kindler, gentler' IM!

A Concluding Note

There is much about IM and HRM left to determine, many parameters yet to establish regarding when and how much IM will impact HRM decisions, and still more theoretical advances to be made. Although the research on IM and HRM is more advanced than the comparable organizational work on individual differences in IM discussed in Chapter 6, we need to remember that this is a field still in its infancy. When considering the longer time period in which performance appraisal, recruitment, and selection models, theories, and mechanisms have been investigated, there is little doubt that the comparative development of IM leaves it at a more basic level.

While this chapter has emphasized areas where IM is important, there clearly are aspects of the HRM arena where IM plays less of an active

Table 7.3	**How IM Can Impact Issues/Processes in HRM**	
Issues/process	Some questions regarding the potential impact of IM	Comments
Performance Appraisal (PA)	• Does the rater use PA to create an impression on the employee, others in the organization, or self? • How effective are IM strategies in impacting PA? • Do IM-related individual difference variables impact PA?	The impact of IM on PA has been reviewed by Villanova and Bernardin (1989), (1991) and Miller and Cardy (2000)
Letters of Recommendation (LR)	• Do differing IM strategies impact the efficacy of the LR? • How is the LR viewed by people with different expectations of what IM strategies should be used?	The impact of IM on LR has been discussed by Steve Knouse (1989)
Resumés	• What IM strategies can be used in resumés? • Are different IM strategies more or less effective, depending on the job sought? • Do high self-monitors manage the impressions of credentials more effectively?	The impact of IM on resumés has been examined by Knouse, Giacalone, and Pollard (1988)
Cover letters	• How might cover letters be written and presented (paper type, fonts, etc.) in order to best manage the impressions sought?	The impact of IM on cover letters has been examined by Knouse, Giacalone, and Pollard (1988)
Training	• What impact does trainer IM ability have on training effectiveness? • How might IM strategies be used to present training material? • What impact does IM have on training evaluations?	Theoretical and empirical work on the impact of IM on training needs to be done
Organization development	• How is IM used to hide or mitigate resistance to change? • What role does IM play in the diagnostic stages of organization development?	Theoretical and empirical work on the impact of IM on organization development needs to be done
Motivation	• How might employee IM concerns be used to increase employee motivation? • How might IM be used organizationally to develop a motivation strategy that takes employee differences into account?	The impact of IM on employee motivation has been addressed by Huber, Latham, and Locke (1989)

▶

Issues/process	Some questions regarding the potential impact of IM	Comments
Employee Assistance Programs (EAPs)	• To what extent might IM concerns prevent employees from using EAPs?	No theoretical or empirical work has been done on IM and EAPs
Anti-social behaviors	• To what extent are the anti-social behaviors an attempt to create a particular impression on supervisors and co-workers? • How might IM be used to neutralize the negative aspects of anti-social behavior at work?	Work has been done on these areas by Payne (1989) on theft, and by Giacalone and Rosenfeld (1987), Giacalone and Knouse (1990) and Giacalone, Riordan and Rosenfeld (1997) on employee sabotage
Leadership	• What strategies do individuals use to acquire and maintain the image of a leader? • How do individual differences in IM factors impact leadership emergence and/or effectiveness?	The impact of IM on leadership has been addressed by Leary (1989), and has been investigated by a number of researchers (e.g., Leary and Schlenker, 1980; Leary et al., 1986; Gardner and Avolio, 1998)

role and operates quietly in the background (Schlenker & Pontari, 2000). For example, contractually required health and medical benefits, promotions and raises based largely on collective bargaining agreements and seniority, and mandatory age-related retirements in dangerous professions (e.g., police, fire department) are HRM activities not greatly impacted by IM factors.

However, while not all HRM-related functions are affected by IM concerns, many core areas are. Thus, it is important for HR managers to evaluate their decisions with a watchful eye, realizing that almost any decision they make which requires that an evaluation be made on an employee *might* be subject to the bias of a managed impression. It is critical that HR managers discern where these biases might occur, as well as where IM might offer refreshing and positive advantages to dated HRM processes.

8 Current, Emerging, and Future Directions

The Final Act

If all the world is really a stage, as the theatrical metaphor we used so often throughout this book to illustrate IM suggests, let us consider this chapter our final act. Following the format of many final acts, we will revisit some key themes presented previously. In the opening chapter, we showed how IM has become popular in organizational behavior, management, social psychology, and communication. In response to questions many people ask about IM, we offered the following conclusions based on research and theory: IM is widespread in social and organizational life. It occurs for a variety of reasons ranging from the purely selfish to the most humanitarian. The same IM behavior can have a number of motives and will be carried out if the estimated benefits of engaging in the behavior exceed the costs. Our discussion showed how IM is not inherently bad, that it is used by everyone to a greater or lesser degree, and we manage many of our impressions automatically and without conscious awareness. Under certain conditions, IM can influence both the audience as well as the IMer. Leary and Kowalski's (1990) model describing how people monitor the impressions they are making, become motivated to IM, and then choose a particular IM tactic, was offered as one potential integrating framework. The principles of that model were further elaborated in the cybernetic model by Bozeman and Kacmar (1997) that emphasized the role that feedback plays in monitoring and modifying IM behaviors to match standards.

In Chapter 2, ingratiation, the most common and most investigated form of acquisitive IM, was described. Ingratiation tactics fulfill the powerful human desire to be liked by others. In Chapter 3, other acquisitive tactics used to create positive impressions were described. These included self-promotion, intimidation, exemplification, and supplication. We also reviewed indirect IM – ways people claim identities as a result of associating with positive and disassociating with negative things or events.

Chapters 4 and 5 summarized protective IM tactics – those we use to repair or protect a spoiled or threatened identity. Predicaments – events which put someone's identity in a bad light – often precipitate protective IM tactics and strategies. The tactics of excuses, justifications, disclaimers, self-handicapping, and apologies are some of the ways individuals extricate themselves from predicaments that have occurred or they fear will happen. As we saw in Chapter 5, protective tactics can also be indirect, such as when individuals try to disassociate or distance themselves from negative events.

In Chapter 6 we looked at how differences among people in their tendencies to manage impressions can be assessed. The Self-Monitoring Scale measures differences in people's attentiveness and responsiveness to social cues. Self-monitoring is related to a person's IM skill and his or her success at it. The Balanced Inventory of Desirable Responding measures the inclination to deceptively IM others, as well as people's tendencies to deceive themselves through exaggerated positive presentations. The Self-Presentational Scale measures people's tendencies to manage positive impressions by attributing very positive characteristics to themselves and by denying negative characterizations. It has yet to be used extensively in organizations. The Measure of Ingratiatory Behaviors in Organizational Settings measures employees' tendencies to use the various forms of ingratiation. Use of these IM measures in organizational settings has been sporadic but new applications for the workplace are proposed. As evidence of the reliability, validity, norms and utility of these measures increases, we may find that IM measures can give us clues to the causes of low employee productivity or poor managerial performance, to those positions in which skilled IMers could be most useful, or to individuals or job groups that would benefit from training in IM.

In Chapter 7, the relevance of IM for HR managers was examined. The possibility that the ability to IM may be added to the list of competencies required for many jobs was raised. That IM plays a key role in employment interviews may have come as no surprise; the finding that IM can outweigh job-related credentials may have. Thus, it is important that interviewers consider following a structured interview format, ask questions about experiences that the interviewee suspects are verifiable, be trained to recognize IM and remember that the interview is probably a good sample of the interviewee's IM abilities which may be very important for success in some jobs. The potential biasing influence of IM in exit interviews and surveys led to recommendations that exit interviews and surveys be conducted so that the identifiability of the exiting employee's responses can be minimized, that some time is allowed to pass after the employee's exit, and the responses of voluntary separators are distinguished from terminated employees. The careerist orientation was discussed as a potentially dysfunctional form of IM because it emphasizes appearances over competency. Studies showed the more subtle forms of IM used by careerists are related to career success. This led to recommendations that organizations attempt to control careerists, including using objective performance appraisal methods whenever possible, linking rewards to cooperative rather than exclusively self-interested actions, and getting organization members to understand the dysfunctional IM of the careerist and call it when they see it.

Some consistent themes emerged throughout this book. The use of IM requires skill. The ingratiator's dilemma illustrates what is often true about IM – when you need it the most is when it is hardest to do effectively. Presumably this is because audiences recognize that when the stakes are high, people may feign an identity to attain an important outcome or avoid a negative one. Throughout the chapters, we offered some advice on the conditions when IM is most likely to be effective, how delivery can increase its effectiveness, and how organizations can begin to reap the positive effects of IM and avoid some of its negative consequences.

More fully understanding issues of effectiveness and ways IM can be used to foster organizational and personal goals will undoubtedly be the subject of sequels to the present book. What will those sequels add to what we know now and have presented here? Below we speculate on areas in theory and research we believe are most likely to be the focus of organizational IM research in the near future. Then we will outline sequels that would be of greatest interest to practitioners.

Sequels in IM Theory and Research

As this book reveals, the field of organizational IM is rapidly growing and is ripe for more research and application. In terms of research, answers to three key questions would greatly extend the utility of IM: How much does IM influence organizational functioning? How much do organizational factors influence IM? How do IM behaviors work together?

How Much Does IM Influence Organizational Behavior?

Organizational IM researchers face the challenge of specifying when and how IM influences behavior in organizations. In order to fully understand organizational behavior, the role of IM needs to be recognized and better understood. One researcher, who has done research in both the laboratory and field is Dr Micki Kacmar. She provides a 'Behind the Scenes' look at her career, work and ambitions for the field of organizational IM.

We know IM is very common, but how much does it actually influence organizational behavior? Studies of people in organizations and experiments simulating organizational processes have shown IM plays a key role. However, most studies were not designed to answer the question of how *much* of an influence it had. There have been a few studies (see Appendix for a discussion) addressing the issue of relative influence of IM on questionnaire responses that have established IM as a subtle influence; not one that overwhelms other factors (Dwight & Feigelson, 2000; Moorman & Podsakoff, 1992). This may well be the case for other aspects of organizational IM – it influences behavior, but its influence is sometimes subtle, resulting in small to moderate changes or selectivity in behavior, rather than wholly altering or producing novel behaviors. Of course, we also have documented that organizational processes such as job interviews and performance evaluations are situations of hyper-IM, where the impact of managing impressions is usually large.

IM may also serve to enhance a number of organizational behaviors. An interesting study that we believe reflects a likely future direction was done by Carpenter and Golden (1997). A key managerial characteristic

> **Behind the Scenes**
>
> *K. Michele Kacmar*
>
> I returned to school to complete a Ph.D. at Texas A&M University in 1986. Upon arrival at A&M, each new Ph.D. student is assigned a senior Ph.D. student as a mentor. Luckily, I was assigned to Sandy Wayne. She had just finished her comprehensive examinations and was busily working on her dissertation proposal in the area of IM. In order to complete her dissertation research she needed a confederate for her laboratory study. I eagerly volunteered. After over 100 hours in the lab repeating the same IM cues over and over, I was hooked!
>
> Since this first exposure to the area, I have found out that IM can be applied to almost every area of business. For example, my research has shown the importance of IM in interviewing, performance appraisal, job search and recruitment, and supervisor, subordinate, and peer relationships. With respect to interviewing, I have found that individuals who are good IMers usually are able to convince someone they are the best candidate, even when they are less qualified than other less vocal applicants. Also, interviewers do not like saying no to good IMers because they like them.
>
> How should organizations deal with IM? Organizations can train interviewers to be aware of and recognize the tactics that IMers use. Utilizing structured interviews that keep the focus of the interview on job relevant areas, and not allowing the applicant to control the topics of discussion, will help select qualified candidates, and not IMers.

is the power *attributed* to the manager, not simply the official power of a particular management position. How managers act, including their IM, influences how much power they are perceived to have. In this study, managers who believed they had a lot of power and then acted like they had power were seen as more powerful than managers who did not use the power image even though the absolute power of their positions was the same. Looking at the dynamic interactions of IM with issues such as power and other organizational behaviors is a promising area for future researchers.

How Do Organizational Factors Influence IM?

Much of the work in IM has been prompted by researchers' awareness that organizational behavior is highly responsive to the social aspects of situations. Throughout the text we discussed: the influence of behavior being public; individuals feeling accountable; the goals IM might help accomplish; the status or attitudes of the audience; and so on. Despite the many demonstrations of situational influences, we still need a richer understanding of how situations influence IM in order to determine how IM will operate in organizational settings. Some key situational factors in organizations are: aspects of organizational culture and policy; the nature of the employment relationships; and the growing prevalence of electronic over other forms of communication. How do these factors affect IM? Do the nature of these factors increase the likelihood and impact of IM or change the very nature of it? A study by Ashford, Rothbard, Piderit, and Dutton (1998) illustrates the complexity of this type of analysis at the same time it shows the value of looking at organizational factors. This study examined how willing female managers were to promote issues of gender equity. Now you might expect the manager's beliefs would be the main predictor of her willingness to be an advocate, but they were not. It was the supportiveness of the organizational climate, including warm and trusting relationships with decision makers, that led these female managers to be willing to advocate for gender equity. Past research has shown IM is responsive to many interpersonal cues. In the future, we expect an even greater emphasis on issues of organizational culture and personnel practices in the understanding of IM in organizations.

The changing employment relationship

In today's workplace, there are more and more people working part-time, as independent contractors and for multiple employers. This means people are working more often with strangers. We suspect that this may increase the IM challenge for individuals as they attempt to influence the image they have in the minds of a more rapidly changing and ever-greater range of individuals. This challenge will be both an informational and emotional one. Individuals are operating under greater uncertainty and must figure out what they are to do as their organizations change around them or they change organizations. They must be more conscious of how they are being perceived, and be adjusting their IM so they are perceived as they desire to be. The novel situations will require much more conscious processing and information seeking from more sources. If the employment relationship continues to become more tentative, the importance of IM will increase as employees seek to maintain good relationships to avoid terminations or layoffs, and because those relationships could be a resource for future positions. The study of organizational IM will need to address these new employment conditions and the new roles and demands placed on the IMer.

The media of the message

An interesting phenomenon in today's organizations that is affecting how we relate to each other is the increasing use of electronic forms of communication. Even a group of the most casual computer users can easily come up with a few horror stories about how a misdirected and widely disseminated email message has caused acute IM problems for the individuals involved. In March 2001, the CEO of Cerner Corporation wrote a stinging email intended for several hundred company managers. The email berated employees for not working hard enough and threatened layoffs unless things changed. The email message was leaked and posted on the Internet causing the company's stock to drop over 20 percent in just three days (Wong, 2001). Individuals in such messy predicaments probably wish we had written a book just on electronic IM, as they contemplated whether it was possible to restore their image after a nasty email about the boss got accidentally forwarded to him. They may have lamented that defensive IM by email or posted to a website, is limited in the feedback the sender receives about how successful the electronic IM was at removing the tarnish from his identity. Along these lines, research suggests that the negotiating of identities may be very difficult in this 'media poor' electronic environment (Riordan, in press).

Electronic forms of communication do more than create additional need for protective IM. Electronic communication offers the opportunity of immediate communications, to a world-wide audience, at very little expense. Personal and corporate webpages will be the subject of some interesting analyses in the future by IM researchers. The combination of webpages, associated keywords and search engines offer the interesting possibility of IMers choosing the keywords they would like associated with their identities (their webpages) and using those keywords to cause their webpages to appear in the results of searches conducted by individuals all over the world.

The forms of IM that occur in virtual work environments and social chat rooms will be of much future interest. Again, the channels of communication are limited, which poses limitations to effective communication, but also offers liberating opportunities for the IMer. Studies of social chat rooms have revealed a significant number of individuals who present themselves as being of the opposite gender. We suspect this phenomenon won't translate to the world of work, but you never know.

How Do IM Behaviors Work Together?

Another future direction for research will be to establish how IM behaviors work together. Some research has shown influence attempts have different effects when used together than when used alone (Barry & Shapiro, 1992). Recall Baron's (1989) job interview study reviewed in Chapter 7, in which he found male interviewers rated females more negatively if they wore perfume and engaged in a lot of nonverbal IM, than if they used either IM tactic alone. This suggests IM can be overdone by using too many tactics or using them too vigorously. Increasingly, researchers will be using sophisticated designs and statistical methods to study a constellation of variables that will lead to richer understandings of how IM behaviors work together and interact with various personal and situational variables.

Future Directions in IM Application and Practice

In this section we address four emerging issues facing contemporary organizations. First, we look at the issue of improving organizational functioning through IM training programs. Second, we consider IM as one means of addressing the challenges of diversity. Third, we discuss the relatively new area of how organizations IM the 'company image'.

Finally, the importance of business ethics to organizational IM will be explored.

IM Training: Self-Help and Formal Approaches

We have learned IM behaviors are widespread in organizations. For many, the next question will be, is it possible to modify IM so it better suits individual and organizational purposes? Should we have IM training programs? Should there be organizational development interventions for IM?

The answer to each of these questions is likely to be 'yes' and there is a growing advocacy that IM is an important skill that can and needs to be trained. The approaches include both self-help and more formal IM training.

Self-help IM training

The book, *Put Your Best Foot Forward* (Dimitrius & Mazzarella, 2000), is an excellent example of a self-help IM training book in the tradition begun by Dale Carnegie. The book, and others like it, aim to teach IM as a skill with applications both to the corporate world and to social settings. Readers are advised by the authors to read *Put Your Best Foot Forward* with a pencil in hand and to note in separate columns – Dos, Antidotes (which counteract negative effects of the Dos) and Don'ts – those things they can do to strengthen their image. Based on survey data that asked people what qualities they found most desirable in others, the authors argue that trustworthiness, caring, humility, and capability are the 'four qualities at the foundation of every great impression' (p. 15) and are the 'compass qualities' they advise readers to develop. Using the metaphor of a color printer that creates multicolor images with tiny dots of only a few colors, images are said to be constructed through incorporation of seven distinct 'colors': personal appearance; body language; voice; communication style; content of communication; actions; and environment or setting. Through chapters on each of these subjects, prescriptions are given for how to create a positive image. These are supplemented by 'magic pills' in the form of handshakes, eye contact, smiling, posture and enthusiasm that the authors claim can be used in any encounter, and 'toxic traits' like offensive physical acts (e.g., bad hygiene), unappealing word usage, insensitive communications, aggressiveness, and pettiness that will consistently cause 'serious, often irreparable, damage to your impression' (p. 127).

Formal approaches

While interesting and provocative, self-help approaches are often based on the author's own experience or a series of anecdotes or case studies. A more formal approach that is better aligned with previous studies of organizational IM has been offered by Mark Martinko's (1991) practitioner's model of the IM process. This could be a useful guide for a formal training curriculum with modules being developed for each step of the process. It is summarized in Figure 8.1.

More recently, Giacalone, Knouse, and Pearce (1998) have described a three-phased IM training of organizational leaders. In the **first phase**, organizational personnel list particular IM behaviors which are specific to various facets of leadership. For example, participants could identify behaviors which indicate that a leader possesses technical and tactical proficiency. This behavioral list of competence indicators could then be evaluated by the participants to gain consensus on which behaviors are indicative of effective leader IM.

In the **second phase**, the list of leader IM effectiveness indicators is appended with Likert rating scales (e.g. 'I have never seen my immediate supervisor do this' to 'I have frequently seen my immediate supervisor do this'). In the **final phase**, members and leaders are surveyed with the instrument and a general skills measure which assesses parallel skills of interest. A good example is the US Army's Leadership Professionalism Assessment Form (LPAF) which allows soldiers to assess the leadership competence in: technical and tactical proficiency; communications; professional ethics; planning; management technology; decision making; teaching and counseling; supervision; team development; clarifying ambiguity; negotiation; development; assessment; consensus building; and evaluation. A comparative analysis is then done to assess the relationship between the rating of the tactics and the parallel rating of competencies (such as the LPAF ratings). This process can help determine the extent to which particular IM behaviors are predictive of perceived individual competencies.

Figure 8.1 **A Practitioner's Guide to Steps in the IM Process**

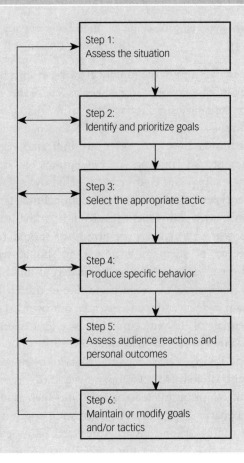

Source: Based on Martinko, 1991

Such process could help to determine what non-performance related behaviors organizational members use to identify leadership competence. Trainers can instruct leaders with the appropriate behavior patterns that augment knowledge and execution of tasks. This would provide an effective way of demonstrating leadership competence by combining competence with IM techniques that verify competence.

IM and Diversity

> The importance of self-presentational concerns may well be culturally relative
> (Baumeister, 1982, p. 22).

The integration of the rapidly growing ethnic, national, gender, and age diversity of the work force is seen as one of the greatest challenges facing many organizations today. We know that people are judged by the groups to which they belong. Race, nationality, gender, and age – probably because they often are indicated visually – are some of the strongest determinants of perceptions of strangers. Even ongoing relationships can be adversely affected by lack of familiarity with, or by stereotypes of, ethnic groups, nationalities, genders, and age groups. People with different backgrounds come to the work place with divergent expectations for how they should be treated, what will be expected of them, and how they should treat others. Differences in diverse backgrounds can be related to differing values relative to the types of images we respect and like in others, our own aspirations for certain images, and, consequently, our own IM behaviors. IM offers the potential of helping individuals and organizations deal with the challenges posed by increasing diversity.

In 1988, Gardner and Martinko noted in their review of organizational IM, 'Comparatively little research has explored the relationships between actor attributes such as race, gender, and age and IM behavior' (p. 334). An interesting study done since that review is one of IM among Asian Americans (Xin, 1997). Grounded in the research that shows that in general Asian Americans in the United States are perceived to be very intelligent and hardworking, Xin raises the question, why are less than one percent of the top level managers in the Fortune 500 companies of Asian descent? IM, specifically the use of self-disclosure, is suggested as one possible reason. Asian cultures, as reflected in the teachings of Confucius, stress maintaining appropriate distance and respect for authority, which would be inconsistent with a high degree of self-disclosure. Since self-disclosure has been related to a number of very positive organizational outcomes, this puts the Asian manager at a disadvantage when it comes to 'moving up the ladder' in companies dominated by American culture. In a study designed to test these ideas, Xin found that Asian Americans used different IM tactics than did the European Americans: they reported significantly less self-disclosure and self-focused tactics than the European Americans studied. Surprisingly, the IM behaviors of the Asian Americans were largely ineffective as shown by the fact that they were not related to how their supervisors felt about them. Such a finding would be consistent with the idea that stereotypes rather than individualized information were determining supervisors' reactions to these Asian American managers.

To more systematically study the relationship between organizational IM and diversity issues, the three authors of this book edited a special issue of the journal the *American Behavioral Scientist*, entitled *IM and Diversity: Issues for Organizational Behavior* (Rosenfeld, Giacalone, & Riordan, 1994). Contributors to the special issue addressed organizational IM as it applied to multi-national (Mendenhall & Wiley, 1994; Giacalone & Beard, 1994), racial/ethnic/cultural (Allison & Herlocker, 1994; Crittenden & Bae, 1994; Rosenfeld, Booth-Kewley, Edwards, & Alderton, 1994) and gender (Kacmar & Carlson, 1994; Wayne, Liden, & Sparrowe, 1994; Riordan, Gross, & Maloney, 1994) issues. As the articles in the special issue demonstrated, there is a good deal of potential for better understanding and for addressing the challenges of diversity through theory, research, and practice in IM.

To illustrate, we explore several issues using the articles that appeared in the special issue, to show how IM topics can address today's diversity challenges.

Training programs that go beyond understanding

> Training aging persons to be aware of the kinds of behaviors that project an 'old' impression and practicing 'acting young' can help them counteract the otherwise natural expectations on the part of others (and themselves) that the aging individual inevitably declines... It is one's youthful or aged image that counts. IM training can help preserve the image
> (Eden, 1991, p. 28).

Understanding cultural and gender differences is the basis for many current diversity training programs: their purpose is to sensitize people to notice and respect others' values, and to understand how subtle aspects of verbal and nonverbal communication can lead to misunderstandings. Sensitivity, respect, and knowledge are very important. However, this approach to training has been faulted for emphasizing differences leading to discomfort and avoidance and for reinforcing passivity (e.g., thinking not doing).

The next phase of diversity training must go beyond merely understanding differences to developing skills to more effectively manage interactions and communications so organization members can work together. Mark Martinko's (1991) model of IM training could be applied to diversity training as well. Special focus would be placed on assessing the situation as individuals with diverse backgrounds do not always share the same perceptions of situations (Riordan, 1993). Careful attention would also have to be paid to the feedback and outcome processes, as described in the cybernetic model (Bozeman & Kacmar, 1997). If feedback and outcomes are monitored closely, certain relationships that can help the IMer succeed in diverse workplaces may become apparent.

Cross-cultural training

Take a basic dilemma faced by all employees regardless of their locale – how to get credit for their successes while avoid being blamed for failures. Giacalone and Beard (1994) have proposed models that outline where and how culturally-based attributions can lead to functional and dysfunctional outcomes. Together, the models strongly recommend new cross-cultural training programs in both culturally bound attributions and IM strategies.

IM skill-building also offers a promising framework for improving cross-cultural training. It has been suggested that individuals who are perceptive and willing to actively IM will be the ones who will be most successful managing identities that help them to be effective working in a foreign culture (Mendenhall & Wiley, 1994). IM training could teach specific techniques, how those operate within a particular culture, and how to read feedback from those who hold key organizational positions.

IM training is likely to provide the additional benefit of helping people to feel more confident and in control of their interactions. This would make them more willing to engage in the necessary trial-and-error learning of cross-cultural IM so they more quickly become effective (Mendenhall & Wiley, 1994). A possible future avenue for IM training is teaching trainees how to redefine situations so they can be more effective. This could be done in the area of diversity training as well. Allison and Herlocker (1994) suggest two ways: (1) develop superordinate goals that everyone is working toward, and (2) have an outside group everyone is working against. IM can play a key role in these actions. For example, Rob, a new manager viewed sceptically by employees, could emphasize in interactions with his department, their long-range departmental goals and his commitment to them, and try to elicit similar claims from them. He could also carefully manage the identity of being a hostile, aggressive manager toward another department who his department is competing with. In this way he can become a member of the **in-group**, and facilitate the types of departmental relationships that will help him be effective.

As mentioned in Chapter 2, the IM tactic of ingratiation may be especially crucial to members of racial/ethnic minority groups, women, immigrants, and expatriates who often need to please majority group members in positions of greater social power. Box 8.1 explores this emerging diversity–ingratiation relationship.

An important consideration in any training program is that there are instances of the same IM behavior having different effects depending on the demographic characteristics of the perceiver and/or performer. This serves to caution us that recommendations about IM may depend on the cultural background of the IMer and the audience. Dr Michael Bond is someone who has had a good deal of personal and professional experience with IM and cultural diversity. He shares some of these experiences in a 'Behind the Scenes' Profile.

Leader–member exchanges, gender, and cultural issues

Wayne, Liden, and Sparrowe (1994) outlined how gender may be related to the development of leader–member exchanges, (e.g., the relationship between an employee and his or her boss). High quality leader–member exchanges have been shown to be related to important organizational outcomes like personal influence, access to information and opportunities for professional development. For someone wanting to have a successful career in an organization, the quality of leader–member exchanges he or she establishes could be critical. For females to counteract some of the potential negative effects of gender on the quality of a relationship with a male supervisor, they may need to be

| Box 8.1 | **Stereotypes, Ingratiation, and Diversity** |

Interpersonal understanding is often negatively affected by stereotypes of race, ethnicity, nationality, or gender. Stereotypes can lead to false assumptions about individuals, especially since the nature of most stereotypes is negative – more negative at least than the characteristics attributed to one's own group. We explain our own behaviors and those of our **in-group** more favorably than we do the actions of **out-group** members (Allison & Herlocker, 1994).

Cognitive social psychologists have found that stereotyping is an often inevitable by-product of the universal human tendencies to categorize, simplify, and group social stimuli. Stereotyping typically involves using a primary category like race or gender. This occurs quickly and can have a restricting influence on the range of characteristics attributed to individuals: they are believed to have the stereotypical characteristics and not other characteristics, that would be inconsistent with the stereotype.

We believe that as organizations grow increasingly diverse and multi-national, the IM tactic of ingratiation may be crucial to members of racial/ethnic minority groups, women, immigrants, and expatriates who may need to please majority group members in positions of greater social power. As we suggested in Chapter 2, by generating liking and feelings of good will, ingratiation may counteract cognitive tendencies to stigmatize, stereotype, and devalue people who are different. Ingratiation may provide a possible 'antidote' to the constricting nature of stereotyping and **out-group stigmatization**.

Because of their lower social power in many organizations, we believe that members of diverse groups may be more likely to use ingratiation – the IM tactic of choice of the powerless. In doing so, minority group members and women may face a dual-edged sword. On the one hand, relatively lower social power of women and minorities in organizational settings results in their frequent use of ingratiation. It is precisely this lack of social power, however, that may hinder the effectiveness of these influence attempts – a case of the ingratiator's dilemma meeting the diverse work force!

Behind the Scenes

Michael Harris Bond

An actor creates an illusion in order to discover reality
(Sir Alec Guiness).

I accept the premise that, 'One cannot not communicate.' If this premise about our lives together is true, then three possible consequences would seem to follow: one may remain unaware of this fact of life, one may choose to ignore it and live life 'naturally', or one may take charge of the power that is ours to communicate – what we wish about ourselves to others.

But what shall we communicate? In organizations it seems that we would be well advised to communicate what is necessary for us to survive, indeed prosper. Given that we are mutually interdependent for our security, those communications must signal some commitment to our colleagues and to the organization itself. As the twentieth century has given way to the twenty-first, these commitments will be towards people and institutions that are more ethnically, linguistically, and culturally diverse than has been the case before.

Many people would like to communicate an open, welcoming stance towards this diversity. Their reasons may be personal, social or political, but they must all answer the question, 'How?' How does one manifest competence, concern, enthusiasm, integrity, steadiness and happiness to people of different backgrounds? How does one escape the prison of the stereotypes into which they will cast us? How can we maintain the harmony of the organization while still honoring the various backgrounds of those people who enliven it?

These are new and testing questions in a post-colonial world. I am a Baha'i committed to the process of forging a unity across cultural lines in practical ways. The world of work is the testing ground for this enterprise, as it is here that people are most likely to cross cultural lines. My experience in consulting for Hong Kong organizations suggests that we need new knowledge, new skills, and new resolve to produce synergy out of this diversity.

All this newness makes us self-conscious. Many people feel they must deliberately stage-manage their behavior across ethnic lines to enhance organizational life. And indeed we must, at least until we ▶

become as unself-consciously fluent in our behavior across ethnic lines as we are with people similar to us. The learning sequence is: unconscious incompetence. After all, our own culture is simply a system of habits and skills we have acquired over our lifespan; we need the same process of plodding acquisition to become bi-cultural, tri-cultural, multi-cultural. So, we become as children again in order to live more effectively as adults.

Personally, I have had to undergo this same struggle. Hong Kong Chinese culture is very different from my Canadian culture of origin. It socializes its members to different values, beliefs, interpersonal styles and ideal personalities. Compromising, turning a blind eye, giving the benefit of the doubt, discovering sources of delight, communicating mindfully and, yes, carefully managing impressions have all been required of me to survive and prosper in this organization people call the Chinese University of Hong Kong. What I have learned, I teach to others. In the process I have come to respect my Canadian heritage and appreciate the Hong Kong Chinese people.

Cultivate the way yourself and your virtue will be genuine
Cultivate it in the realm and the realm will flourish
(Lao Tzu, Tao Te Ching).

more active IMers, skillfully using acquisitive IM tactics as many of their male co-workers do. We suspect many of the recommendations for females might well apply to any individual working in a situation in which the organizational power structure is composed primarily of individuals of different backgrounds.

On a related note, Kacmar and Carlson (1994) theorize that in the job interview process men and women tend to use self- and other-promotional tactics at different rates. Self-promotional tactics focus on the applicant's own qualities and credentials whereas other-promotional tactics include things like complimenting the company and asking questions about the interviewer. They contend that women may benefit in the job search process from the use of subtle other-focused tactics, and additional training in the use of self-focused tactics.

These studies point to how difficult male–female interactions among individuals raised in the same country can be. Imagine how confused things can get when the diversity in assumptions, perceptions, IM styles, and life experiences is even greater! Take the situation of an individual working for a company owned and operated in another country with a very different culture. Studies of different cultures have shown substantial differences among them in people's reactions to IM strategies and their preferences for certain identities. In a series of studies, Crittenden and Bae (1994) had individuals in four Asian cultures evaluate scenarios describing how a fictitious person explained his or her successes and failures. Not surprisingly, the cultures differed markedly in their evaluations of an individual who took a great deal of credit for his success and blamed his failures on external factors. They found that individuals in some collectivist cultures do not automatically devalue individuals who take credit for their successes. Across the Asian cultures they studied, individuals who gave self-enhancing explanations were seen as smarter and as having higher achievement; those making more modest attributions were seen as having a greater sense of social responsibility but as being less productive. Thus, it seems that acquisitive IM is needed even in collectivist cultures. However, self-enhancing IM tactics are risky. This would be especially true if the culture is not well understood by the prospective IMer.

How Do Organizations Manage Their Images?

This book has focused largely on how individuals manage impressions of themselves. But IM can also involve managing the impressions of organizations. An area ripe for future work is understanding how individuals and groups manage images of organizations (Ginzel, Kramer, & Sutton, 1993).

One example of the new direction involves the IM strategies of two international radical social groups studied by Elsbach and Sutton (1992). Earth First! is associated with using confrontational tactics as means of protecting wilderness areas and the wildlife that lives there. Driving spikes into trees in an old growth forest is one of the approaches attributed to them. The other group studied, ACT UP (AIDS Coalition to Unleash Power), targets governmental agencies and businesses that it feels obstruct or slow medical treatment for individuals with AIDS. ACT UP is associated with confrontational tactics like having members lie under the wheels of targeted drug company trucks to prevent them from moving freely. By employing an IM perspective, Elsbach and

Sutton were able to find similarities in how these two organizations maintained a positive public image.

Following an incident like those described above, the organizations would respond in very rational terms and in a manner consistent with how mainstream organizations are expected to respond to such charges. In this way, the organization was perceived as being more credible because it responded as more reputable organizations would be expected to respond. They would also claim individuals who committed the acts were merely fringe elements acting on their own, without any direction from the organization. By these claims, the organizations also distanced themselves from the perpetrators.

After credibility was established, and the perpetrators disassociated, the organizations impression managed by using protective followed by acquisitive IM tactics. The organizations justified the actions by citing the greater wrongs being committed by the targeted groups (i.e., destroying the forests and slowing the treatment of individuals with AIDS). Entitlements and enhancements were then used, focusing on the potential positive consequences of the actions and how their organizations had been responsible for 'what little' progress that had been made on these issues.

Can these same IM techniques be seen in more mainstream organizations? Elsbach and Sutton (1992) have speculated that mainstream organizations adopt a strategy similar to that of radical social groups. In the early 1990s the book *Satanic Verses* was pulled from the shelves of Walden Book Stores in United States. Its author, Salman Rushdie, was the target of death threats for supposedly insulting the Muslim religion, and bookstores were afraid of being targets of terrorist violence themselves. Because some perceived this as unwarranted censorship, Walden Books' action was called into question. In responding to criticism, Walden Books denied they had stopped selling the books, claimed that the book was just temporarily sold out, that they had removed the books because of concerns for employee safety, and that employees deserved a lot of credit for working despite bomb threats. This sequence is a good example of how organizations often offer a series of accounts, not all of which are consistent with each other, to manage their corporate image.

Gail Russ (1991) has looked at the ways organizations and organizational members manage the image of the company through company annual reports, letters to stockholders, press releases, and similar written archival materials. Using these materials, Russ analyzed how companies manage stakeholders' impressions of the company and key figures within it. She points out, for instance, that organizational leaders do not just give the financial figures that are required by law, but spend a great deal of effort and resources to present a positive picture of the company. Expensive brochures with glossy paper and attractive graphics are common. Events affecting the company are interpreted in ways that will lead the organization to be perceived in positive ways, such as attributing failure to external causes. Self-promotion and enhancement are common (e.g., 'everyone is a hero in our company' quoted in Russ, 1991, p. 234).

Linda Ginzel and her colleagues have looked at how top leadership manages the identity of the company at times when its image is threatened (Ginzel, et al., 1993). They too argue the process is much like the protective IM process used by individuals (see Chapters 4 and 5). In situations where a company's image is threatened, the leadership engages in a damage-control process, relying heavily on accounts (e.g., excuses, justification, apologies, denials) much as individuals do. Their analysis emphasizes the iterative nature of accounts by organizations in crisis. Often company leadership will test and then offer a sequence of accounts – sometimes quite different in form and content – until it finds an account or set of accounts important audiences will accept as satisfactory explanations for events.

> The cycle of interlocked behavior continues until organizational actors and their audiences have reduced, or eliminated, perceived equivocality regarding the event. As audience members become satisfied, the salience of the predicament decreases... In such cases, top management and their organizational audiences have achieved a 'settlement' regarding the final interpretation to be placed on the event
>
> *(Ginzel, et al., 1993, p. 246–7).*

As our understanding of how the impressions of organizations are managed increases, it will be interesting to contrast the management of individual identities with the management of organizational identities. Organizations may have a more difficult time IMing because they are likely to have more audiences and those audiences may have very different interests (e.g., competitors versus stockholders) that may also be very political (Pfeffer, 1981). It is not uncommon for additional predicaments to arise for companies as they attempt to satisfy different audiences. Because companies are abstract entities (not people with feelings, families, etc.) audiences may feel freer to doubt and harshly criticize companies in public. This may require organizations to be more active IMers.

It also may be why many large organizations have individuals on staff who are trained in IM and have responsibility for maintaining the company's image. While helpful most of the time, having professional public relations staff may lead management to ignore implications of their own actions for public relations because they think someone else will handle that (Ginzel, et al., 1993).

Ethics and Organizational IM

We began this book with a discussion of the expansive view of IM and an insistence that we move beyond the view of IM as a self-centered and manipulative form of interpersonal behavior. Appropriately, we return in this last act to a discussion of the potentially ethical or unethical use of IM in business settings. Although IM is an integral part of daily life in organizations, engaged in for one reason or another by all organizational members, and carried out for the widest range of motives, it can also be used for unethical purposes. As organizations manage their impressions to cover up unethical deeds or deceive the public, our sensitivity to this fact is heightened.

Anecdotal and popular press evidence confirms that the process of IM and business ethics are interrelated. But as Knouse and Giacalone (1992) have noted, there are few scientific studies of the role that IM may play in business ethics. Although a few articles discussing the issues of IM and ethics by individuals at work can be found in the literature (Giacalone & Payne, 1995; Payne & Giacalone, 1990), the role that IM plays in business ethics has not been empirically studied. However, with the growing concern that business has developed for ethical behavior, the role that IM may play in creating or thwarting the maintenance of an ethical work environment would appear to be of growing and future interest.

The literature that does exist would lead us to conclude that future investigations of the roles IM might play in business ethics could be focused in two different directions. On one hand, the focus could be on ethically evaluating the use of IM at work, and focusing on its appropriateness, fairness, and moral repercussions. Conversely, the focus might also be on the use of IM tactics following ethical infractions and corporate wrongdoing.

Making wrong look right (or not too bad)

What happens when an individual worker, or an organization as a whole, is accused or found guilty of behaviors that are unethical or dangerous? The IM literature says the individuals or the company representatives would attempt to make themselves appear more favorable by using protective tactics such as excuses and justifications. The ability to create a less negative impression of an unethical act may allow an employee to moderate the perception of that act, and thereby impact the degree of punishment that management doles out. In such cases, the employee's use of IM is an attempt to provide some disciplinary relief which will lessen long-term financial or political repercussions (Payne & Giacalone, 1990).

Some work has looked at how organizations use IM to get others (in and out of the organization) to redefine unethical behavior to make it appear more positive. Giacalone and Payne (1995) reported that IM behaviors, in the service of lessening the appearance of unethical behavior, can be found in simple press reports. They provided a series of actual examples in which organizations used denials, disassociation, scapegoating, accounts, and apologies as means of recasting their questionable behaviors. In his book on corporate doublespeak, Lutz (1989) provides a good example of such an IM attempt by National Airlines. Because one of the company's airplanes crashed while attempting to land in Pensacola, Florida in 1978, National received an after-tax insurance benefit of $1.7 million. While National had to account for this money in its annual report, it did not want to do so by discussing a topic as uncomfortable as an airline crash. Instead, the report contained a footnote that attributed the income to 'the involuntary conversion of a 727' (p. 4). What the company was trying to do was manage the impression of being profitable without appearing to be a dangerous airline.

Given the growing pressure from the public for greater organizational accountability, and the intertwined ethical concerns of the companies themselves, the role that IM plays in the ethical conduct and identity management of organizations will likely expand even further.

A Concluding Note

Because the field of organizational IM is still relatively new, we suspect that this book has raised as many questions as it has answered regarding how people build and enhance their reputations at work. That is as it should be. The chapters in this book characterize the basic nature of IM and how it operates in organizations. They illustrate how IM is measured and review much of the research to date on organizational IM. Our projections throughout the text on how IM can be used by individuals working in organizations and by organizations themselves are the areas where we and other experts in the field have the most questions. We suspect those may be where your questions lay too. We hope they will be addressed in future research, theory, and practice.

When the three authors of this book first met as graduate students in Jim Tedeschi's lab in Albany, New York over 20 years ago, the concept of organizational IM existed only as a very rough plot line (with a strong fantasy component!). Even though we were studying IM in the highly controlled social psychology laboratory, few had thought to apply IM to organizations. If someone had told us then we would write entire books on this topic we (and our professors) would have laughed in disbelief. Now that we have finished the present volume, we hope you have found our effort to be plausible and that the basic message of our work comes through clearly: IM is a pervasive process – integral to the functioning and success of today's organizations and their members.

Appendix: IM Research Methodologies

Although many people assume that IM can be studied through casual observation or by using common sense, researchers depend on more systematic techniques called **research methodologies**. These research methodologies are the formalized conditions a researcher establishes under which he or she observes or measures behavior. Methodologies employed by IM researchers reflect the journey of the field through the behavioral and organizational sciences. By looking at studies grouped by methodological approaches, we can capture a sense of the breadth of the field and how the research on IM has progressed and evolved.

Observational Studies

Goffman and other symbolic interactionists studied IM through the use of **observational studies**. This methodology involves the researcher observing many and varied interactions, looking for patterns, and then summarizing the patterns in a narrative. Goffman and others working at about the same time used observational studies to learn about IM processes in career progress (Becker & Strauss, 1956), being labeled as 'crazy' (Rosenhan, 1973), acting 'sick' (Braginsky, Braginsky, & Ring, 1969), interactions between practitioner and client (Kuhn, 1964), street life (Whyte, 1943), families (Goffman, 1964) and even in the career of funeral director (Habenstein, 1962).

Weaknesses of observational studies are that they tend to be less objective and conclusions drawn using this approach are not as open to verification and replication by others. Observational researchers carrying out observational studies do attempt to be as structured and scientific in their collection and analysis of data as possible within the limitations of this method. A study by Gardner and Martinko (1988), for example, had observers record school administrators' verbal statements which researchers then related to the characteristics of the audience hearing the statements. One conclusion the researchers reached was that administrators engaged in more IM when they were addressing their supervisors than when they were addressing other types of audiences.

Experiments

When psychologists began studying IM, they used a methodology popular in psychology – the **laboratory experiment**. With this method, the researcher sets up a highly controlled situation in a laboratory in which an **independent variable** is manipulated and another variable – the **dependent variable** – is observed and measured. Usually there are at least two conditions: an **experimental condition** that includes the independent variable, and a **control condition** that does not. If the dependent variable changes when the independent variable is present, it is assumed to be the result of the independent variable.

Sandy Wayne and Gerald Ferris (1990) provide a good example of a laboratory experiment that has organizational relevance. In their study, undergraduate students played the role of a 'supervisor' who interacted with a 'subordinate' (who was actually a confederate of the experimenter) as they carried out an assigned task: processing mail orders for a catalogue marketing firm. As they worked, the confederate engaged in different types of IM (e.g., giving compliments; doing favors for the supervisor) or no IM (a control condition). Thus, the type of IM was an independent variable. At the end of the work session, the researcher gave the student playing the role of supervisor information that indicated the subordinate had high, average, or low performance on the mail order processing task. This was the second independent variable.

Student supervisors were then asked to evaluate the subordinate. The findings of this study indicated that IM worked: subordinates who used it were seen as more productive than those who did not, even though all supervisors had been told the subordinates' performance had been the same.

Three of the most common independent variable manipulations used in IM experiments are: changing the audience characteristics, having a behavior occur publicly or privately, and having participants use a simulated lie detector called the bogus pipeline. We will describe these for you now.

Changing the audience characteristics

As we discussed in Chapter 2, Edward E. Jones was one of the most influential of all IM theorists. Many of Jones' laboratory studies manipulated audience characteristics to determine their impact on IM behaviors. He, his students, and colleagues, demonstrated under a variety of conditions that people would change their behavior based on what they had been told about an audience and/or the target of their IM (Jones, 1964). For example, when research participants role-playing a job interview thought the interviewer liked domineering people, they acted in more domineering ways than participants who had been told the interviewer liked passive people, or those not told anything about the interviewer's preferences (cited in Jones, 1964).

Public–private manipulations

Public conditions are those in which individuals feel they are identifiable and that someone may be watching their behavior. Private conditions are those in which people feel more anonymous – they do not feel they can be identified or associated with their actions. Use of this experimental paradigm is based on the assumption that if an experimental setting differs in no other way, and research participants under public conditions engage in a behavior and those under private conditions do not, the behavior is assumed to be a form of IM since it occurs only when there is an audience. If a behavior occurs whether or not an audience is present, it is assumed likely to result from something more than just IM – being the result of the person's personality or deeply-held core convictions for example. It could, of course, also be automatic IM that is occurring without conscious awareness.

Take an experiment by Forsyth, Riess, and Schlenker (1977) in which research participants spent 20 minutes doing a really boring task (no, it wasn't reading this Appendix!). They were then asked to evaluate the task on a questionnaire that they either signed (public) or did not sign (private). As you might expect, their ratings were more positive in the public conditions when they knew they could be identified and therefore were concerned about the impression they were making. While this effect was obtained with college students, you can imagine how much putting names on company surveys – especially those dealing with sensitive information – could influence employees' responses. This has led some to recommend guaranteeing anonymity and confidentiality as standard policy on organizational surveys – especially those that contain sensitive topics (Rosenfeld, Booth-Kewley, & Edwards, 1993; Edwards, Thomas, Rosenfeld, & Booth-Kewley, 1997).

The bogus pipeline

The bogus pipeline (BPL) is an elaborate piece of electronic equipment represented to research participants as being a powerful lie detector. The BPL has been used as a means of measuring the influence of IM on various behaviors (Jones & Sigall, 1971; Roese & Jamieson, 1993). The reasoning is that people will be more truthful and less likely to engage in deceptive IM when they believe their 'real' feelings can be detected by a machine. For example, in an experiment conducted at the time when the BPL was very popular, one student in a pair of students role-playing workers, received much more pay than the other student, even though their work output had been the same (Rivera, 1976). When students who had been 'overpaid' were asked on a questionnaire how satisfied they were with the money they received, they did not say they were pleased with the extra money. However, when other overpaid students were hooked up to the BPL, rather than given a questionnaire, they 'admitted' they were pleased when asked the same question. Presumably, students were afraid they would appear greedy if they acknowledged they were pleased to receive a large payment at the other student's expense, so they managed a more positive identity in their response to the questionnaire. However students hooked up to the BPL feared their real feelings would be detected by the machine anyway, so they admitted their pleasure at receiving the extra money.

While the BPL produced many interesting findings in social psychological studies, it is not likely to be used in organizational research. The BPL was used in these social psychology experiments in ways analogous to how some companies have used lie detectors with their employees. However, claims for the polygraph's ability to weed out liars from truth tellers have been overstated and its use in many organizations has been severely limited (see Bashore & Rapp, 1993; Steinbrook, 1992; Saxe, 1991). Thus, even if the BPL really did live up to its lie-detecting potential, it would likely meet with stiff resistance both as a research and practical tool in organizational settings.

Field Studies

A common research strategy used to study organizational IM is the **field study**. In a field study, relationships among naturally occurring organizational characteristics, personal variables, and various behaviors are explored. For example, Wayne and Ferris (1990) gave employees at two banks a questionnaire asking them the extent to which they had engaged in a given behavior over the previous three months. They also asked employees' supervisors to rate them. They found employees who used supervisor-focused IM were rated more positively by their supervisors than employees who used IM that was either self-focused or job-focused.

A comparison of this field study with the experimental study by Wayne and Ferris discussed earlier shows the relative advantages of each approach. The experiment used undergraduate students acting as employees, whereas the field study used actual employees in the work setting. Thus, findings of field studies may be more generalizable to people working in organizations. However, there are two common features of field studies that limit conclusions drawn from them. First, the researcher rarely if ever will be able to say that groups of employees being compared have been randomly assigned to these groups. Without random assignment, it may be that the groups differ even before the study begins and so the differences observed could be due to those initial differences rather than the variables being studied. Secondly, the researcher in a field study has less control over the introduction of the independent variable and the measurement of the dependent variable than in an experiment. Again, taking the Wayne and Ferris field study, two questionnaires were filled out and their results correlated. The researcher only knows these variables are related, not necessarily that the variable of interest (i.e., IM strategies) actually causes the other (i.e., supervisor evaluations). Despite these shortcomings, field methodologies are very valuable to the organizational researcher because they deal with work-related and organization-related variables that are often difficult to simulate or otherwise study in the laboratory.

Field studies also can answer another set of important questions: does IM actually occur in real life or is it a figment of our experimentation? Does the IM used in everyday life look anything like the IM psychologists have studied so closely in the laboratory? There have been many laboratory experiments of simulated job interviews that have found the use and powerful effects of IM. However, it was not until relatively recently that the IM of real job candidates going through actual interviews and evaluations was studied. Stevens and Kristoff (1995) looked at college students being interviewed at their campus career offices for professional positions. Data were collected by questionnaires given to student interviewees and the company personnel who interviewed them, and through tape recordings of the actual interviews. As you might imagine, IM researchers were very reassured to learn that real interviewees were using IM in forms that had been studied so extensively in the laboratory. Yet, in the field setting interviewees used far more self-promotion than ingratiation in their IM; a result that had not been observed in laboratory studies and so serves as a reminder of why field studies can be so valuable. Field studies are often of great interest because they involve people in real settings and therefore help us see how we might apply the findings to understanding our everyday lives.

Longitudinal Studies

Longitudinal studies are ones in which the same people are tracked across time. These studies have the advantage of seeing changes in a single individual's IM across time and in various situations. A longitudinal study is valuable because of its focus on individuals and changes across time. However, because it is time-consuming and expensive, it is an underutilized research methodology. There has been at least one longitudinal study of organizational IM that can serve as an illustration of its value. This study showed that a supervisor's liking and perceived similarity to employees at one time predicted performance ratings by the supervisor at a later time (Wayne & Liden, 1995). The authors argued that IM behaviors that produced liking and perceived similarity were active ingredients in producing positive outcomes for the IMer. It would have been difficult and not very meaningful to measure all of these variables at one time in a real work setting. However, taking the measurements at two different times could be done as part of other ongoing activities, not appear so contrived, and show how even though separated in time, IM and performance appraisals are related.

Scenario Studies

A problem that occurs when studying IM is that it can be impractical or unethical to manipulate or find naturally occurring instances of certain variables (e.g., fraud, sabotage, aggression). To get around this, IM researchers sometimes choose to conduct **scenario studies**. One kind of scenario study has research participants read about people using IM in an imaginary situation and then give their reactions. In one study discussed previously, research participants read scenarios of a fictitious US senator who had accepted a bribe or solicited the services of a prostitute (Riordan, Marlin, & Kellogg, 1983). The scenario included the senator's explanation for his actions: either an excuse or a justification (see Chapter 4). To find out how people evaluate actions in light of excuses and justifications, research participants answered questions about what they thought about the senator and his action. One interesting finding of this study was that senators who excused their actions by claiming some temporary debilitating condition (e.g., drunkenness) were seen in a more positive light than senators who tried to minimize the gravity of their action (e.g., claiming the action was carried out for reputable reasons and was not really what it seemed). Many scenario studies have a similar focus – how do audiences react to IM tactics? The key disadvantage of this approach is that the researcher cannot be sure that people react to scenarios the same way they would if they were really observing the situation. Yet, these studies are relatively easy to perform and are often interesting for the participants involved.

Individual Difference Measures

As we saw in Chapter 6, people differ in the degree to which they use IM, the type of IM behaviors they engage in, and how good they are at it. Another way to study IM is by focusing on these differences in IM styles. In a typical study, participants take a test that measures how much or how little of an IM-related trait such as self-monitoring (Snyder, 1974), need for approval (Crowne & Marlowe, 1964), or fear of negative evaluation (Watson & Friend, 1969) they have. They are then placed in an experimental setting that should affect people who are either high or low in that trait more than others, or their scores on the test measuring the trait are correlated with their behavior. In one study, research participants worked on a boring task with a group leader who clearly appreciated hard work or did not (Watson & Friend, 1969). Participants with a high fear of negative evaluation worked harder than other participants. Another example is a study that showed bank employees who scored high on tests measuring their tendencies to engage in IM and to deceive others were more effective in influencing their supervisors than other types of employees (Deluga, 1991).

Response Bias

Some studies have been generated by researchers concerned that responses to organizational questionnaires are contaminated by too much IM. If people manage their impressions by answering questionnaires so that they 'look good', how can researchers know if their questionnaire results reflect anything about the topic they want to be studying? This is especially a problem if people are asked sensitive questions about things such as drug and alcohol use, organizational theft, and sexual harassment (Hosseini & Armacost, 1993).

To address this issue Moorman and Podsakoff (1992) used a powerful statistical technique called **meta-analysis** in which the findings from many related studies are analyzed simultaneously so that general conclusions can be drawn about the topic of interest. The two researchers looked at the results of 33 studies and found that managing a socially desirable identity was a significant factor on many questionnaires, meaning that respondents were trying to manage a positive impression with their questionnaire responses by distorting them somewhat. However, the authors were able to show that the questionnaires were also measuring real differences among people in job satisfaction, personal control, role conflict, and role ambiguity, and not just people's attempts to look good. Similar conclusions regarding the potential biasing effects of IM have been drawn in recent studies using other methodologies. Barrick and Mount (1996), for example, found evidence of IM in the relationships between personality measures and job performance. However, when they used statistical techniques to remove the influence of IM, they still saw a relationship between personality and job performance. Thus, IM was an ingredient, but it didn't make the whole performance pie.

Another methodology being used more extensively to look at response bias or the degree to which IM is influencing responses is based on the finding that truthful responses come more quickly than false responses (Tetrick, 1989). In scientific terms, this means that the **response latency** of truthful responses is shorter in duration than falsified responses. Some researchers have extended this reasoning to suggest that when respondents engage in deceptive IM they will take longer to respond than when being accurate (Vasilopoulus, Reilly, & Leaman, 2000).

A Contemporary Approach: Studying IM in its Own Right

Today, IM is studied in its own right, not just as an after-the-fact reinterpretation of experimental or questionnaire responses such as was popular among social psychologists during the 1970s (Rosenfeld & Giacalone, 1991). A great variety in methodologies and findings have emerged: people's motivation to engage in IM is heightened by including incentives for the management of particular impressions or by leading respondents to anticipate or create a negative identity for themselves (Ashford & Northcraft, 1992; Daubman & Heatherington, 1992). Other studies look at what identities subjects try to construct as a function of their personalities and values, the identities they desire, or role constraints inherent in the situation (Kumar & Beyerlein, 1991; Leary, 1992). Research also shows how organizations are managing identities in ways not unlike those used by individuals (Crane, 2000; Conlon & Murray, 1996; Elsbach, Sutton, & Principe, 1998) Studies are now considering the consequences of IM for audiences as well as the IMer (Abdolmohammadi & Shanteau, 1992; Jones, Brenner, & Knight, 1990).

Given the recent increase in citations in the psychological, organizational, and sociological literatures, it is clear that research specifically designed to investigate IM is growing dramatically. Years ago, when it was difficult to publish articles about IM in the professional literature, the present authors used to joke that we wished there was a 'Journal of IM' that would accept our work. Now, as the field continues to so rapidly expand, this pipedream of the late 1970s may become a reality in the twenty-first century.

References

Abdolmohammadi, M. J., & Shanteau, J. (1992). Personal attributes of expert auditors. *Organizational Behavior and Human Decision Processes, 53,* 158–172.

Abdullah, H. S. (1997). Impression management concept. *New Straits Times* (Malaysia), September 17, p. 14.

Abrams, G. (1991). All smiles: The Dale Carnegie brand of optimism is still winning friends and influencing people. *Los Angeles Times,* June 14, pp. E1, E16–E17.

Albas, D., & Albas, C. (1988). Aces and bombers: The post-exam impression management strategies of students. *Symbolic Interaction, 11,* 289–302.

Allen, R. W., Madison, D. L., Porter, L. W., Renwick, P. A., & Mayes, B. T. (1979). Organization politics: Tactics and characteristics of the actors. *California Management Review, 22,* 77–83.

Allison, S. T., & Herlocker, C. E. (1994). Constructing impressions in demographically diverse organizational settings: A group categorization analysis. *American Behavioral Scientist, 37,* 637–52.

Anderson, L. R., & Thacker, J. (1985). Self monitoring and sex as related to assessment center ratings and job performance. *Basic and Applied Social Psychology, 6,* 345–61.

Anderson, L. R., & Tolson, J. (1989). Group members' self-monitoring as a possible neutralizer of leadership. *Small Group Behavior, 20,* 24–36.

Anderson, N. R. (1991). Decision making in the graduate selection interview: An experimental investigation. *Human Relations, 44,* 403–17.

Anti-Scud Duds (1993). *Newsweek,* November 29, p. 7.

Argyle, M. (1988). *Bodily Communication.* London: Methuen & Co. Ltd.

Arkin, R. (1981). Self-presentation styles. In J. T. Tedeschi (Ed.). *Impression Management and Social Psychological Research* (pp. 311–33). New York: Academic Press.

Arkin, R. M., & Shepperd, J. A. (1989). Self-presentation styles in organizations. In R. A. Giacalone & P. Rosenfeld (Eds), *Impression Management in the Organization* (pp. 125–39). Hillsdale, NJ: Lawrence Erlbaum Associates.

Arkin, R. M., & Shepperd, J. A. (1990). Strategic self-presentation: An overview. In M. J. Cody & M. L. McLaughlin (Eds), *The Psychology of Tactical Communication* (pp. 175–93). Clevedon, UK: Multilingual Matters Ltd.

Arvey, R. D., & Renz, G. L. (1992). Fairness in the selection of employees. *Journal of Business Ethics, 11*, 331–40.

Aryee, S., Wyatt, T., & Stone, R. (1996). Early career outcomes of graduate employees: The effect of mentoring and ingratiation. *Journal of Management Studies, 33*, 95–118.

Ashford, S. J., & Northcraft, G. B. (1992). Conveying more (or less) than we realize: The role of impression management in feedback-seeking. *Organizational Behavior and Human Decision Processes, 53*, 310–34.

Ashford, S. J., Rothbard, N. P., Piderit, S. K., & Dutton, J. E. (1998). Out on a limb: The role of context and impression management in selling gender-equity issues. *Administrative Science Quarterly, 43*, 23–57.

Ashforth, B. E., & Lee, R. T. (1990). Defensive behavior in organizations: A preliminary model. *Human Relations, 43*, 621–48.

Austin, W., & Utne, M. K. (1977). Sentencing: Discretion and justice in judicial decision-making. In B. D. Sales (Ed.), *Psychology in the Legal Process* (pp. 163–94). New York: Spectrum.

Ave, C. (1994). It's time to tell your best-worst boss tale. *San Diego Union Tribune*, June 5, p. D–12.

Baker, H. G., & Spier, M. S. (1990). The employment interview: Guaranteed improvement in reliability. *Public Personnel Management, 19*, 85–90.

Barker, K. A. (1992). Changing assumptions and contingent solutions. The cost and benefits of women working full- and part-time. *Sex Roles, 28*, 47–71.

Baron, R. A. (1986). Self-presentation in job interviews: When there can be 'too much of a good thing.' *Journal of Applied Psychology, 16*, 16–28.

Baron, R. A. (1989). Impression management by applicants during employment interviews: The 'too much of a good thing' effect. In R. W. Eder & G. R. Ferris (Eds), *The Employment Interview: Theory, Research, Practice* (pp. 204–15). Newbury Park, CA: Sage Publications.

Baron, R. A. (1990). Countering the effects of destructive criticism: The relative efficacy of four interventions. *Journal of Applied Psychology, 75*, 235–45.

Barrick, M. R., & Mount, M. K. (1996). Effect of impression management and self-deception on the predictive validity of personality constructs. *Journal of Applied Psychology, 81*, 261–2.

Barry, B., & Shapiro, D. L. (1992). Influence tactics in combination: The interactive effects of soft versus hard tactics and rational exchange. *Journal of Applied Social Psychology, 22*, 1429–41.

Bashore, T. R., & Rapp, P. E. (1993). Are there alternatives to traditional polygraph procedures? *Psychological Bulletin, 113*, 3–22.

Baumeister, R. F. (1982). A self-presentational view of social phenomena. *Psychological Bulletin, 91,* 3–26.

Baumeister, R. F. (Ed.). (1986). *Public Self and Private Self.* New York: Springer-Verlag.

Baumeister, R. F. (1989). Motives and costs of self-presentation in organizations. In R. A. Giacalone & P. Rosenfeld (Eds), *Impression Management in the Organization* (pp. 57–85). Hillsdale, NJ: Lawrence Erlbaum Associates.

Baumeister, R. F. (2000). Ego depletion and the self's executive function. In A. Tesser, R. B. Felson and J. M. Suls (Eds). *Psychological Perspectives on Self and Identity* (pp. 9–34). Washington D.C.: American Psychological Association.

Baumeister, R. F., & Hutton, R. F. (1987). Self-presentation theory: Self-construction and audience pleasing. In B. Mullen & G. R. Goethals (Eds), *Theories of Group Behavior* (pp. 71–87). New York: Springer-Verlag.

Baumeister, R. F., & Jones, E. E. (1978). When self-presentation is constrained by the target's knowledge: Consistency and compensation. *Journal of Personality and Social Psychology, 36,* 608–18.

Baumeister, R. F., Kahn, J., & Tice, D. M. (1990). Obesity as a self-handicapping strategy: Personality, selective attribution of problems, and weight loss. *Journal of Social Psychology, 130,* 121–3.

Becker, H. S., & Strauss, A. (1956). Careers, personality and adult socialization. *American Journal of Sociology, 62,* 253–63.

Becker, T. E., & Martin, S. L. (1995). Trying to look bad at work: Methods and motives for managing poor impressions in organizations. *Academy of Management Journal, 38,* 174–99.

Beeman, D. R., & Sharkey, T. W. (1987). The use and abuse of corporate politics. *Business Horizons,* March–April, 26–30.

Berglas, S., & Jones, E. E. (1978). Drug choice as a self-handicapping strategy in response to non-contingent success. *Journal of Personality and Social Psychology, 36,* 405–17.

Bernstein, D. A. (1993). Excuses, excuses. *APS Observer, 6,* 4.

Bies, R. J., Shapiro, D. L., & Cummings, L. L. (1988). Causal accounts and managing organizational conflict: Is it enough to say it's not my fault? *Communication Research, 15,* 381–99.

Bies, R. S., & Sitkin, S. B. (1992). Explanation as legitimation: Excuse-making in organizations. In M. L. McLaughlin, M. J. Cody, & S. J. Read (Eds), *Explaining One's Self to Others: Reason-Giving in a Social Context* (pp. 183–98). Hillsdale, NJ: Lawrence Erlbaum Associates.

Bleifuss, J. (1994). New angles from the spin doctors. *New York Times,* March 20, p. F–13.

Bohra, K. A., & Pandey, J. (1984). Ingratiation toward strangers, friends, and bosses. *Journal of Social Psychology, 122,* 217–22.

Booth-Kewley, S., Edwards, J. E., & Rosenfeld, P. (1992). Impression management, social desirability, and computer administration of attitude questionnaires: Does the computer make a difference? *Journal of Applied Psychology, 77,* 562–6.

Booth-Kewley, S., Rosenfeld, P., & Edwards, J. E. (1992). Impression management and self-deceptive enhancement among Hispanic and non-Hispanic White Navy recruits. *Journal of Social Psychology, 132,* 323–9.

Bornstein, R. F., Riggs, J. M., Hill, E. L., & Calabrese, C. (1996). Activity, passivity, self-denigration, and self-promotion: Toward an interactionist model of interpersonal dependency. *Journal of Personality, 64,* 637–73.

Bozeman, D. P., & Kacmar, K. M. (1997). A cybernetic model of impression management processes in organizations. *Organizational Behavior and Human Decision Processes, 69,* 9–30.

Braaten, D. O., Cody, M. J., & DeTienne, K. B. (1993) Account episodes in organizations: Remedial work and impression management. *Management Communication Quarterly, 6,* 219–50.

Braginsky, B. M., Braginsky, D. D., & Ring, K. (1969). *Methods of Madness: The Mental Hospital as Last Resort.* New York: Holt.

Briggs, S.R., & Cheek, J.M. (1988). On the nature of self-monitoring: Problems with assessment, problems with validity. *Journal of Personality and Social Psychology, 54,* 663–78.

Briggs, S. R., Cheek, J. M., & Buss, A. H. (1980). An analysis of the self-monitoring scale. *Journal of Personality and Social Psychology, 38,* 678–86.

Brown, P., & Levinson, S. C. (1987). *Politeness: Some Universals in Language Use.* Cambridge, England: Cambridge University Press.

Butcher, L. (1989). *Accidental Millionaire: The Rise and Fall of Steve Jobs.* New York: Paragon House.

Byrne, D. (1971). *The Attraction Paradigm.* New York: Academic Press.

Cain, R. (1994). Managing impressions of an AIDS service organization: Into the mainstream or out of the closet? *Qualitative Sociology, 17,* 43–61.

Caldwell, D. F., & O'Reilly, C. A. (1982). Boundary spanning and individual performance: The impact of self-monitoring. *Journal of Applied Psychology, 67,* 124–7.

Callister, R. R., Kramer, M. W., & Turban, D. B. (1999). Feedback seeking following career transitions. *Academy of Management Journal, 42,* 429–38.

Carnegie, D. (1936). *How to Win Friends and Influence People.* New York: Simon & Schuster.

Carnegie, D. (1973). *How to Win Friends and Influence People.* New York: Pocket Books.

Carpenter, M. A., & Golden, B. R. (1997). Perceived managerial discretion: A study of cause and effect. *Strategic Management Journal, 18,* 187–206.

Cascio, W. F. (1975). Accuracy of verifiable biographical information blank responses. *Journal of Applied Psychology, 60,* 767–9.

Cavanagh, G. F., Moberg, D. J., & Valasquez, M. (1981). The ethics of organizational politics. *Academy of Management Review, 6*, 363–74.

Christie, R., & Geis, F. (1970). *Studies in Machiavellianism*. New York: Academic Press.

Cialdini, R. B. (1989). Indirect tactics of image management: Beyond basking. In R. A. Giacalone & P. Rosenfeld (Eds), *Impression Management in the Organization* (pp. 45–56). Hillsdale, NJ: Lawrence Erlbaum Associates.

Cialdini, R. B. (1993). *Influence: The Psychology of Persuasion*. New York: William Morrow and Company, Inc.

Cialdini, R. B., Borden, R. J., Thorne, A., Walker, M. R., Freeman, S., & Sloan, L. R. (1976). Basking in reflected glory: Three (football) field studies. *Journal of Personality and Social Psychology, 34*, 366–75.

Cialdini, R. B., & De Nicolas, M. E. (1989). Self-presentation by association. *Journal of Personality and Social Psychology, 57*, 626–31.

Cialdini, R. B., Finch, J. F., & De Nicolas, M. E. (1990). Strategic self-presentation: The indirect route. In M. J. Cody & M. L. McLaughlin (Eds), *The Psychology of Tactical Communication* (pp. 194–206). Clevedon, UK: Multilingual Matters Ltd.

Cialdini, R. B., & Richardson, K. D. (1980). Two indirect tactics of impression management: Basking and blasting. *Journal of Personality and Social Psychology, 39*, 406–15.

Clark, T., & Salaman, G. (1998). Creating the 'right' impression: Towards a dramaturgy of management consultancy. *The Service Industries Journal, 18*, 121–38.

Clary, E. G., & Shaffer, D. R. (1980). Effects of evidence withholding and defendant's prior record on juridic decisions. *Journal of Psychology, 112*, 237–45.

Cobb, A. T. (1986). Political diagnosis: Applications in organizational development. *Academy of Management Review, 11*, 482–96.

Conlon, D. E., & Murray, N. M. (1996). Customer perceptions of corporate responses to product complaints: The role of explanations. *Academy of Management Journal, 39*, 1040–56.

Cooley, C. H. (1964). *Human Nature and the Social Order*. New York: Schocken Books.

Cooper, J., & Jones, E. E. (1969). Opinion divergence as a strategy to avoid being miscast. *Journal of Personality and Social Psychology, 13*, 23–40.

Craig, D., & Rosato, D. (1994). Portfolio managers spark market's volatility. *USA Today*, April 1, p. B–1.

Crane, A. (2000). Corporate greening as amoralization. *Organization Studies, 21*, 673–96.

Crant, J. M. (1996). Doing more harm than good: When is impression management likely to evoke a negative response? *Journal of Applied Social Psychology, 26*, 1454–71.

Crant, J. M., & Bateman, T. S. (1993). Assignment of credit and blame for performance outcomes. *Academy of Management Journal, 36*, 7–27.

Crawford, K. S., Thomas, E. D., & Funk, J. J. (1980). Pygmalion at sea: Improving the work effectiveness of low performers. *Journal of Applied Behavioral Science, 16*, 482–505.

Crittenden, K. S., & Bae, H. (1994). Self-effacement and social responsibility: Attribution as impression management in Asian cultures. *American Behavioral Scientist, 37*, 653–71.

Crowne, D. P. (1979). *The Experimental Study of Personality.* Hillsdale, NJ: Lawrence Erlbaum Associates.

Crowne, D. P., & Marlowe, D. (1960). A new scale of social desirability independent of psychopathology. *Journal of Consulting and Clinical Psychology, 24*, 349–54.

Crowne, D. P., & Marlowe, D. (1964). *The Approval Motive.* New York: Wiley.

Daubman, K. A., Heatherington, L., & Ahn, A. (1992). Gender and the self-presentation of academic achievement. *Sex Roles, 27*, 187–204.

DeGree, C. E., & Snyder, C. R. (1985). Alder's psychology of use today: Personal history of traumatic life events as a self-handicapping strategy. *Journal of Personality and Social Psychology, 48*, 1512–19.

Delery, J. E., & Kacmar, K. M. (1998). The influence of applicant and interviewer characteristics on the use of impression management. *Journal of Applied Social Psychology, 28*, 1649–69.

Deluga, R. J. (1991). The relationship of upward-influencing behavior with subordinate impression management characteristics. *Journal of Applied Social Psychology, 21*, 1145–60.

Deluga, R. J., & Perry, J. T. (1994). The role of subordinate performance and ingratiation in leader-member exchanges. *Group and Organization Management, 19*, 67–86.

DePaulo, B. M. (1992). Nonverbal behavior and self-presentation. *Psychological Bulletin, 111*, 203–43.

DePaulo, B. M., & Bell, K. L. (1996). Truth and investment: Lies are told to those who care. *Journal of Personality and Social Psychology, 71*, 703–16.

Deutschman, A. (2000). *Second Coming of Steve Jobs.* New York: Broadway Books.

Dimitruis, J., & Mazzarella, M. (2000). *Put Your Best Foot Forward: Make a Great Impression by Taking Control of How Others See You.* New York: Scribner.

Dobbins, G. H., Farh, J. L., & Werbel, J. D. (1993). The influence of self monitoring on inflation of grade point averages for research and selection purposes. *Journal of Applied Social Psychology, 2*, 321–34.

Dobbins, G. H., Long, W. S., Dedrick, E. J., & Clemons, T. C. (1990). The role of self-monitoring and gender on leader emergence: A laboratory and field study. *Journal of Management, 16*, 609–18.

Drost, D. A., O'Brien, F. P., & Marsh, S. (1987). Exit interviews: Master the possibilities. *Personnel Administrator, 32*, 104–10.

DuPont, de Nemours and Company (1952). *Du Pont, the Autobiography of an American Enterprise*. Wilmington, Delaware: E. I. Du Pont de Nemours & Company.

Dwight, S. A., & Feigelson, M. E. (2000). A quantitative review of the effect of computerized testing on the measurement of social desirability. *Educational and Psychological Measurement, 60*, 340–60.

Eden, D. (1991). Applying impression management to create productive self-fulfilling prophecy at work. In R. A. Giacalone & P. Rosenfeld (Eds), *Applied Impression Management: How Image-Making Affects Managerial Decisions* (pp. 13–40). Newbury Park, CA: Sage Publications.

Eder, R. W., & Ferris, G. R. (Eds). (1989). *The Employment Interview: Theory, Research, Practice*. Newbury Park, CA: Sage Publications.

Edwards, J. E., Thomas, M. D., Rosenfeld, P., & Booth-Kewley, S. (1997). *How to Conduct Organizational Surveys: A Step-by-Step Approach*. Newbury Park, CA: Sage Publications.

Ehrenhalt, A. (2001). Hypocrisy has it virtues. *New York Times*, February 6, p. A25.

Elsbach, K. D., & Kramer, R. M. (1996). Members' responses to organizational identity threats: Encountering and countering the *Business Week* rankings, *Administrative Science Quarterly, 41*, 442–76.

Elsbach, K. D., & Sutton, R. I. (1992). Acquiring organizational legitimacy through illegitimate actions: A marriage of institutional and impression management theories. *Academy of Management Review, 35*, 699–738.

Elsbach, K. D., Sutton, R. I., & Principe, K. E. (1998). Averting expected challenges through anticipatory impression management: A study of hospital billing. *Organization Science, 9*, 68–86.

Eppler, D. D., Honeycutt, E. D., & Ford, J. B. (1998). The relationship of self-monitoring and adaptiveness to the performance of real estate sales professionals. *The Journal of Business and Economic Studies, 4*, 37–51.

Eylon, D., Giacalone, R. A., and Pollard, H. G. (2000). Beyond contractual interpretation: Bias in arbitrators' case perceptions and award recommendation, *Journal of Organizational Behavior, 21*, 513–24.

Fandt, P. M., & Ferris, G. R. (1990). The management of information and impressions: When employees behave opportunistically. *Organizational Behavior and Human Decision Processes, 45*, 140–58.

Feldman, D. C. (1985). The new careerism: Origins, tenets, and consequences. *Industrial-Organizational Psychologist, 22*, 39–44.

Feldman, D. C. (1988). *Managing Careers in Organizations*. Glenview, IL: Scott, Foresman.

Feldman, D. C. (1990). Risky business: The recruitment, selection, and socialization of new managers in the twenty-first century. *Journal of Organizational Change Management, 2*, 16–29.

Feldman, D. C., & Klich, N. (1991). Impression management and career strategies. In R. A. Giacalone & P. Rosenfeld (Eds), *Applied Impression Management: How Image-Making Affects Managerial Decisions* (pp. 67–80). Newbury Park, CA: Sage Publications.

Feldman, D. C., & Weitz, B. A. (1990). *From the Invisible Hand to the Glad Hand: Understanding the Antecedents and Consequences of a Careerist Orientation to Work*. Unpublished manuscript.

Ferrari, J. R. (1991). A preference for favorable public impression by procrastinators: Selecting among cognitive and social tasks. *Personality and Individual Differences, 12*, 1233–7.

Ferrari, J. R. (1992). Procrastinators and perfect behavior: An exploratory factor analysis of self-presentation, self-awareness, and self-handicapping components. *Journal of Research in Personality, 26*, 75–84.

Ferrari, J. R., & Tice, D. M. (2000). Procrastination as a self-handicap for men and women: A task-avoidance strategy in a laboratory setting. *Journal of Research in Personality, 34*, 73–83.

Ferris, G. R., Judge, T. A., Rowland, K. M., & Fitzgibbons, D. E. (1994). Subordinate influence and the performance evaluation process: Test of a model. *Organizational Behavior and Human Decision Processes, 58*, 101–35.

Ferris, G. R., King, T. R., Judge, T. A., & Kacmar, K. M. (1991). The management of shared meaning in organizations: Opportunism in the reflection of attitudes, beliefs, and values. In R. A. Giacalone & P. Rosenfeld (Eds), *Applied Impression Management: How Image-Making Affects Managerial Decisions* (pp. 41–66). Newbury Park, CA: Sage Publications.

Ferris, G. R., & Mitchell, T. R. (1987). The components of social influence and their importance for human resources research. In K. M. Rowland & G. R. Ferris (Eds), *Research in Personnel and Human Resources Management* (pp. 103–28). Greenwich, CT: JAI Press.

Ferris, G. R., Russ, G. S., & Fandt, P. M. (1989). Politics in organizations. In R. A. Giacalone, & P. Rosenfeld (Eds), *Impression Management in the Organization* (pp. 143–70). Hillsdale, NJ: Lawrence Erlbaum Associates.

Finch, J. F., & Cialdini, R. B. (1989). Another indirect tactic of (self-) image management: Boosting. *Personality and Social Psychology Bulletin, 15*, 222–32.

Fletcher, C. (1989). Impression management in the selection interview. In R. A. Giacalone & P. Rosenfeld (Eds), *Impression Management in the Organization* (pp. 269–81). Hillsdale, NJ: Lawrence Erlbaum Associates.

Fletcher, C. (1990). The relationship between candidate personality, self-presentation strategies, and interviewer assessments in selection interviews: An empirical study. *Human Relations, 43*, 739–49.

Fletcher, C. (1992). Ethical issues in the selection interview. *Journal of Business Ethics, 11*, 362–7.

Food Lyin (1997) *McNeil-Lehrer News Hour*, January 15, Corporation for Public Broadcasting.

For California cow, one caricature too many (1993). *New York Times*, December 12, p. A–12.

Forsyth, D. R., Riess, M., & Schlenker, B. R. (1977). Impression management concerns governing reactions to a faulty decision. *Representative Research in Social Psychology, 8,* 12–22.

Fraser, J. A. (2001). They don't call it a cell for nothing: Phone, fax, and laptop keep us tied to our jobs. *Washington Post*, February 4, p. B–2.

Freiberg, P. (1991). Black men may act cool to advertise masculinity. *APA Monitor, 22,* March, 30.

Frink, D. D., & Ferris, G. R. (1998). Accountability, impression management, and goal setting in the performance evaluation process. *Human Relations, 51,* 1259–83.

Furnham, A. (1992). *Personality at Work: The Role of Individual Differences in the Workplace.* London: Routledge.

Gabrenya, W. K., & Arkin, R. M. (1980). Factor structure and factor correlates of the self-monitoring scale. *Personality and Social Psychology Bulletin, 6,* 13–22.

Gangestad, S. W., & Snyder, M. (2000). Self-monitoring: Appraisal and reappraisal. *Psychological Bulletin, 126,* 530–55.

Gardner, W. L., & Avolio, B. (1998). The charismatic relationship: A dramaturgical perspective. *Academy of Management Review, 23,* 32–58.

Gardner, W. L., & Martinko, M. J. (1988). Impression management in organizations. *Journal of Management, 14,* 321–8.

Garland, H., & Beard, J. F. (1979). The relationship between self-monitoring and leader emergence across two task situations. *Journal of Applied Psychology, 64,* 72–6.

Garretson, P., & Teel, K. S. (1982). The exit interview: Effective tool or meaningless gesture? *Personnel, 4,* 70–7.

Garrison, L., & Ferguson, J. (1977). Separation interviews. *Personnel Journal, 56,* 438–42.

Geier, T., & Hawkins, D. (1993). Outlook: Eye on the '90s. *US News & World Report*, December 20, p. 12.

Giacalone, R. A. (1985). On slipping when you thought you had put your best foot forward: Self-promotion, self-destruction, and entitlements. *Group and Organization Studies, 10,* 61–80.

Giacalone, R. A. (1987). Management, sex, and symbolic association/disassociation following success and failure. *Basic and Applied Social Psychology, 1&2,* 45–56.

Giacalone, R. A. (1988). The effects of administrative accounts and gender on the perception of leadership. *Group and Organization Studies, 13,* 195–207.

Giacalone, R. A. (1989). Image control: The strategies of impression management. *Personnel*, May, 52–5.

Giacalone, R. A., & Beard, J. W. (1994). Impression management, diversity and international management. *American Behavioral Scientist, 37*, 621–36.

Giacalone, R. A., & Duhon, D. (1991). Assessing intended employee behavior in exit interviews. *Journal of Psychology: Interdisciplinary and Applied, 125*, 83–90.

Giacalone, R. A., Elig, T. W., Ginexi, E. M., & Bright, A. J. (1995). The impact of identification and type of separation on measures of satisfaction and missing data in the exit survey process. *Military Psychology, 7*, 235–52.

Giacalone, R. A., & Falvo, R. (1985). *Self-presentation, Self-monitoring, and Organizational Commitment.* Paper presented at the 93rd Annual Meeting of the American Psychological Association, August, Los Angeles, CA.

Giacalone, R. A., & Knouse, S. B. (1988). Males' attitudes toward women and symbolic association/disassociation with female managers. *Basic and Applied Social Psychology, 9*, 289–300.

Giacalone, R. A., & Knouse, S. B. (1989). Farewell to fruitless exit interviews. *Personnel, 66*, 60–2.

Giacalone, R. A., & Knouse, S. B. (1990). Justifying wrongful employee behavior: The role of personality in organizational sabotage. *Journal of Business Ethics, 9*, 55–61.

Giacalone, R. A., Knouse, S. B., & Ashworth, D. N. (1991). Impression management and exit interview distortion. In R. A. Giacalone & P. Rosenfeld (Eds), *Applied Impression Management: How Image-Making Affects Managerial Decisions* (pp. 97–107). Newbury Park, CA: Sage Publications.

Giacalone, R. A., Knouse, S. B., & Pearce, C. L. (1998). The education of leaders: Impression management as a functional competence. *Journal of Management Systems, 10*, 67–80.

Giacalone, R. A., & Payne, S. L. (1995). Evaluation of employee rule violations: Impression management effects in historical context. *Journal of Business Ethics, 14*, 477–87.

Giacalone, R. A., & Pollard, H. G. (1989). Comparative effectiveness of impression management tactics on the recommendation of grievant punishment: An exploratory investigation. *Forensic Reports, 2*, 147–60.

Giacalone, R. A., & Pollard, H. G. (1990). Acceptance of managerial accounts for unethical supervisory behavior. *Journal of Social Psychology, 130*, 103–11.

Giacalone, R. A., Pollard, H. G., & Brannen, D. (1989). The role of forensic factors and grievant impression management on labor arbitration decisions. In R. A. Giacalone & P. Rosenfeld (Eds), *Impression Management in the Organization* (pp. 315–26). Hillsdale, NJ: Lawrence Erlbaum Associates.

Giacalone, R. A., Pollard, H. G., & Eylon, D. (2000). Beyond contractual interpretation: Bias in arbitrators' case perceptions and award recommendations. *Journal of Organizational Behavior, 21*, 513–24.

Giacalone, R. A., Reiner, M. L., & Goodwin, J. (1992). Ethical concerns in grievance arbitration. *Journal of Business Ethics, 11*, 267–72.

Giacalone, R. A., & Riordan, C. A. (1990). Effect of self-presentation on perceptions and recognition in an organization. *Journal of Psychology, 124*, 25–38.

Giacalone, R. A., & Riordan, C. A., & Rosenfeld, P. (1997). Employee Sabotage. In R. A. Giacalone & J. Greenberg (Eds), *Antisocial Behavior in Organizations* (pp. 109–29). Thousand Oaks, CA: Sage.

Giacalone, R. A., & Rosenfeld, P. (1984). The effect of perceived planning and propriety on the effectiveness of leadership accounts. *Social Behavior and Personality, 12*, 217–24.

Giacalone, R. A., & Rosenfeld, P. (1986). Self-presentation and self-promotion in an organizational setting. *Journal of Social Psychology, 126*, 321–6.

Giacalone, R. A., & Rosenfeld, P. (1987). Justification and procedures for implementing institutional review boards in organizations. *Journal of Business Ethics, 6*, 5–17.

Giacalone, R. A., & Rosenfeld, P. (Eds). (1989). *Impression Management in the Organization.* Hillsdale, NJ: Lawrence Erlbaum Associates.

Giacalone, R. A., & Rosenfeld, P. (Eds). (1991). *Applied Impression Management: How Image-Making Affects Managerial Decisions.* Newbury Park: Sage Publications.

Gilbert, D. T., & Jones, E. E. (1986). Exemplification: The self-presentation of moral character. *Journal of Personality, 54*, 593–615.

Gilbert, D. T., & Krull, D. S. (1988). Seeing less and knowing more: The benefits of perceptual ignorance. *Journal of Personality and Social Psychology, 54*, 193–202.

Gilmore, D. C., & Ferris, G. R. (1989a). The effects of applicant impression management tactics on interviewer judgments. *Journal of Management, 15*, 557–64.

Gilmore, D. C., & Ferris, G. R. (1989b). The politics of the employment interview. In Eder, R. W., & Ferris, G. R. (Eds), *The Employment Interview: Theory, Research, Practice* (pp. 195–203). Newbury Park, CA: Sage Publications.

Ginzel, L. E. (1994). The impact of biased inquiry strategies on performance judgments. *Organizational Behavior and Human Decision Processes, 57*, 1–19.

Ginzel, L. E., Kramer, R. M., & Sutton, R. I. (1993). Organizational impression management as a reciprocal influence process: The neglected role of organizational audience. *Research in Organizational Behavior, 15*, 227–66.

Godfrey, D. K., Jones, E. E., & Lord, C. G. (1986). Self-promotion is not ingratiating. *Journal of Personality and Social Psychology, 50*, 106–15.

Goffman, E. (1959). *The Presentation of Self in Everyday Life.* Garden City, NY: Doubleday Anchor.

Goffman, E. (1964). On cooling out the mark: Some aspects of adaptation to failure. In A. M. Rose (Ed.), *Human Behavior and Social Processes: An Interactionist Approach* (pp. 482–505). Boston: Houghton Mifflin Company.

Goffman, E. (1971). *Relations in Public*. New York: Harper & Row.

Gold, G. J., & Weiner, B. (2000). Remorse, confession, group identity, and expectancies about repeating a transgression. *Basic & Applied Social Psychology, 22*, 291–300.

Goldstein, I. L. (1971). The application blank: How honest are the responses? *Journal of Applied Personality, 55*, 491–2.

Good, L. R., & Good, K. C. (1973). An objective measure of the motive to avoid appearing incompetent. *Psychological Reports, 32*, 1075–7.

Goodale, J. G. (1982). *The Fine Art of Interviewing*. Englewood Cliffs, NJ: Prentice-Hall.

Goodwin, C., & Ross, I. (1992). Consumer responses to service failures: Influence of procedural and interactional fairness perceptions. *Journal of Business Research, 25*, 149–63.

Gordon, R. A. (1996). Impact of ingratiation on judgments and evaluations: A meta-analytic investigation. *Journal of Personality and Social Psychology, 71*, 54–70.

Gordon, L. V., & Stapleton, E. S. (1956). Fakability of a forced-choice personality test under realistic high school employment conditions. *Journal of Applied Psychology, 40*, 258–62.

Gould, S., & Penley, L. E. (1984). Career strategies and salary progression: A study of their relationships in a municipal bureaucracy. *Organizational Behavior and Human Performance, 34*, 244–65.

Gouldner, A. W. (1960). The norm of reciprocity: A preliminary statement. *American Sociological Review, 25*, 161–78.

Gove, W. R., Hughes, M., & Geerkin, M. R. (1980). Playing dumb: A form of impression management with undesirable side effects. *Social Psychology Quarterly, 43*, 89–102.

Greenberg, J. (1990). Employee theft as a reaction to underpayment inequity: The hidden cost of pay cuts. *Journal of Applied Psychology, 75*, 561–8.

Greenberg, J. (1996). 'Forgive me, I'm new': Three experimental demonstrations of the effects of attempts to excuse poor performance. *Organizational Behavior and Human Decision Processes, 66*, 165–78.

Greenberg, J., Bies, R. J., & Eskew, D. E. (1991). Establishing fairness in the eye of the beholder: Managing impressions of organizational justice. In R. A. Giacalone & P. Rosenfeld (Eds) *Applied Impression Management: How Image-Making Affects Managerial Decisions* (pp. 111–32). Newbury Park, CA: Sage Publications.

Habenstein, R. W. (1962). Sociology of occupations: The case of the American funeral director. In A. M. Rose (Ed.), *Human Behavior and Social Processes: An Interactionist Approach* (pp. 225–46). Boston: Houghton Mifflin Company.

Halle, L. J. (1965). *The Society of Man*. New York: Harper & Row.

Hamashige, H. (1994). Club's ongoing success speaks volumes. *Los Angeles Times*, October 29, pp. A1, A16, A18.

Harrell-Cook, G., Ferris, G. R., & Dulebohn, J. H. (1999). Political behaviors as moderators of the perceptions of organizational politics–work outcome relationships. *Journal of Organizational Behavior, 20,* 1093–105.

Harrison, J. K., Chadwick, M., & Scales, M. (1996). The relationship between cross cultural adjustment and the personality variables of self efficacy and self monitoring. *International Journal of Intercultural Relations, 20,* 167–88.

Harrison, A. W., Hochwarter, W. A., Perrewe, P. L., & Ralston, D. A. (1998). The ingratiation construct: An assessment of the validity of the Measure of Ingratiatory Behaviors in Organizational Settings (MIBOS). *Journal of Applied Psychology, 83,* 932–43.

Hatton, D. E., Snortum, J. R., & Oskamp, S. (1971). The effects of biasing information and dogmatism upon witness testimony. *Psychonomic Science, 23,* 425–7.

Heatherington, L., Burns, A. B., & Gustafson, T. B. (1998). When another stumbles: Gender and self-presentation to vulnerable others. *Sex Roles, 38,* 889–913.

Hedges, S. J., Walsh, K. T., & Headden, S. (1994). The Whitewater files. *US News and World Report,* January 17, p. 43.

Henderson, M., & Hewstone, M. (1984). Prison inmates' explanations for interpersonal violence: Accounts and attributions. *Journal of Consulting and Clinical Psychology, 52,* 789–94.

Hendricks, M., & Brickman, P. (1974). Effects of status and knowledgeability of audience on self-presentation. *Sociometry, 37,* 440–9.

Heneman, H. G., III, and Sandver, M. G. (1983). Arbitrator's backgrounds and behavior. *Journal of Labor Research, 4,* 115.

Henneberger, M. (2000). Is what we've got here a compulsion to exaggerate?, *New York Times,* October 15, section 4, pp. 1, 3.

Hewitt, J. P., & Hall, P. M. (1973). Social problems, problematic situations, and quasi-theories. *American Sociological Review, 38,* 367–74.

Hewitt, J., & Stokes, R. (1975). Disclaimers. *American Sociological Review, 40,* 1–11.

Hewstone, M., & Brown, R. (Eds). (1986). *Contact and Conflict in Intergroup Encounters.* Oxford/New York: Basil Blackwell.

Hiestand, M. (1991, January 15). Even reputations can be insured. *USA Today,* p. C2.

Hill, M. F., Jr., & Sinicropi, A. V. (1987). *Evidence in Arbitration.* BNA Books, Arbitration Series.

Hinkin, T. R., & Schriesheim, C. A. (1989). Development and application of new scales to measure the French and Raven (1959) bases of social power. *Journal of Applied Psychology, 74,* 561–7.

Hinrichs, J. H. (1975). Measurement of reasons for resignation of professionals: Questionnaire versus company and consultant exit interviews. *Journal of Applied Psychology, 60,* 530–2.

Hodgins, H. H., Liebeskind, E., & Schwartz, W. (1996). Getting out of hot water: Facework in social predicaments. *Journal of Personality and Social Psychology, 71*, 300–14.

Hollander, E. P. (1958). Conformity, status, and idiosyncrasy credit. *Psychological Review, 65*, 117–27.

Holtgraves, T. (1992). The linguistic realization of face management: Implications for language production and comprehension, person perception, and cross-cultural communication. *Social Psychology Quarterly, 55*, 141–59.

Hosseini, J. C., & Armacost, R. L. (1993). Gathering sensitive data in organizations. In P. Rosenfeld, J. E. Edwards & M. D. Thomas, *Improving Organizational Surveys: New Directions, Methods and Applications* (pp. 29–50). Newbury Park: Sage Publications.

Howard, J. L., & Ferris, G. R. (1996). The employment interview context: Social and situational influences on interviewer decisions. *Journal of Applied Social Psychology, 26*, 112–36.

Hu, D. H. (1944). The Chinese concepts of face. *American Anthropologist, 46*, 45–64.

Huber, V., Latham, G., & Locke, E. (1989). The management of impressions through goal setting. In R. A. Giacalone & P. Rosenfeld (Eds), *Impression Management in the Organization* (pp. 203–18). Hillsdale, NJ: Lawrence Erlbaum Associates.

Iacocca, L. (1984). *Iacocca: An Autobiography.* Toronto: Bantam Books.

Ickes, W., Reidhead, S., & Patterson, M. (1986). Machiavellianism and self-monitoring: As different as 'me' and 'you'. *Social Cognition, 4*, 58–74.

Jablonsky, W. A. (1975). How useful are exit interviews? *Supervisory Management, 20* (5), 8–14.

James, W. (1890). *Principles of Psychology.* New York: Holt.

Jellison, J. M., & Gentry, K. W. (1978). A self-presentation interpretation of the seeking of social approval. *Personality and Social Psychology Bulletin, 4*, 227–30.

Jenkins, J. M. (1993) Self-monitoring and turnover: The impact of personality on intent to leave. *Journal of Organizational Behavior, 14*, 83–91.

Johnson, D. (1987) At 75, Carnegie's message lives on. *New York Times*, December 13, p. A28.

Jones, E. E. (1964). *Ingratiation: A Social Psychological Analysis.* New York: Appleton-Century-Crofts.

Jones, E. E. (1990). *Interpersonal Perception.* W. H. Freeman & Company: New York.

Jones, E. E., Brenner, K. J., & Knight, J. S. (1990). When failure elevates self-esteem. *Personality and Social Psychology Bulletin, 16*, 200–09.

Jones, E. E., Gergen, K. J., Gumpert, P., & Thibaut, J. W. (1965). Some conditions affecting the use of ingratiation to influence performance evaluation. *Journal of Personality and Social Psychology, 1*, 613–25.

Jones, E. E., Jones, R. G., & Gergen, K. J. (1963). Some conditions affecting the evaluation of a conformist. *Journal of Personality, 31,* 270–88.

Jones, E. E., & Pittman, T. S. (1982). Toward a general theory of strategic self-presentation. In J. Suls (Ed.), *Psychological Perspectives on the Self* (Vol. 1) (pp. 231–62). Hillsdale, NJ: Lawrence Erlbaum Associates.

Jones, E. E., & Sigall, H. (1971). The bogus pipeline. A new paradigm for measuring affect and attitudes. *Psychological Bulletin, 76,* 349–64.

Jones, E. E., & Rhodewalt, F. (1982). *The Self-Handicapping Scale.* Unpublished scale, Princeton University.

Judge, T. A., & Bretz, R. D. (1994). Political influence behavior and career success. *Journal of Management, 20,* 43–65.

Jung, J. (1987). Anticipatory excuses in relation to expected versus actual task performance. *Journal of Psychology, 121,* 413–21.

Kacmar, K. M., & Carlson, D. S. (1994). Using impression management in women's job search process. *American Behavioral Scientist, 37,* 682–96.

Kacmar, K. M., & Carlson, D. S. (1999). Effectiveness of impression management tactics across human resource situations. *Journal of Applied Social Psychology, 29,* 1293–315.

Kacmar, K. M., Delery, J. E., & Ferris, G. R. (1992). Differential effectiveness of applicant impression management tactics on employment interview decisions. *Journal of Applied Social Psychology, 22,* 1250–72.

Kacmar, K. M., & Valle, M. (1997). Dimensionality of the Measure of Ingratiatory Behaviors in Organizational Settings (MIBOS) scale. *Educational and Psychological Measurement, 57,* 314–28.

Kacmar, K. M., Wayne, S. J., & Wright, P. M. (1996). Subordinate reactions to the use of impression management tactics and feedback by the supervisor. *Journal of Managerial Issues, 8,* 35–53.

Kalab, K. A. (1987). Student vocabularies of motive: Accounts for absence. *Symbolic Interaction, 10,* 71–83.

Kalven, H., & Zeisel, H. (1966). *The American Jury.* Chicago: University of Chicago Press.

Kashy, D. A., & DePaulo, B. M. (1996). Who lies? *Journal of Personality and Social Psychology, 70,* 1037–51.

Kelly, A. E. (2000). Helping construct desirable identities: A self-presentational view of psychotherapy. *Psychological Bulletin, 126,* 475–94.

Kilduff, M., & Day, D. V. (1994). Do chameleons get ahead? The effects of self monitoring on managerial careers. *Academy of Management Journal, 37,* 1047–60.

Kipnis, D., & Vanderveer, R. (1971). Ingratiation and the use of power. *Journal of Personality and Social Psychology, 17,* 280–6.

Knapp, M. L., Stafford, L., & Daly, J. A. (1986). Regrettable messages: Things people wish they hadn't said. *Journal of Communication, 36,* 40–59.

Knouse, S. B. (1989). Impression management and the letter of recommendation. In R. A. Giacalone & P. Rosenfeld (Eds), *Impression Management in the Organization* (pp. 283–96). Hillsdale, NJ: Lawrence Erlbaum Associates.

Knouse, S. B. (1996). *Human Resource Management Perspectives on TQM: Concepts and Practices*. Milwaukee, WI: ASQ Quality Press.

Knouse, S. B., & Giacalone, R. A. (1992). Discussion willingness in the exit interview. *Canadian Journal of Administrative Sciences, 9*, 24–9.

Knouse, S. B., & Giacalone, R. A. (1992). Ethical decision-making in business: Behavioral issues and concerns. *Journal of Business Ethics, 11*, 369–72.

Knouse, S. B., Giacalone, R. A., & Pollard, H. G. (1988). Impression management in the resumé and its cover letter. *Journal of Business and Psychology, 3*, 242–9.

Knouse, S. B., Rosenfeld, P., & Culbertson, A. L. (Eds). (1992). *Hispanics in the Workplace*. Newbury Park, CA: Sage Publications.

Korda, M. (1975). *Power: How To Get It, How To Use It*. New York: Ballantine.

Kuhn, M. H. (1964). The interview and the professional relationship. In A. M. Rose (Ed.), *Human Behavior and Social Processes: An Interactionist Approach* (pp. 193–297). Boston: Houghton Mifflin Company.

Kumar, K., & Beyerlein, M. (1991). Construction and validation of an instrument for measuring ingratiatory behaviors in organizational settings. *Journal of Applied Psychology, 76*, 619–27.

Larwood, L. (1991). Start with a rational group of people... Gender effects of impression management in organizations. In R. A. Giacalone & P. Rosenfeld (Eds), *Applied Impression Management: How Image Making Affects Managerial Decisions* (pp. 177–94). Newbury Park, CA: Sage Publications.

Latham, V. M. (1985). *The Role of Personality in the Job Search Process*. Paper presented at the annual meetings of the Midwestern Psychological Association, May, Chicago, IL.

Lautenschlager, G. J., & Flaherty, V. L. (1990). Computer administration of questions: More desirable or more social desirability? *Journal of Applied Psychology, 75*, 310–14.

Leary, M. R. (1983a). A brief version of the fear of negative evaluation scale. *Personality and Social Psychology Bulletin, 9*, 371–6.

Leary, M. R. (1983b). Social anxiousness: The construct and its measurement. *Journal of Personality Assessment, 47*, 66–75.

Leary, M. R. (1989). Self-presentational processes in leadership emergence and effectiveness. In R. A. Giacalone & P. Rosenfeld (Eds), *Impression Management in the Organization* (pp. 363–74). Hillsdale, NJ: Lawrence Erlbaum Associates.

Leary, M. R. (1992). Self-presentational processes in exercise and sport. *Journal of Sport and Exercise Psychology, 14*, 339–51.

Leary, M. R. (1993). The interplay of private self processes and interpersonal factors in self-presentation. In J. Suls (Ed.), *Psychological Perspectives on the*

Self: The Self in Social Perspective, Vol. 4 (pp. 127–55). Hillsdale, NJ: Lawrence Erlbaum Associates.

Leary, M. R., & Kowalski, R. M. (1990). Impression management: A literature review and two component models. *Psychological Bulletin, 107*, 34–47.

Leary, M. R., & Kowalski, R. M. (1993). The interaction anxiousness scale: Construct and criterion-related validity. *Journal of Personality Assessment, 61*, 136–46.

Leary, M. R., & Schlenker, B. R. (1980). Self-presentation in a task-oriented leadership situation. *Representative Research in Social Psychology, 11*, 152–9.

Leary, M. R., Robertson, R. B., Barnes, B. D., & Miller, R. S. (1986). Self-presentation of small group leaders as a function of role requirements and leadership orientation. *Journal of Personality and Social Psychology, 51*, 742–8.

Lee, S. J., Quigley, B. M., Nesler, M. S., Corbett, A. B., & Tedeschi, J. T. (1999). Development of a self-presentation tactics scale. *Personality and Individual Differences, 26*, 701–22.

Lefkowitz, J., & Katz, M. L. (1969). Validity of exit interviews. *Personnel Psychology, 22*, 445–5.

Lennox, R., & Wolfe, R. (1984). A revision of the self-monitoring scale. *Journal of Personality and Social Psychology, 46*, 1348–64.

Levine, S.P., & Feldman, R. S. (1997). Self presentational goals, self monitoring, and nonverbal behavior. *Basic and Applied Social Psychology, 19*, 505–18.

Levinson, D. J. (1978). *The Seasons of a Man's Life.* New York: Ballantine.

Liden, R. C., Martin, C. L., & Parson, C. K. (1993). Interviewer and applicant behaviors in employment interviews. *Academy of Management Journal, 36*, 372–86.

Liden, R. C., & Mitchell, T. R. (1988). Ingratiatory behaviors in organizational settings. *Academy of Management Review, 13*, 572–87.

Lipsky, M. (1980). *Street-Level Bureaucracy: Dilemmas of the Individual in Public Services.* New York: Russell Sage Foundation.

Luthans, F., & Kreitner, R. (1985). *Organizational Behavior Modification and Beyond.* Glenview, Ill.: Scott Foresman.

Lutz, W. (1989). *Doublespeak.* New York: Harper/Perennial.

Maddux, J. E., Norton, L. W., & Leary, M. R. (1988). Cognitive components of social anxiety: An investigation of the integration of self-presentation theory and self-efficacy theory. *Journal of Social and Clinical Psychology, 6*, 180–90.

Markman, K. D., & Tetlock, P. E. (2000). 'I couldn't have known': Accountability, foreseeability and counterfactual denials of responsibility. *British Journal of Social Psychology 39*, 313–25.

Markoff, J. (2001). Thinking revolution, talking evolution at Apple. *New York Times Week in Review*, January 21, section 4, p. 4.

Martinko, M. J. (1991). Future directions: Toward a model for applying impression management strategies in the workplace. In R. A. Giacalone & P. Rosenfeld (Eds), *Applied Impression Management: How Image-Making Affects Managerial Decisions* (pp. 259–77). Newbury Park, CA: Sage Publications.

McCall, M. W., Lombardo, M. M., & Morrison, A. M. (1988). *The Lessons of Experience*. Lexington, MA: Lexington.

McCroskey, J. C. (1992). Reliability and validity of the willingness to communicate scale. *Communication Quarterly, 40*, 16–25.

McGraw, K. M. (1991). Managing blame: An experimental test of the effects of political accounts. *American Political Science Review, 85*, 1133–57.

Mendenhall, M. E., & Wiley, C. (1994). Strangers in a strange land: The relationship between expatriate adjustment and impression management. *American Behavioral Scientist, 37*, 605–20.

Merton, R. K. (1948). The self-fulfilling prophecy. *Antioch Review, 8*, 193–210.

Mexican president's resumé is erroneous (2001). *USA Today*, January 26, p. 10A.

Miller, A. (1969). *Arthur Miller's Collected Plays with an Introduction*. New York: Viking Press.

Miller, J. S., & Cardy, R. L. (2000). Self monitoring and performance appraisal: Rating outcomes in project teams. *Journal of Organizational Behavior, 21*, 609–26.

Miller, L. E., & Grush, J. E. (1986). Individual differences in attitudinal versus normative determination of behavior. *Journal of Experimental Social Psychology, 22*, 190–202.

Miller, A., Smith, V. E., & Mabry, M. (1992). Shooting the messenger?: How Food Lion handled a damaging TV exposé. *Newsweek*, November 23, p. 51.

Millham, J., & Jacobson, L. I. (1978). The need for approval. In H. London & J. E. Exner (Eds), *Dimension of Personality* (pp. 365–90). New York: Wiley.

Mills, C. W. (1940). Situation identities and vocabularies of motive. *American Sociological Review, 5*, 904–15.

Mohamed, A. A., Gardner, W. L., & Paolillo, J. G. (1999). A taxonomy of organizational impression management tactics. *Advances in Competitiveness Research, 7*, 108–30.

Molloy, J. T. (1978). *Dress for Success*. New York: Warner.

Montagliani, A., & Giacalone, R. A. (1998). Impression management and cross-cultural adaption. *Journal of Social Psychology, 138*, 598–608.

Moorman, R. H., & Podsakoff, P. M. (1992). A meta-analytic review and empirical test of the potential of confounding effects of social desirability response sets in organizational behavior research. *Journal of Occupational and Organizational Psychology, 65*, 131–49.

Morgan, D. F. (1987). Varieties of administrative abuse: Some reflections on ethics and discretion. *Administration & Society, 19*, 267–84.

Nelson, N. E., & Curry, E. M., Jr, (1981). Arbitrator characteristics and arbitral decisions. *Industrial Relations, 20,* 316.

O'Brien, G. (1993). Sucking up: Today getting ahead is a rearguard action. *Playboy, 40,* pp. 144, 146.

Odom, M. (1993). Kissing up really works on boss. *San Diego Union-Tribune,* August 12, p. E–12.

Orbuch, T.L. (1997). People's accounts count: The sociology of accounts. *Annual Review of Sociology, 23,* 455–78.

Ornstein, S. (1989). Impression management through office design. In R. A. Giacalone & P. Rosenfeld (Eds), *Impression Management in the Organization* (pp. 411–26). Hillsdale, NJ: Lawrence Erlbaum Associates.

Overstreet, J. (1994), How to be a better negotiator. *USA Today,* October 17, p. 2B.

Palmer, R. J., Walker, R. B., Campbell, T. L., & Magner, N. R. (2001). Examining the impression management orientation of managers. *Journal of Managerial Psychology, 16,* 35–49.

Pan, P. (2000). Pilot error is blamed for crash in Taipei. *Washington Post,* November 4, p. A20.

Pandey, J., & Kakkar, S. (1982). Supervisor's affect: Attraction and positive evaluation as a function of other-enhancement. *Psychological Reports, 50,* 479–86.

Pandey, J., & Rastogi, R. (1979). Machiavellianism and ingratiation. *Journal of Social Psychology, 108,* 221–5.

Pandey, J., & Singh, P. (1987). Effects of Machiavellianism, other-enhancement, and power-position on affect, power-feeling, and evaluation of the ingratiator. *Journal of Psychology, 12,* 287–300.

Parkinson, M. G. (1979). *Language Behavior and Courtroom Success.* Paper presented at the Annual Meeting of the British Psychological Society, July, Bristol.

Paulhus, D. L. (1984). Two-component models of social desirable responding. *Journal of Personality and Social Psychology, 46,* 598–609.

Paulhus, D. L. (1988). *Assessing Self-Deception and Impression Management in Self-Reports: The Balanced Inventory of Desirable Responding.* Unpublished manual. University of British Columbia, Vancouver, Canada.

Paulhus, D. L. (1991). Measurement and control of response bias. In J. P. Robinson, P. R. Shaver, & L. S. Wrightsman (Eds), *Measurement of Personality and Social Psychological Attitudes* (pp. 17–59). San Diego: Academic Press.

Paulhus, D. L., Graf, P., & VanSelst, M. (1989). Attentional load increases the possibility of self-presentation. *Social Cognition, 7,* 389–400.

Payne, S. L. (1989). Self-presentational tactics and employee theft. In R. A. Giacalone & P. Rosenfeld (Eds), *Impression Management in the Organization* (pp. 397–408). Hillsdale, NJ: Lawrence Erlbaum Associates.

Payne, S. L., & Giacalone, R. A. (1990). Social psychological approaches to the perception of ethical dilemmas. *Human Relations, 43,* 649–665.

Perlez, J. (2001). State Dept's work rules: Powell's free and easy guide. *New York Times,* January 26, p. A3.

Peters, T. J., & Waterman, R. H. (1982). *In Search of Excellence: Lessons from America's Best Run Companies.* New York: Harper and Row.

Petras, R., & Petras, K. (1994). *The 776 Even Stupider Things Ever Said.* New York: HarperCollins.

Pfeffer, J. (1981). *Power in Organizations.* Boston: Pitman.

Pinker, S. (1994). Is there a gene for compassion? *New York Times Book Review,* September 25, pp. 3, 34.

Poniewozik J. (2000). Operating system, *New York Times Book Review,* October 8, p. 38.

Pryor, B., & Buchanan, R. W. (1984). The effects of a defendant's demeanor on juror perceptions of credibility and guilt. *Journal of Communication, 24,* 92–9.

Rafaeli, A., & Pratt, M. G. (1993). Tailored meanings: On the meaning and impact of organizational dress. *Academy of Management Review, 18,* 32–55.

Raia, A. (1985). Power, politics, and the human resource professional. *Human Resource Planning, 4,* 200–5.

Ralston, D. A. (1985). Employee ingratiation: The role of management. *Academy of Management Review, 10,* 477–87.

Ralston, D. A., & Elsass, P. M. (1989). Ingratiation and impression management in the organization. In R. A. Giacalone & P. Rosenfeld (Eds), *Impression Management in the Organization* (pp. 235–49). Hillsdale, NJ: Lawrence Erlbaum Associates.

Rao, A., Schmidt, S. M., & Murray, L. H. (1995). Upward impression management: Goals, influence strategies, and consequences. *Human Relations, 48,* 147–67.

Ray, M. C., & Simons, R. L. (1987). Convicted murderers' accounts of their crimes: A study of homicide in small communities. *Symbolic Interaction, 10,* 57–70.

Rehmus, C. M. (1984). *Writing the Opinion.* Ithaca, NY: ILR Press.

Rhodewalt, F., Saltzman, A. T., & Wittmer, J. (1984). Self-handicapping among competitive athletes: The role of practice in self-esteem protection. *Basic and Applied Social Psychology, 5,* 197–210.

Riechmann (2001). And now, a prebuttal by FLOTUS' husband. *Albany Times Union,* February 11, p. A6.

Riess, M., & Rosenfeld, P. (1980). Seating preferences as nonverbal communication: A self-presentational analysis. *Journal of Applied Communications Research, 8,* 22–30.

Riggio, R. E., & Friedman, H. S. (1986). Impression formation: The role of expressive behavior. *Journal of Personality and Social Psychology, 50,* 421–7.

Rind, B., & Bordia, P. (1996). Effect of restaurant tipping of male and female servers drawing a happy, smiling face on the backs of customers' checks. *Journal of Applied Social Psychology, 26*, 218–25.

Ringer, R. J. (1976). *Winning Through Intimidation*. Greenwich, CT: Fawcett.

Riordan, C. A. (1989). Images of corporate success. In R. A. Giacalone & P. Rosenfeld (Eds), *Impression Management in the Organization* (pp. 87–104). Hillsdale, NJ: Lawrence Erlbaum Associates.

Riordan, C. A. (1993). A study of campus climate: Methodology and results. In J. Q. Adams & J. R. Welsch (Eds), *Multicultural Education: Strategies for Implementation in Colleges and Universities*, (pp. 113–24). Illinois Staff and Curriculum Developers Association.

Riordan, C. A. (in press). Groupware and decision-making. In L. F. Monplaisir & N. Singh (Eds). *Collaborative Engineering Design in Production and Development*. Stevenson Ronch, LA: American Scientific Publishers.

Riordan, C. A., Gross, T., & Maloney, C. C. (1994). Self-monitoring, gender and the personal consequences of impression management. *American Behavioral Scientist, 37*, 715–25.

Riordan, C. A., James, M. K., & Runzi, M. J. (1989). Explaining failures at work: An accounter's dilemma. *The Journal of General Psychology, 116*, 197–205.

Riordan, C. A., Marlin, N. A., & Kellogg, J. T. (1983). The effectiveness of accounts following transgression. *Social Psychology Quarterly, 46*, 213–19.

Rivera, A. N. (1976). Public versus private reactions to positive inequity. *Journal of Personality and Social Psychology, 34*, 895–900.

Robins, R. W., & Paulhus, D. L. (2001). The character of self-enhancers: Implications for organizations. In B. W. Roberts & R. Hogan (Eds), *Personality Psychology in the Workplace*, (pp. 193–222). Washington D.C.: American Psychological Association.

Roese, N. J., & Jamieson, D. W. (1993). Twenty years of bogus pipeline research: A critical review and meta-analysis. *Psychological Bulletin, 113*, 363–75.

Rosenfeld, P. (1993). *Impression Management, Fairness and the Employment Interview*. In R. D. Arvey (Chair), Perceptions, theories and issues of fairness in the employment interview. Symposium presented at the 101st meeting of the American Psychological Association, Toronto, Canada, August.

Rosenfeld, P. (1997). Impression management, fairness, and the employment interview. *Journal of Business Ethics, 16*, 801–8.

Rosenfeld, P., Booth-Kewley, S., & Edwards, J. E. (1993). Computer-administered surveys in organizational settings. *American Behavioral Scientist, 36*, 485–511.

Rosenfeld, P., Booth-Kewley, S., Edwards, J. E., & Alderton, D. L (1994). Linking diversity and impression management: A study of Hispanic, Black and White Navy Recruits. *American Behavioral Scientist, 37*, 672–81.

Rosenfeld, P., Booth-Kewley, S., Thomas, M. D., & Edwards, J. E., (1996). Responses on computer surveys: Impression management, social desirability, and the big brother syndrome. *Computers in Human Behavior, 12*, 263–74.

Rosenfeld, P., & Edwards, J. E., & Thomas, M. D. (Eds). (1993). *Improving Organizational Surveys: New Directions, Methods and Applications.* Newbury Park, CA: Sage Publications.

Rosenfeld, P., & Garrison, M. (1991). *Instructor's Resource Manual to Accompany 'Psychology Today'* (7th edition) New York: McGraw Hill.

Rosenfeld, P., & Giacalone, R. A. (1991). From extreme to mainstream: Applied impression management in organizations. In R. A. Giacalone and P. Rosenfeld (Eds), *Applied Impression Management: How Image-Making Affects Managerial Decisions* (pp. 3–12). Newbury Park: Sage Publications.

Rosenfeld, P., Giacalone, R., & Bond, M. (1983). The cross-cultural efficacy of entitlements in American and Hong Kong Chinese students. In J. B. Deregowski, S. Dziurawiec, & R. C. Annis (Eds), *Explications in Cross-cultural Psychology* (pp. 266–9). Swets & Zeitlinger: Lisse.

Rosenfeld, P., Giacalone, R. A., & Riordan, C. A. (1994). Impression management theory and diversity: Lessons for organizational behavior. *American Behavioral Scientist, 37*, 601–4.

Rosenfeld, P., Giacalone, R. A., & Riordan, C. A. (1995). Impression management. In N. Nicholson (Ed.), *Blackwell Dictionary of Organizational Behavior.* Oxford, UK: Blackwell Publishers.

Rosenhan, D. L. (1973). On being sane in insane places. *Science, 179*, 250–8.

Rosenstein, B. (2001). Author: Don't avoid office politics; become a master. *USA Today*, February 12, p. 6B.

Rosenthal E. (2001). For a fee, Chinese company will beg pardon for anyone. *New York Times*, January 3, pp. A1, A4.

Rosenthal, R., & Jacobson, L. (1968). *Pygmalion in the Classroom.* New York: Holt, Rinehart & Winston, Inc.

Ross, C. E., & Mirowsky, J. (1984). Socially desirable response and acquiescence in a cross-cultural survey of mental health. *Journal of Health and Social Behavior, 25*, 189–97.

Roth, D. L., Harris, R. N., & Snyder, C. R. (1988). An individual differences measure of attributive and repudiative tactics of favorable self-presentation. *Journal of Social and Clinical Psychology, 6*, 159–70.

Roth, D. L., Snyder, C. R., & Pace, L. M. (1986). Dimensions of favorable self-presentation. *Journal of Personality and Social Psychology, 51*, 867–74.

Rumsey, M. (1976). Effects of defendant background and remorse on sentencing judgments. *Journal of Applied Social Psychology, 6*, 247–59.

Russ, G. S. (1991). Symbolic communication and image management in organizations. In R. A. Giacalone & P. Rosenfeld (Eds), *Applied Impression Management: How Image-Making Affects Managerial Decisions* (pp. 219–40). Newbury Park: Sage Publications.

Savitsky, J., & Sim, M. (1974). Trading emotions: Equity theory of reward and punishment. *Journal of Communication, 24,* 140–7.

Saxe, C. (1991). Science and the CQT Polygraph: A theoretical critique. *Integrative Physiological and Behavioral Science, 26,* 223–31.

Schlenker, B. R. (1980). *Impression Management: The Self-Concept, Social Identity, and Interpersonal Relations.* Monterey, CA: Brooks/Cole.

Schlenker, B.R. (1987). Threats to identity: Self-identification and social stress. In C. R. Snyder & C. E. Ford (Eds), *Coping with Negative Life Events: Clinical and Social Psychological Perspectives* (pp. 273–321). New York: Plenum Press.

Schlenker, B.R. (2000). Impression Management. In A. F. Kazdin (Ed. in Chief), *Encyclopedia of Psychology.* Washington D.C.: American Psychological Association Books.

Schlenker, B.R. (in press). Self-presentation. In M. R. Leary & J. P. Tangney (Eds), *Handbook of Self and Identity.* New York: Guildford.

Schlenker, B. R., & Britt, T. W. (1999). Beneficial impression management: Strategically controlling information to help friends. *Journal of Personality and Social Psychology, 76,* 559–73.

Schlenker, B. R., Britt, T. W., & Pennington, J. W. (1996). Impression regulation and management: A theory of self-identification. In R. M. Sorrentino and E. T. Higgins (Eds). *Handbook of Motivation and Cognition: The Interpersonal Context* (Vol. 3) (pp. 118–47). New York: Guilford Press.

Schlenker, B. R., & Darby, B. W. (1981). The use of apologies in social predicaments. *Social Psychology Quarterly, 44,* 271–8.

Schlenker, B. R., & Pontari, B. A. (2000). The strategic control of information: Impression management and self-presentation in daily life. In A. Tesser, R. B. Felson, and J. M. Suls (Eds). *Psychological Perspectives on Self and Identity* (pp. 199–232), Washington D.C.: American Psychological Association.

Schlenker, B. R., & Weigold, M. F. (1992). Interpersonal processes involving impression regulation and management. *Annual Review of Psychology, 43,* 133–68.

Schmit, J., & Jones, D. (1994). How USAir coped with the crash. *USA Today,* September 12, pp. B1–B2.

Schonbach, P., & Kleibaumhuter, P. (1990). Severity of reproach and defensiveness of accounts. In M. J. Cody & M. L. McLaughlin (Eds) *The Psychology of Tactical Communication* (pp. 229–43). Clevedon, UK: Multilingual Matters Ltd.

Schriesheim, C. A., & Hinkin, T. R. (1990). Influence tactics used by subordinates: A theoretical and empirical analysis and refinement of the Kipnis, Schmidt, and Wilkinson subscales. *Journal of Applied Psychology, 75,* 246–57.

Schutz, A. (1997). Self-presentational tactics of talk-show guests: A comparison of politicians, experts and entertainers. *Journal of Applied Social Psychology, 27,* 1941–52.

Scott, M. B., & Lyman, S. M. (1968). Accounts. *American Sociological Review, 33*, 46–62.

Scully, D., & Marolla, J. (1984). Convicted rapists' vocabulary of motive: Excuses and justifications. *Social Problems, 31*, 530–44.

Serial killer (1994). *USA Today*, March 30, p. 3A.

Shaffer, D. R., & Sadowsky, C., (1979). Effects of withheld evidence on juridic decisions, II: Locus of withholding strategy. *Personality and Social Psychology Bulletin, 5*, 40–3.

Shapiro, L. (1994). Sexual desk jockeying. *Newsweek*, October 10, p. 59.

Shem, S. (1978). *The House of God*. New York: Dell.

Sherwood, A. (1983). Exit interviews: Don't just say goodbye. *Personnel Journal, 62*, 744–50.

Sias, P. M., Kramer, M. W., & Jenkins, E. (1997). A comparison of the communication behaviors of temporary employees and new hires. *Communication Research, 24*, 731–54.

Singh, V., & Vinnicombe, S. (2001). Impression management, commitment and gender: Managing others' good opinions. *European Management Journal, 19*, 183–94.

Smith, J. L., Berry, N. J., & Whitely, P. (1997). The effect of interviewer guise upon gender self-report responses as a function of interviewee's self-monitoring position. *European Journal of Social Psychology, 27*, 237–43.

Smith, A., & Davidson, J., Jr. (1983). *Personality and Situational Variables in the Evaluation Screening Process*. Unpublished manuscript, Boston University and University of Utah.

Smith, T. W., Snyder, C. R., & Perkins, S. C. (1983). The self-serving function of hypochondriacal complaints: Physical symptoms as self-handicapping strategies. *Journal of Personality and Social Psychology, 44*, 787–97.

Smith, D. S., & Strube, M. J. (1991). Self-protective tendencies as moderators of self-handicapping impressions. *Basic and Applied Social Psychology, 12*, 63–80.

Snyder, M. (1974). Self-monitoring of expressive behavior. *Journal of Personality and Social Psychology, 30*, 526–37.

Snyder, M. (1987). *Public Appearances, Private Realities: The Psychology of Self-Monitoring*. New York: W. H. Freeman.

Snyder, M., Berscheid, E., & Matwychuk, A. (1988). Orientations toward personnel selection: Differential reliance on appearance and personality. *Journal of Personality and Social Psychology, 54*, 972–9.

Snyder, M., & Copeland, J. (1989). Self-monitoring processes in organizational settings. In R. A. Giacalone & P. Rosenfeld (Eds), *Impression Management in the Organization* (pp. 7–19). Hillsdale, NJ: Lawrence Erlbaum Associates.

Snyder, M., & Gangestad, S. (1982). Choosing social situations: Two investigations of self-monitoring processes. *Journal of Personality and Social Psychology, 43*, 123–5.

Snyder, C. R., Higgins, R. L., & Stucky, R. J. (1983). *Excuses: Masquerades in Search of Grace*. New York: Wiley.

Snyder, C. R., Lassegard, M., & Ford, C. E. (1986). Distancing after group success and failure: Basking in reflected glory and cutting off reflected failure. *Journal of Personality and Social Psychology, 51*, 382–8.

St Antoine, T. J. (1984). *Arbitration and the Law*. Ithaca, NY: ILR Press.

Steinbrook, R. (1992). The polygraph: A flawed diagnostic method. *New England Journal of Medicine, 327*, 122–3.

Stengel, R. (2000). *You're Too Kind: A Brief History of Flattery*. New York, NY: Simon & Schuster.

Stephens, M. (1992). To thine own selves be true. *Los Angeles Times Magazine*, August 23, pp. 40–2, 60–2.

Stevens, C. K. (1997). Effects of pre-interview beliefs on applicants' reactions to campus interviews. *Academy of Management Journal, 40*, 947–66.

Stevens, C. K., & Kristof, A. L. (1995). Making the right impression: A field study of applicant impression management during job interviews. *Journal of Applied Psychology, 80*, 587–606.

Stokes, R., & Hewitt, J. P. (1976). Aligning actions. *American Sociological Review, 41*, 838–49.

Strube, M. J. (1986). An analysis of the self-handicapping scale. *Basic and Applied Social Psychology, 7*, 211–24.

Strutton, D., Pelton, L. E., & Lumpkin, J. R. (1995). Sex differences in ingratiatory behavior: An investigation of influence tactics in the salesperson–customer dyad. *Journal of Business Research, 34*, 35–45.

Sykes, G., & Matza, D. (1957). Techniques of neutralization: A theory of delinquency. *American Journal of Sociology, 22*, 664–70.

Szwajkowski, E. (1992). Accounting for organizational misconduct. *Journal of Business Ethics, 11*, 401–11.

Tannen, D. (1994). *Talking from 9 to 5*. New York: Morrow.

Tata, J. (2000). Implicit theories of account-giving: Influence of culture and gender. *International Journal of Intercultural Relations, 24*, 437–54.

Tennen, H., & Affleck, G. (1991). Blaming others for threatening events. *Psychological Bulletin, 108*, 209–32.

Tetlock, P. E., & Manstead, A. S. R. (1985). Impression management versus intrapsychic explanations in social psychology: A useful dichotomy? *Psychological Review, 92*, 59–77.

Tetrick, L. E. (1989). An exploratory investigation of response latency in computerized administrations of the Marlowe-Crowne Social Desirability Scale. *Personality & Individual Differences, 10*, 1281–7.

Tice, D. M., & Baumeister, R. F. (1990). Self-esteem, self-handicapping, and self-presentation: The strategy of inadequate practice. *Journal of Personality, 58*, 443–64.

Tuohy, W. (1993). BBC to air Mao documentary over China's objections. *Los Angeles Times*, December 19, p. A–4.

Turban, D. B., & Dougherty, T. W. (1994). Role of protege personality in receipt of mentoring and career success. *Academy of Management Journal*, *37*, 688–702.

Turnley, W. H., & Bolino, M. C. (2001). Achieving desired images while avoiding undesired images: Exploring the role of self-monitoring in impression management. *Journal of Applied Psychology, 86*, 351–60.

Tyre, P. (2001). Improving on history. *Newsweek*, July 2, p. 34.

Ungar, S. (1981). The effects of others' expectations on the fabrication of opinions. *The Journal of Social Psychology, 114*, 173–85.

Vasilopoulos, N. L., Reilly, R. R., & Leaman, J. A. (2000). The influence of job familiarity and impression management on self-report measure scale scores and response latencies. *Journal of Applied Psychology, 85*, 50–64.

Velasquez, M., Moberg, D. J., & Cavanaugh, G. F. (1983, Autumn). Organizational statesmanship and dirty politics: Ethical guidelines for the organizational politician. *Organizational Dynamics*, 65–80.

Villanova, P., & Bernardin, H. J. (1989). Impression management in the context of performance appraisal. In R. A. Giacalone & P. Rosenfeld (Eds), *Impression Management in the Organization* (pp. 299–314). Hillsdale, NJ: Lawrence Erlbaum Associates.

Villanova, P., & Bernardin, H. J. (1991). Performance appraisal: The means, motive and opportunity to manage impressions. In R. A. Giacalone & P. Rosenfeld (Eds), *Applied Impression Management* (pp. 81–96). Newbury Park, CA: Sage Publications.

von Baeyer, C. L., Sherk, D. L., & Zanna, M. P. (1981). Impression management in the job interview. *Personality and Social Psychology Bulletin, 7*, 45–51.

Vonk, R. (1998). The slime effect: suspicion and dislike of likeable behavior toward superiors. *Journal of Personality and Social Psychology, 74*, 849–64.

Watson, O., & Friend, R. (1969). Measurement of social evaluative anxiety. *Journal of Consulting and Clinical Psychology, 33*, 448–57.

Watt, J. D. (1993). The impact of the frequency of ingratiation on the performance evaluation of bank personnel. *The Journal of Psychology, 127*, 171–7.

Wayne, S. J., & Ferris, G. R. (1990). Influence tactics, affect and exchange quality in supervisor-subordinate interactions: A laboratory experiment and field study. *Journal of Applied Psychology, 75*, 487–99.

Wayne, S. J., & Kacmar, K. M. (1991). The effects of impression management on the performance appraisal process. *Organizational Behavior and Human Decision Processes, 48*, 70–88.

Wayne, S. J., & Liden, R. C. (1995). Effects of impression management on performance ratings: A longitudinal study. *Academy of Management Journal, 38*, 232–60.

Wayne, S. J., Liden, R. C., & Sparrowe, R. T. (1994). Developing leader member exchanges: The influence of gender and ingratiation. *American Behavioral Scientist, 37*, 697–714.

Weatherly, K., & Beach, L. R. (1994). Making the right impression. *Contemporary Psychology, 39*, 416–17.

Weber, S. J., & Cook, T. D. (1972). Subject effects in laboratory research: An examination of subject roles, demand characteristics, and valid inference. *Psychological Bulletin, 77*, 273–95.

Weiner, B., Amirkhan, J., Folkes, V. S., & Verette, J. A. (1987). An attributional analysis of excuse giving: Studies of naive theory of emotion. *Journal of Personality and Social Psychology, 52*, 316–24.

Weinstein, E. A., & Deutschberger, P. (1963). Some dimensions of altercasting. *Sociometry, 26*, 454–66.

Welch, J. (1999). How to.... Fill in the gaps on your CV. Go on be a devil and create the right impression without selling your soul. *The Guardian*, October 23, Section: Guardian Rise, p. 4.

Wexler, M. N. (1986). Impression management and the new competence. *Et cetera, 20*, 247–58.

Whrenberg, S. (1980). The exit interview: Why bother? *Supervising Management, 5*, 20–5.

Whyte, W. F. (1943). *Street Corner Society.* Chicago: The University of Chicago Press.

Wong, E. (2001). A stinging office memo boomerangs; Chief executive is criticized after upbraiding workers by email. *New York Times*, April 5, p. C–1.

Wood, R. E., & Mitchell, T. E. (1981). Manager behavior in a social context: The impact of impression management on attributions and disciplinary actions. *Organizational Behavior and Human Performance, 28*, 356–78.

Woods, R. H., & Macaulay, J. F. (1987). Exit interviews: How to turn a file filler into a management tool. *Cornell Hotel and Restaurant Administration Quarterly, 28*, 39–46.

Wortman, C. B., & Linsenmeier, J. A. W. (1977). Interpersonal attraction and techniques of ingratiation in organizational settings. In B. M. Staw and G. R. Salancik (Eds), *New Directions in Organizational Behavior* (pp. 133–78). Chicago, IL: St Clair Press.

Wosinska, W., Dabul, A. J., Whetstone-Dion, R., & Cialdini, R. B. (1996). Self-presentational responses to success in the organization: The costs and benefits of modesty. *Basic and Applied Social Psychology, 18*, 229–42.

Wright, J. P. (1979). *On a Clear Day You Can See General Motors.* New York: Avon.

Xin, K. R. (1997). Asian American managers: An impression gap? *Journal of Applied Behavioral Science, 33*, 335–55.

Yandell, B. (1979). Those who protest too much are seen as guilty. *Personality and Social Psychology Bulletin, 5*, 44–7.

Zack, A. M. (1989). *Grievance Arbitration.* Boston: Lexington Books.

Zarandona, J. L., & Camuso, M. A. (1985). A study of exit interviews: Does the last word count? *Personnel, 62,* 47–8.

Zerbe, W. J., & Paulhus, D. L. (1987). Socially desirable responding in organizational behavior: A reconception. *Academy of Management Review, 12,* 250–64.

Index

If you have enjoyed reading this book, why not read other titles in the same series.

Managing Employee Performance
Design and Implementation in Organizations

Richard S Williams, *Principal Psychology, Assessment and Consultancy Unit, The Home Office*

- Clearly describes the key approaches to designing, implementing and managing an effective performance management system, and sets these approaches within the broader context of the organization.
- Covers the importance of mission and strategy, reviewing and rewarding performance, and the controversies surrounding performance-related pay.
- Relevant to all those who have a responsibility for designing, introducing or managing a performance management system.

Thomson Learning 2002, 296pp, 1-86152-780-2, Paperback

Managing Innovation and Change
A Critical Guide for Organizations

Nigel King, *University of Huddersfield* and **Neil Anderson,** *Professor of Work Psychology, Goldsmith's College, University of London*

- Discusses the origins of creativity, group approaches to innovation, managing innovative teams and how to manage organizations.
- Describes the psychological principles, theories and techniques applied in these areas.
- Enables managers to improve organizational strategies and their responses to change.

Thomson Learning 2002, 264pp, 1-86152-783-7, Paperback

Creating the Healthy Organization
Well-being, Diversity and Ethics at Work

Sue Newell, *Professor of Management, Royal Holloway College, University of London*

- Explores the impact of work organizations on individual employees, groups and the wider community.
- Argues that the creation of working environments which promote positive well-being and eliminate unfair discrimination is the key to long term sustainability.
- Relevant to all those who are involved in maintaining a policy of good human relations while achieving competitive success.

Thomson Learning 2002, 264pp, 1-86152-784-5, Paperback

Managing Teams
A Strategy for Success

Nicky Hayes, *University of Bradford*

- Explores our knowledge about how teams work, how and why they become effective and how they influence an organization.
- Uses practical examples, organizational experience and the psychological mechanisms underlying teams and team management.
- Describes how managers at all levels can improve teamworking.

Thomson Learning 2002, 240pp, 1-86152-782-9, Paperback

Recruitment and Selection
A Framework for Success

Dominic Cooper, *B-Safe Ltd*, **Ivan T Robertson**, *Professor of Occupational Psychology, Manchester School of Management, UMIST* and **Gordon Tinline**, *Managing Consultant, Robertson Cooper Ltd*

- Offers a framework for action to assist selectors in accurately predicting employees' future behaviour at work.
- Identifies customer needs, establishes the necessary evaluative and decision-making standards and optimizes the return on investment.
- Describes and discusses selection methods.

Thomson Learning 2002, 288pp, 1-86152-781-0, Paperback

To order any of these titles:

UK
Tel: +44 (0)1264 342 932
Fax: +44 (0)1264 342 761
E-mail: thomsonlearning.orders@itps.co.uk

International
Tel: +44 (0)1264 343 022
Fax: +44 (0)1264 342 761
E-mail: thomsonlearning.orders@itps.co.uk